RESERVATIONS IN INDIA
Myths and Realities

About the Author

Mulchand S. Rana is a social thinker, scholar and writer on various vital social issues of contemporary nature and larger relevance. Basically a post-graduate in management, he started his career as a probationary officer in a nationalized bank in 1977 and rose to the senior managerial position when he resigned in 2000. All along his bright banking career, he was also associated with quite a few premier academic and training institutes and reputed voluntary organizations.

He joined Gujarat Public Service Commission as a member for six years till 2006. He, while being associated with this prestigious Constitutional Institution, had a very useful exposure of dealing and deciding in recruitment, promotions as various personnel and HRD matters pertaining to state government employees/officers.

RESERVATIONS IN INDIA
Myths and Realities

Mulchand S. Rana

CONCEPT PUBLISHING COMPANY, NEW DELHI-110 059

Cataloging in Publication Data—DK
Courtesy: D.K. Agencies (P) Ltd. <docinfo@dkagencies.com>

Rana, Mulchand S.
Reservations in India : myths and realities / Mulchand S. Rana.
p. cm.
Includes bibliographical references.
Includes index.
ISBN 13: 9788180695605
ISBN 10: 8180695603

1. Reverse discrimination—India. 2. Reverse discrimination—Law and legislation—India. 3. People with social disabilities—Government policy—India. I. Title.

DDC 305.560 954 22

ISBN-13: 978-81-8069-560-5
ISBN-10: 81-8069-560-3

First Published 2008

Published and Printed by
Ashok Kumar Mittal
Concept Publishing Company
A/15-16, Commercial Block, Mohan Garden
New Delhi (INDIA)

Phones : 25351460, 25351794
Fax : 091-11-25357103
Email : publishing@conceptpub.com

Preface and Acknowledgements

Reservation in India, Myths and Realities is an integrated study of various aspects around reservation; a measure initiated in India after independence for the emancipation of socially deprived and economically backward people of the nation who are known as scheduled castes (SC), scheduled tribes (ST) and other backward classes (OBC). The discussion and coverage mainly centers around 'Reservation' the focus point of State initiatives launched for these communities. Reservation resorted to as an urgent and immediate measure, did work well during all these years having brought about a significant positive and clearly visible result that none can deny.

Sixty years of implementation of any specific socio-economic measure like reservation needs its evaluation since the whole world has undergone a fast sea change during this period. Reservation system also needs to be re-examined in light of economic reforms in the era of liberalization, privatization and globalization, as also number of judicial pronouncements, constitutional modifications etc. and simultaneously also taking into serious consideration, on and often uproarings from the society, changing political considerations, increasing judicial activism all around reservation.

Indian reservation system has remained under constant debates and attacks. There are lot of misconceptions and misunderstandings prevailing around reservation or say positive discrimination. Recently published reports of Justice Rajinder Sachar Committee and Justice Rang Nath Mishra Commission, Gurjar agitations in Rajasthan etc. all have kept the issue of reservation alive in media and society at large. It has simultaneously also evoked lot of confusions and concerns on both the sides. As rightly observed by Marc Galenter, "The Society is unfortunately not only divided into pro-reservationists and anti-reservationists or sometimes retentionalists and abolitionists, it has also acentuated the caste consciousness making caste the biggest party in India".

Social tension in the country has been accentuating with the gradual realization of frustration of those deprived and of a sense of loss to those entrenched. The violent reactions in the country have been deepening on caste lines, which are bound to have serious implications for Indian society. Gruesome incidents like Kumher massacre in Rajasthan, Tsundur in Andhra Pradesh, frightening crimes in Gohana and Jhajjar in Haryana, Kherlanji brutal killings in Maharashtra, discriminations in prestigious institutions like All India Institute of Medical Science, New Delhi and Indian Institute of Technology, Chennai, and going little ahead, historic anti-reservation agitations in Gujarat, all are the painful stories of extreme forms of caste hatreds prevailing even today in the Hindu upper caste mind-set. Many of those who deny this ground reality in principle, operate it in practice. Life moves in the frontiers of caste and cultured men speak in soft tones against this irrational, illogical and equally inhuman system while its rejection in action just does not occur to them.

The Indian social system is structured on the primises of perceptional purity and pollution. The Indian social system has not changed some of its obsolete and outdated tenets which have ridiculously kept spirit of casteism very much in its own ugly characteristics. Some apparent changes in people's behavioural manifestations should not be considered as caste disappearance from society. The study also reveals that the experience of removing untouchability has been slow, halting and uneven in different parts of the country. Practice of manual scavenging still sizeably exists amidst all technological advancements.

Growing intolerance of the upper castes and the aspirations of the lower castes are glaring indications that the Indian road to social equality is bound to be marked by bloody clashes between different castes, if a definite design of policy is not attempted to achieve balance in society. The days of false promises and rosy hopes are over. The future would be difficult if imperceptible discrimination is not checked in time and with commitment. A measure like reservation has to be viewed in its effectiveness in abridging these social divides.

A time has ripen when the whole issue of upliftment of these masses has to be considered through a holistic approach. This won't materialize merely by arguments for and against the continuance of reservation. It has to be instrumental in breaking caste barriers, and provides the maximum benefits to the left out fraction of the oppressed. The issue of upliftment of entire backward communities is a multi-dimensional social issue calling for an honest and sincere concern with a long-term vision.

This could include provision of free or cheap good quality education in schools, land reforms by giving land to the actual landless cultivators, strict implementation of minimum wages, and a complete stoppage of all kinds of discriminatory behaviour whether in villages or in corporate sector. This will have to be viewed not from bare statistical yardsticks like so much of increase in the per capita income of the people, or reduction in number of families below poverty line as per the government jargons and definitions, but looking at these people for their whole-hearted uplifting out of miseries of social discriminations and abysmal poverty both of which are hand in gloves relationship. If all these were religiously implemented, there would be perhaps no need for reservations for any section of population.

This typical Indian problem also calls for a sensitized State Administration. The fact that as India's socio-political ambience is still caste ridden, caste is still a millstone round the neck of many officials in the administration and their mind-set militates against rising above caste. Constitutional provisions covering reservation etc. *per se* are like a rule book. If officials go by its alphabets and letters without understanding the spirit underlying the provisions, they cannot do much, and what they do may even be detrimental to the spirit of Constitution of India. This may be more so particularly in case of lower echelon bureaucracy.

Something on the other hand also needs to be looked at equally with deep concern. Recent demands of Gurjars for higher reservation from existing OBC quota to ST category, movement of including converted Christians and Arzal Muslims to SC reservation and like that everyday more and more communities are pouring into and queuing up for their inclusion in the list of reservation beneficiaries. The reservation that was supposed to be by itself of a self-destructive in nature sees now no bounds, no horizons. Perhaps the very noble objective of reservation is forgotten in this race of gaining some short-term individualistic benefits by playing with the casteism. Unfortunately, this important tool has turned out to be perceived as vote catcher device by the shortsighted power centered politicians.

What is our national goal? It is undoubtedly establishing a harmonious egalitarian society through socio economic engineering and accelerating the process of upward mobility of more and more backward castes/class families. The Constitution of India has also vowed to promote with special care by the State to improve the present position of SCs, STs and OBCs. The real power could be shared by the weakest sections only if the doors of the upper decks were opened to them. The strength of a chain lies with its weakest part.

In the words of Justice Krishna Iyer, "The real solution to the issue of reservation lies in 'Growth' *i.e.* to enlarge the size of the cake. The vast human potential of the Harijans and Girijans, the one-fifth of the Idnian people goes to thistles and every communal effort to twist the politics of power for promoting chances of getting jobs becomes inevitable, caste being a deep rooted pathology in our country.

To recall Dr. Ambedkar, "On the social plane, we have in India a society based on privileges of graded inequality which means elevation for some and degradations for the others. On the economic plane, we have a society in which there are some who have immense wealth as against the many who are living in abject poverty. On the 26th January 1950, we are going to enter into a life of contradictions. In politics, we will have equality and in social and economic life, we will have inequality.

We must remove this contradiction at the earliest possible moment, or else those who suffer from inequality will blow up the structure of political democracy which this Assembly has so laboriously built up.

Acknowledgements

I am thankful to all those friends and well-wishers who have continuously provided all sorts of assistance as and when required. I am heartily indebted to Indubhai Jani, Chandubhai Maheria and Bhagyeshbhai for their pioneering inspirations and providing me with lot of materials on the subject. I also thank Devang, my son-in-law and Hitesh for all time computer and net assistance, Chetan Rathod, Avani Shrivastav and Dr. Vijay Jhala, for surveys, tabulations and editing, Vijay Parmar for proof reading and finally, advocates Jayesh Bhairavia, Digant Joshi for interactive law related inputs.

Before concluding, I owe to all time support of my family members, but for which, I could not have been able to have satisfaction for this accomplishment. My wife Indu, Himanshu, Mimansha, Chandrakant, Hetal, Devang and Anil Kumar all have been an abounding source of inspiration to all my such social contributions.

Mulchand S. Rana

Ahmedabad
26th January, 2008

E-mail: mulchandrana@yahoo.co.in

Contents

List of Tables

PART I

Reservation Amidst Indian Social Conditions

This part covers mainly prevailing Indian social conditions under which the idea of reservation came into existence. This status was granted with a view to bringing change in the treatment to these downtroddens from untouchability, and other social equality norms. It also covers impact of reservation policy during last sixty years of its implementation, focusing on relevance of reservation in today's conditions, subsequent addition of OBC reservations creating a major uproar in the Indian social life against reservation and eruptions of anti-reservation movements in some part of the country particularly Gujarat in the last quarter of the 20th century.

1

Reservation: An Ever Lauding Debate

Discourse on welfare of backward classes which always centers around reservation has engaged every one at the local to national and the international level in an unprecedented manner drawing the attention of social reformists, intellectuals, voluntary action groups, human right activists, the political dispensation and at times in global perspective as well. Reservation is one of the most talked about subjects now-a-days. There will be no newspaper, periodical journal or electronic media without something about reservation. One day, it will be regarding reservations in IITs/IIMs, the other day regarding private sector reservation, Sachar Committee Report, Creamy layer, reservation for females, reservation in case of religious converts and so on.

Reservation is a mechanism of protective discrimination, as a social policy of the state enshrined in the Constitution to ensure the participation of the traditionally neglected section of the society involving fixation of quota in the electoral, employment and educational institutions.

If one recalls those post-independence days, every body was concerned about the need for an integrated and harmonious society free of social antagonism. There was a firm determination for the uplifting of those who were left bigoted because of the prevailing social practices since centuries. Accordingly, there was a heart felt sympathy and a feeling of accommodation towards the intended beneficiaries of reservation who were inflicted with lot of hardships and inhuman treatment. Accordingly, need for the reservation was accepted as a common consensus and national loyalty in those days. With passage of time, this feeling of accommodation and sympathy has shattered taking almost a negative turn and has now created a situation of hatred. What changes during these years took place that contributed in such a drastic perceptional 'U' turn in the minds of the common people? Has the root cause for which reservation was introduced been completely eradicated? Have the social inequalities dwindled to a redundant level? It is high time for introspection of all these basic questions, the society is confronted with.

Marc Galenter renowned sociologist who has worked in depth on inequalities prevailing in the Indian society says, as regards reservation," The problem of reservational protective discrimination is multi-dimensional involving formidable burdens of policy making and administration in a developing nation. The compensatory or protective discrimination in favour of backward section of society once recognized as unparallel experiment betoking a generosity and farsightedness rare among the nations has developed into one of the most notorious provisions of the constitution."

He remarks," The Society is unfortunately not only divided into pro-reservationists and anti-reservationists or sometimes retentionalists and abolitionists, it has also accentuated the caste consciousness making caste the biggest party in India." *(Competing Equalities 1983 Galanter Marc)*

Origin of Reservation

The thought of reservation has its roots way back in the year 1902, when Chhatrapati Shahuji Maharaj a small ruler in the then Kolhapur State in Maharastra in pre-independence days introduced Reservation in the jobs in his small Kingdom for the 'Antayaj' i.e. hither to known as Shudras or the backwards. This was followed by another little larger State of Mysore in South India introducing reservation in the State in the year 1921, on the basis of report of Millar Committee idea of reservation which covered scheduled castes, backward classes and most of non-Brahmin castes. Incidentally, Millar Committee appointed in 1918, was the first Committee/

Commission appointed in India for suggesting upliftment measures for the socially deprived people. Immediately, thereafter in 1921 itself, the sprawling Madras Presidency introduced reservation for the backward classes including scheduled castes and most of non-Brahmin castes, many of which are not even in the present list of OBCs. The large Bombay Presidency initiated the process in 1931 following the report of the State Committee for the depressed classes and some backward castes such as nomadic communities.

Government of India Act, 1935

This was the first Statute during the British Regime, which incorporated the provisions for reservation to scheduled castes and scheduled tribes and many other backward castes. The Indian constitution after independence, not only regularized these provisions through its various articles, but also cast a duty bound obligation on the State to look after their overall development through numerous welfare measures for these categories who have legged behind for centuries together due to peculiar social inequalities deeply rooted in the country.

However, the objective of the Britishers behind the reservation provisions and the one by our own constitution framers was quite different. The Britishers were interested merely in maintaining the balance of power in society to facilitate their rule. They had double standards in values and objectives. They were liberal and also followed principle of social justice in the society but were not concerned with equality and social justice in their colonies. They simply used the device of reservation as a tool to manage the then mounting social tensions along with penetrating fight for freedom. Bristishers cleverly focused on managing agitating forces, broadening their shakening base and thereby to perpetuate their own rule in India. Thus, reservation policy during colonial regime was half hearted, short sighted and ill motivated, besides lacking its need-based coverage. It included number of minorities which never suffered social discrimination, but surprisingly ignored inclusion of those tribes deserted from the mainstream society and living in mountains and forests in a very pitiable condition. It was never so in the hearts and minds of our visionary framers of constitution who were very well aware of the barbaric conditions of the downtroddens known as scheduled castes and scheduled tribes who were alienated from social mainstream, economic justice and human freedom since centuries. These great visionaries were of the firm opinion that the Nation cannot progress equitably undermining the woeful conditions of this one-fifth fraction of the society.

Thus, Reservation is not a number game of apportioning a percentage of vacancies for the eligible community candidates. But it is a mission of abscission of deeply rooted abject social animosity. Social backwardness is not insurmountable and establishing a social harmony wherein every citizen of the nation irrespective of his/her caste, creed or religion shall have an open, impartial and abundant opportunity as also vowed in our constitution.

What is an Inbuilt Consideration Behind Reservation System?

Reservation is not a mere allocation of few seats or a percentage quota for the backward castes/classes. It is a constitutional support to those who are deprived of adequate opportunity and equal treatment from the rest of the society for centuries. Indian society was so typically divided that bond of inequalities got further strengthened with more and more backing of religious sanctions, social beliefs, occupational rigidities and so on. Breaking these strong barriers was certainly a Herculean task. But on the other side were the determined will and now a constitutional intervention also to skirmish this hard hit handicap. Position after these sixty years clearly shows a marked impact of all these collective efforts.

Reservation is not a poverty alleviation programme as is generally misunderstood, but a revolutionary campaign of establishing social harmony and with that one nationhood.

The policy is often identified as 'Protective Discrimination' or Compensatory Discrimination. According to *Marc Galanter,* reservation constitutes protective or say compensatory discrimination in favour of the backward classes, which is envisaged to be used for the purpose of mitigating inequalities. *Marc Galenter* states, "Compensatory Discrimination may be advocated not as a devise to ensure fairness to individuals, but as means to produce desired social customs, e.g. to reduce group disparities, afford representation, encourage development of social talent and so forth. He has examined the utility of reservations as a device for reparation. He further adds, "In some cases, compensatory policies have another root that a history of individious treatment has resulted in accumulated disabilities which are carried by certain groups. No matter, how fair and unbiased the measures now employed for distributing benefits, the victims of past injustice will fair well, in terms of current performance. To distribute benefits by neutral standards, will perpetuate and amplify unjust exactions and exclusions of the past. Fairness then, demands that present distribution be arranged to undo and offset old biases, not to perpetuate them".

Reservation is also known as '**Discrimination in Reverse**'. While affirming the constitutional oath to consider all the citizens as equal, the constitution also provides for some protective umbrella of ensuring a portion of the cake for those who are otherwise unable to avail off. Reasons for their inability are many. But the sum total is that they do need such protection. This may tantamount to discrimination i.e. instead of leaving the full cake for its availment as per one's individual capacity, here a small portion of cake is put aside for those who are not only hungry, but are equally unable to claim their due share out of the total cake.

Compartalized Indian Caste System

Indian social system is set up on ancient Vernashram system fixed with graded ladders of caste consideration. Indian social mind is strongly influenced by the ideology derived from caste system, which assigns a person's status by birth. Hindu social order known as Vernashram, is divided into graded inequality in four different hierarchical segments, i.e. Brahmin at the top, next Kshatriya, then Vaishya and Shudra at the bottom. The Shudras are today's other backward castes (OBC). And still subservient portion is Ati Shudra also known as Pancham, outcastes, untouchables etc. These Ati Shudras are in present day context recognized as scheduled castes (SC) and scheduled tribes (ST). This last ranked bottom of the society is the center point of all the talks around reservation. Of course, reservation at present is more engrossed with controversies around other backward castes (OBC) also known as Socially and Economically backward classes (SEBC).

The whole Hindu society broadly speaking from occupational view point was divided into two parts. One; Mainstream society and rest viz. supplementary society. People under the main stream were associated primarily with agriculture and such other respectful economic activities. The castes under the mainstream include Brahmins, Kshatriyas and Vaishyas as enumerated in the Vernashram system set out from ancient times. While supplementary castes consist Shudras and Ati Shudras i.e. carpenters, blacksmiths, barbers, sweepers etc. who were supposed to provide a sort of ancillary services to the main stream. Inter relationship between these two segments were that of Host or *Yajman* type. Under this relationship, the supplementary communities serve the main stream community through out the year and get in turn food grain and other agriculture produce on seasonal basis in return of their services. The relationship later on developed into a sort of permanent dependence of the lower castes i.e. Shudras and Ati Shudras on the upper castes viz. Brahmin, Kshatriyas and Vaishyas.

Occupation Forked as Impervious Zone in Indian Caste System

As the occupation was directly attached to caste regimentation and the castes in turn were split into a ladder of purity and pollution, a sort of complex perceiving the upper castes as superiors and the lower castes as inferior and untouchables percolated to the respective caste affiliated occupations, they were carrying out. Accordingly, the work of hair cutting, sweeping, toilet cleaning, dead animal lifting, tanning, weaving etc. were considered to be demeaning vocations. Nowhere through out in the world such position prevails. A barber in Britain or a sweeper in America or a blacksmith in Australia commands an equal respect and dignity for his respective vocation. And in our country? A barber whether cutting hair on the roadside in a hutment or in his air conditioned saloon is considered by all means a lower caste person and to be looked down by the people of the upper strata of the society. A sweeper cleaning the toilet is not allowed an entry in the houses of the upper societies even today; least he pollutes the whole house. As noted in the National Geography Survey during their survey in the year 2003 in India, it was pointed out that the poor sweeper engaged in these unclean occupations would not even be offered a soap and a bucket of water for cleaning his body full of mud and filths. What a grotesque approach and hypocritic attitude seen in an Indian society! Why So? Why a scavenging work, which is very much necessary for keeping the society neat, clean and hygienic, is considered so quarantined and contemptible? Functioning of which ethos and philosophies in Hindu society has severed these so called upper castes from the rational and human behaviour in such situations?

Jawaharlal Nehru, the then Prime Minister while addressing the Congress Parliamentary Party on 2nd November 1954 stated, "The conception and practice of caste embodied the aristocratic ideal and was obviously opposed to democratic conceptions. It had its strong sense of noblesse oblige provided people kept their hereditary stations and did not challenge the established order. India's success and achievements were on the whole confined to the upper classes, those lower down in the scale had very few chances and their opportunities were strictly limited. These upper classes were not small limited groups but large in numbers and there was also diffusion of power, authority and influence. Hence, they carried on successfully for a very long time. But the ultimate weakness and falling of the caste system and the Indian social structure were such that they degraded a mass of human being and gave them no opportunities to get out of that condition educationally, culturally or economically. That degradation brought the deterioration all along the line including in its scope even the upper classes. It led to the petrification which became a dominant feature of India's economy and life".

With such a callous attitude and malice treatment from their counter parts in upper society, these so called supplementary communities have lost their self-dignity. They have accepted their pitiable condition as a punishment of sins of their earlier life, what is again and again thrust upon them in the name of religion to which these unfortunates have the highest degree of faith and loyalty. Inferiority complex, separate inhabitation outside the village, starvation, illiteracy coupled therewith unhygienic living etc. have added to their miseries over a period of time. This has equally disturbed the development of the nation as a whole. The low credential to the different but indispensable jobs in the society eliminated the environment of innovations and advancements in such jobs. The people engaged in the socially low rated jobs with assured clientele and experiencing social juxtapose were lacking the element of right man for the right job. As against this, the person engaged in temple rituals and worshippings viz. *Pooja/Archna* and almost contributing nothing to the economy was respected so high in the society. This work is kept in tact for being performed by a segment placed at the top of the social hierarchy even today.

Then, what is the way out that a sweeper's son, a barber's daughter and similar other lacs of new generation youngsters can be pushed forward towards upward mobility through higher education and careers as an officer or Tehsildar or a doctor and so on? Reservation is a sort of interventional support that ensures this transformation. A comparative table in the succeeding chapter exhibits marked improvement in creating lot of doctors, engineers and government employees/officers in the government. A revolutionary transformation into the lives of these deprived masses has become a visible reality as a result of the constitutionally provided reservation system implemented since last sixty years.

Equality Yet a Dream

Every body accepts need of providing equal opportunities to the oppressed section of the society living in sub-human conditions. The Indian constitution too has immediately after embodying equal opportunities to all the citizens of the nation without discrimination on the ground of caste, creed, religion or anything else, has stipulated special provisions for these unequals so as to bring them to a level of the other advanced sections who are already in a better competing level. How is it possible? Leaving all equals and unequals on the same footing without verifying their existing level of competence will not serve the purpose and will lead to perpetuating existing century old situation of inequality. It is not that universally accepted economic parameters like GDP, GNP etc. highlighting the state of economic progress of any nation has not grown in our country. Likewise it is also not that employment and educational opportunities have not recorded upward growth in the country. It has manifold, but unfortunately, its unequated and unjust way of distribution that has neglected a section of the population keeping them amidst the state of exploitation, oppression, injustice, inequality, hunger and diseases. The ultimate goal of any civilized society has to be social justice in the Nation i.e. to make all its citizens able and efficient and raise the level of merit and efficiency. If a small section of society is not upto the general standard of merit and efficiency because of some historical reasons, appropriate environment and adequate opportunities should be created to raise the level of merit and efficiency of this section of society.

The domineering and detracting living condition of these depressed classes is very appropriately described by Justice Sahai in *Indra Sahney* vs. *Union of India case* "The frail and emaciated section of the people living in poverty, rearing in obscurity, possessing no wealth or influence, having no education or much less higher education are suffering from social repression and oppression."

The Justice further states, "Living below poverty line and suffering from social ostracism, the undignified social status and sub-human living conditions, appalling situation and the pathetic condition, their birth in low castes, their demeaning occupation, their degeneration and deprivation caused by prior and continuing discrimination, exploitation, neglect, poverty, disease, isolation, bondage and humiliation, their roots in the lowest of the low segments of society, their affiliation with what are traditionally regarded as demeaning occupations, their humiliating and inescapable segregation and chronic isolation from rest of the population, their social and educational deprivation and helplessness, their abysmal poverty and degenerating backwardness are the classes of the citizens incapable of uplifting themselves in order to join the mainstream of upward mobility.

The description narrated by Justice Sahai is by and large a ground reality seen in respect of these masses belonging to the scheduled castes, scheduled tribes and other backward classes.

Social Justice in Real Perspective

Constitutional Bench consisting of Chief Justice Y.K. Sababarwal, Justice K.G. Balkrishnan and others have stated in *M. Nagraj and Others,'* Equality of opportunity has two different and distant concepts. There is conceptual distinction between a non-discrimination principle and affirmative action under which the State is obliged to provide level playing field to the oppressed classes. Affirmative action in the above sense seeks to move beyond the concept of non-discrimination towards equalizing results with respect to various groups. They further added 'Social justice is one of the sub-divisions of the concept of justice. It is concerned with the distribution of benefits and burdens throughout a society, as it results from social institutions, property system, public organizations etc.'

The problem is what should be the basis of distribution? Writers like Raphael, Mill and Hume defines, 'Social Justice' in terms of rights. Other writers like Hayek and Spencer define 'Social Justice' in terms of deserts. Socialist writers define 'Social Justice' in terms of need. Therefore, there are three criteria to judge the basis of distribution, namely rights, deserts and needs. These three criteria can be put under two concepts of equality—'**Formal Equality**' and '**Proportional Equality**' means that law treats everyone equal and does not favour anyone either because he belongs to the advantaged or disadvantaged section of the society. Concept of 'Proportional Equality' expects the States to take affirmative action in favour of disadvantaged sections of the society within the framework of liberal democracy.

Under the Indian constitution, while basic liberties are guaranteed and individual initiative is encouraged, the State has got the role of ensuring that no class prospers at the cost of the other class and no person suffers because of drawbacks which is not his, but social.

Unwritten; Unofficial Reservations

Reservation as such is not a new thing in India. Though, it might not have been known in its exact nomenclature as reservation, Reservations *de facto* as well de-jure are already in existence and practised every where in the Indian Society in many different ways since time immemorial, most of which are not opposed at all since they especially benefit the rich and middle classes.

Family inheritance right is one such example. Upon death of parent why a son and rarely a daughter automatically gets the property of the parent? No merit of the recepient getting the benefit of this reservation is assessed before passing on the property. Agriculture land in India is another example. In most of the cases, the skilled agricultural labourer does not get the property, but an unskilled absentee landlord living in a city gets access through inheritance to the agricultural land from his parent. Inheritance rights in most of the cases reward those who do not necessarily deserve.

Another awesome case is practice found among most of our large, medium and small business persons who are now heard raising their voice against reservation in the private sector. In India, in case of most businesses, including those where outside shareholders and financial institutions hold the majority stake, management would always be by inheritance whether you take Ambanis, Birlas or most other mercantile and corporate house families. There are few exemplary exceptions also like Narayan Murthi, Deepak Parekh, and Sunil Mittal who have said that they will not pass on management and control to their children, but will consider or have already handed over the management control to professionals who have the merit and ability. How many of those opposing reservation speak out against business and management inheritance? Rahul Bajaj the strong opponent of reservation while taking his son as CEO in his Company argues that his son has been groomed. But then question is, what prevented him from grooming a non-family competent professional member?

Bajaj asked for a level playing field when it comes to competition from MNCs, but does not believe in a level playing field when it comes to the underprivileged. Dhoot of Videocon publicly states that his company does not take women at the executive level. Similarly, how many of the women members of Birla, Bajaj or Ambani families are permitted to participate in core administration in the group companies? This is a clear exclusion or say reverse discrimination. Informal survey states that it is easy to find out that in many companies, most of the staff belongs to the Company owners' or apex management executives' caste, community, gender, religion or linguistic group.

Management Quota

Management quota in admission to self-finance educational institutions is yet a type of **reservation based on ability to pay.** There are hundreds of privately run professional colleges where one may have very good marks, but if he cannot afford to pay donations or high fees, doors of such institutions are closed for him. These admissions on exorbitant fees are justified in the name of euphemism of 'Management Quota'. Under this, in many states in India, students are admitted to engineering colleges with 35% as the minimum marks. Those who have low percentage but enough money get seats. Hardly any of these colleges have even adequate loan or scholarship schemes for their needy students. One does not hear anyone complaining against the seats going to non-merit candidates under **the realm of back door reservation**. In fact, there is such an oversupply position in these seat selling in so called self finance educational institutions that despite the low eligibility marks, thousands of seats go vacant every year. More elaboration on this is available in Part II, Chapter 11, Section C on **'Reservation in Self Finance Education System.'** of this book.

And lastly, 85 per cent reservation of all educational admission seats in Government run educational institutes are reserved for natives, those who are domiciled in that state. There are certain political parties advocating going for bringing language based reservation in such educational admissions. And yet almost none in India thinks of this system as unfair or discriminatory and as undermining merit in the society.

Reservation: A Charity or a Parity?

Task of implementation of reservation which was taken as a national spirit in the beginning in fulfillment of bringing about social assimilation as early as possible, has of late been regarded now as a charity i.e. an obliging act on these people. Reservation is never a charity to these people. It is a national necessity for ensuring equitable and invincible development of the nation. It is an exonerating compensation of the past wrongs done to these communities. It aims at putting them to a parity level.

This was a term used by the Justice Chenappa Reddy in the Supreme Court case of *Akhil Bharatiya Shoshit Karmachari Sangh, Karnataka.* He said, "The backward classes are in search of aid. They need facility; they need launching; they need populism; their needs are their demands; the demands are matter of right and not of philanthrope they ask for parity; not charity." He further added; "Therefore, we see that when posts whether at the stage of initial appointment or at the stage of promotion are reserved or other preferential treatment is accorded to the members of the scheduled castes and the scheduled tribes and other socially and economically backward classes, it is not a concession or privilege extended to them; it is in recognition of their undoubted fundamental right to equality of opportunity and in discharge of the constitutional obligation imposed upon the State to secure to all its citizens 'Justice'—social, economical and political—and quality of status and opportunity to assure the dignity of the individual among all citizens, to promote with special care the educational and economic interests of the weaker sections of the people to ensure their share in the power and participation on equal basis in the administration of the country and generally to foster the ideal of a **"Sovereign, Socialist, Secular Democratic Republic."**

Reservation is not a charity but a parity. It is not a charity since it is a compensation of the age-old injustice made to these communities. It is a parity because it is an effort to bring the unequal to a desired level with the equal and thereby making all as equals.

Reverse Discrimination or Preferential Treatment

This terminology connotes that reservation, which works as a protection to the reserved categories i.e. scheduled castes, scheduled tribes and other backward classes, acts as a reverse discrimination against the upper castes. It is argued that a seat which should have otherwise gone to upper caste person with the same merit goes to a reserved category person. This is nothing but reverse discrimination and is unjust and irrational. It may sound so in isolation. But it has to be examined in totality viz.

First, Reservation is a small quota of the whole lot i.e. the remainder portion is a reverse reservation for the higher castes, which is operated on the same line and norms amongst the higher caste competitors. A person fulfilling the criteria upto the last available seat will stand for a chance provided his merit comes under the bracket of available quota meant for them. *Second;* the reservation provision is one of the measures of putting an unequal giving little push with the equal with an ultimate intention of bringing about total equalities in the society. Once this is done, i.e. when a general situation of equality is established in the nation, the push by way of reservation would be no more required. *Third;* the wording like protective or reverse discrimination denotes a feeling of obligation on these deprived section. This is also not the intent under the constitution. It is a constitutional arrangement of equalizing the unequals of the society.

Reverse Discrimination: A Term Coined During Colonial Regime

The virus of discrimination is the intelligent product of British Regime. They floated this terminology with the inflammatory ill intention, the idea of discrimination as a part of their Divide and Rule Policy and launched reservation for scheduled castes and few minorities from the year 1935. The purpose of introduction of reservation by Britishers was never aimed at redressing the chronic social inequalities in the nation. Theirs was the policy of reverse discrimination in its true sense. The uproaring protests against the British Rule were catching momentum from the laymen of the nation on an enmass scale. The British rulers with an idea of diffusing the growing unrest against them from all the corners of the society, all of a sudden took the recourse of reservation for the first time for the scheduled castes and few minorities in 1935. It is surprising that they had all of a sudden started thinking for doing something for the downtroddens of the country after ruling for over a hundred of years? Provisions for the reservation in our post-independence period never intended for such reverse discrimination. The constitution aims at addressing chronic social inequalities with upbringing of those having remained behind because of the typical social conditions prevailing in the country.

Caste Matters Everywhere

The country has crossed a landmark of 100 crores population now. Such big population by itself creates huge self employment and small business type subsistence level living/earning opportunities to number of people. The so engaged people relieve the burden of present day chronic situation of unemployment to quite a good extent. To encourage such self employment type economic activities, various socio-economic upliftment schemes of training and micro finance have been introduced by the government for providing impetus to backward community youth viz. scheduled castes, scheduled tribes etc. The scheme includes vegetable vendoring, pan shops, tea hawking, and similar other consumer goods type unorganized occupations.

The new generation particularly of scheduled castes who have not experienced the suffering of core untouchability as was practised in the society few decades ago did dare to take up such occupations with assistance of the government sponsored bankable schemes with high hopes and enthusiasm. But the experience by the majority of them reveals that once the upper and middle class residents come to know about the caste origin of such hawker or vendor, they switch over to somewhere else There are instances, where a family in the present day unemployment situation plans out for their kin putting all their super annuations at stake for a small business enterprise and start a new business shop. As narrated earlier, barcade of acceptability of a lower caste person in business and dogmatic casteism leads to failure of such ambitious venture and compels the entrepreneur subsequently for winding up of the ventures.

One will not readily believe this acrimonious reality in the present 21st century. But it is a matter of one's own self assessment on the spot any where in six lacs villages and small towns of this vast and varied country rather than arriving at some conclusion out of a four wall academic debate. Small business entrepreneurship by a lower caste is still a tough task in the caste ridden Indian society. Had this been possible, a sole pressure on reservational jobs as the only source of their livelihood would have not have persisted, which would have also in turn led to desired emancipation of these oppressed in the right direction.

Limitations of Reservation System

Reservation has always been under attacks from many corners in wake of certain inherent limitations of the system. Utility of reservation system is restricted only to those handful people of the reserved categories i.e. scheduled castes, scheduled tribes and other backward classes who have persued study at least upto HSC, so as to be eligible for applying for the job supposedly reserved for them. For a poor student belonging to these categories, government scholarships do not suffice to peruse/complete the study because of the pitiful condition of the family. Because of this hard reality, school droppage ratio among these communities tends to be alarmingly at a very high score. There are thousands of families belonging to these categories, living almost in a condition of starvation. Their priority obviously remains just meeting two ends every day in and day out. Thus inability of these communities to acquire minimum educational requirement keeps them away to avail of the reservational benefits and thereby to come out from vicious cycle of social and economic backwardness. Moreover, the whole cluster of these communities remain cut off from minimum awareness of availing advantage under reservation and other socio economic upliftment programmes launched by the government, hence, provisions of reservation for these unfortunate families are still beyond reach.

Those who oppose the policy of reservation operate primarily with the argument. Perception of 'victimhood' and creation of democratically undesirable identity politics. Another limitation of reservation is that it has led in creation of inequalities within the specified communities, which allow a ' creamy layer' to take advantage of the reservations and benefit unduly while depriving fellows of their own community. Aspects of 'creamy layer are discussed in Part II, Chapter 10 on **'Creamy Layer'.**

Another limitation of reservation system is its rigid and inflexible nature. The instrument of reservation does not allow for more creative modes of affirmative action and hence tends to privileging of some caste-based discrimination while ignoring others and possibly more undesirable forms of exclusion. And lastly, reservation compresses the notion of social justice into just job quota, instead of encompassing broader socio economic policies such as land reforms and other asset redistribution and strategies of income generation so as really to bring the depressed classes at par with other general mass. Such possible alternatives are suggested in Part IV Chapter 20 on 'Beyond a Reservation Percentage'.

Reservations are applicable in case of recruitments in Government sector only. Fresh recruitment in the government has now come to a saturation level and existing jobs at this front are also dismantling because of multiple factors. Therefore, present reservation policy is becoming redundant day by day in view of marginalizing scope of recruitment where reservation can come to the help of its beneficiaries. More details on this aspect of limitation of reservation are available in Part II at Chapter 11, Section C on' **Reservation in Private Sector.'**

And finally, reservation as a policy of positive discrimination should have been exceptional and self-destructive. Originally, earlier reservations were provided only to the untouchables and hence it was exceptional. Subsequently, reservation tended becoming pervasive. While the element of self-destructiveness was not expressly provided, it was implicit. If society ceased to discriminate against *Dalits*, reservation could be abolished. Unfortunately, this vision or philosophy was not properly documented. Reservation therefore is viewed merely as one of the administrative measures of social justice. Apart from the considerations of electoral politics, reservation came handy for diverting attention of people from the deepening unemployment and under employment problem associated with the liberalization policies after 1991, when the policy thrust of globalization tended to severely diminish the reservation pie itself, there is spurt in demands for a larger share of this pie. There are pending demands from backward Muslims, *Dalit* Christians and now political parties have also echoed inclusion of economically poor of the upper castes. It is inconceivable how on earth anyone could devise system to accommodate growing claims of communities for reservations unless of course the entire pie is summarily distributed to all the castes and communities in the proportion, as they are constituted in the total population. Impracticable as this intrinsically is, such a system, instead of solving the problem, will further aggravate it because enlarged domain of reservation would generate as many claims and counterclaims. Ignoring the differential resource base of castes, to institute pervasive reservations for them would itself negate the concept of social justicc, which the entire exercise is seeking to achieve. A system pervasive reservation in any case would be meaningless.

Notwithstanding a few limitations, the reservation has contributed in bringing about a desired social change in the country needing of course its uninterrupted continuance with some modifications so as to refit its suitability to more needy and deserving downtroddens.

Initial Reservations and Subsequent Inclusions

The issue of reservation has to be understood in the broader perspective of the noble aim and objective behind it. Reservation initially launched and its subsequent expansion horizontally and vertically has created such a mess that at times it has evoked lot of misunderstandings and ill feelings about it. Implementation of reservation has two facets as under:

1. Initial reservations arising out of centuries old social discrimination and caste inequalities in the country. Beneficiaries under this, covers communities considered untouchables since time immemorial and now known as scheduled castes (SCs) and those tribes having remained away from the main stream society and now identified as scheduled tribes (STs).

The object of the framers of the constitution was to wipe out the cancer of casteism from Hindu Society. Hence, upon independence, task of attaining social equalities was the matter of great concern and top most priority in the minds of the framers of the constitution and also those who were entrusted with the reign of the nation for governance through democratic system This led to the idea of reservation for the scheduled castes and scheduled tribes right from the beginning of the constitution. Idea behind this initially implemented reservation was towards upbringing of those who were socially deprived, discarded from the main stream and considered untouchables by the rest of the upper caste society. Their social backwardness put them to a miserable economic backwardness too.

Scheduled Castes

The scheduled caste category comprises of those groups isolated and disadvantaged by their untouchability i.e. their lowest status in the traditional Hindu caste hierarchy. Criteria for inclusion of communities under 'Scheduled Castes' was primarily untouchability measured by the incidence of disabilities in economic, occupational, educational, residential and religious tests. More detail on SCs is incorporated in the later chapters of the book.

Scheduled Tribes

People under Scheduled Tribe though were not subject to untouchability and social hatred unlike scheduled castes, there socio-economic condition was abymissal and pathetic deserving protective discrimination for their assimilation in the general stream society. Common criteria for inclusion of tribes under this category were their tribal origin and characteristic, primitive traits and way of life, remote habitation and geographic isolation. Categorisation of scheduled tribes also differs from scheduled castes in that no religious test has been specified in respect of scheduled tribe unlike that in case of scheduled castes.

Reservation meant for scheduled tribes are also distinct from that of scheduled castes not only in their scope but also in their intent. In case of reservation meant for scheduled castes, it is hoped that disabilities and disadvantages that separate these communities from their counterparts will be overcome by the preferential treatment. i.e. aim of the reservation policy is to eliminate their distinctiveness by dispelling all of the differences that set them apart from rest of the society. The aim of reservation policy meant for scheduled tribes is to bring improvement in their condition and a degree of assimilation with preservation of their distinctiveness and a measure of autonomy.

There is no much of dispute so far reservation for these groups is concerned in view of the fact that still more time is required for eradication of this thousand years' old social problem.

2. Subsequent additions arising out of economic backwardness backed by political considerations. (OBCs).

With passage of time, after independence, a need was later on felt that there is still one more sabotaged fraction of the society living in a forlorn condition needing to be included under the existing scheme of positive discrimination. This fraction includes those other castes, which were not untouchables and socially discarded castes. But their living conditions have been almost at par or sometimes worse than scheduled castes and scheduled tribes. The predicament of these people collectively known as other backward castes (OBC) or socially and economically backward class (SEBC) is attributed with their educational backwardness and followed with it, their economic backwardness. A need for reservation was considered necessary for them too similar in line with initial reservation provided for the scheduled castes and scheduled tribes with some modifications and aberrations.

There were political considerations also behind inclusion of other backward castes (OBC) under the umbrella of reservation. Though pattern of reservation for both these categories is same; the idea behind each of this reservation was thus altogether different.

Reservation for OBCs started being implementation of Mandal Commission recommendations in nineties. This reservation policy is under constant attacks and controversies right from the beginning and still has not come out as having settled in its final shape.

Reservation for OBC is separately discussed at length under Chapter No. 6 on **'OBC Reservation'.**

To sum up, OBC reservation has to be understood in socio-economic perspective free from all political considerations, it is surrounded with. A thin line of difference between OBC reservation and SC/ST reservation has also to be clearly drawn to obviate a common misunderstanding prevailing due to inter mixing of the two.

REFERENCES

Marc Galenter, *Competing Equalities*, 1983, p. 3.

Jawaharlal Nehru Addressing Congress Parliamentary Party on 2nd November, 1954, p. 5.

2

Reservation: Aspirations and Achievements

The provisions of reservation are almost completing sixty years of its implementation. Therefore, it is the high time for its evaluation with a view to examining whether it has accomplished the goal set at the time of adoption of the constitution which was primarily economic justice and social equalities. Provisions for reservation include admission in educational institutions and government/public sector recruitments and electoral as well. One practical difficulty in evaluation of impact of reservation or any other such stigmatic social dynamics, there is a lack of adequate, authentic and reliable studies or surveys. Though we have world's most sophisticated statistical system i.e. census, we have been strangely reluctant to include social parameters. The probable reason for lack of such studies could be that though we very much wish to have a casteless society, we do not accept the ground reality of the day that caste system still exists in the society. There are however, some sources of secondary data. Based on such data, evaluation of impact of reservation has been made.

First, let us see the change that has been achieved with the help of providing reservation in admission in educational institutions.

Education

Education is the backbone in the development of any society. Education and coming therefrom skill development and know how are the 21st century dividends which people will leverage to raise themselves out of poverty and climb the human capital ladder. The nation having remained under the slavery regime of British rule, education and economic development were the most neglected areas by these alien rulers during their all those black days of long hundred and fifty years' ruling over the nation. Literacy at the independence was much below 20 per cent. Hence a boost was given after independence for enhancement in overall literacy and also for qualitative development of education, education was one of the thrust area under the post-independence economic planning. All this started being seen in overall literacy rate steadily going up from sixties. As per the available literacy data, while the overall literacy rate has gone up from 23 per cent in 1961, to nearly 65 per cent, in 2001. Thus, 40 per cent growth in forty years all along lot many constraints is not a small achievement.

As regards educational development in general, we had 50 Universities in 1950, now the number is 327. Number of colleges also went up from 500 in 1950 to about 18,000. Added to this, are about 50 research institutes and 8/10 Management Institutes of international repute. Thus there has been a marked development of education quantitatively as well qualitatively in the country.[1]

However, in spite of all this, there is still required much to be done. As per Government of India, HRD survey of 2005, 19.4 crores children of the age group 6-14 years are not attending the school of whom as much 68.3 per cent have not been at all enrolled for primary education and rest took drop before standard four. Of this 19.4 crores illiterates or near to alliterates, highest are from Muslim communities, next to it from scheduled castes (SC), followed by other backward classes (OBC), and at the bottom, scheduled tribes (ST).

As regard, literacy rate in respect of scheduled castes, it has undoubtedly recorded phenomenal swing from mere 10.27 per cent in 1961, to 54.69 per cent in 2001. i.e. four times growth in 40 years! This reveals that the position of literacy in respect of scheduled castes has definitely improved phenomenally because of overall educational facilities set up in the country and special thrust through reservational priorities accorded to these groups. Data in respect of other categories i.e. scheduled tribes and other backward classes have not been available. However, it is gathered that literacy rate in case of scheduled tribes is still as low as 28.8 per cent, the lowest among all the categories in the country. And still more perturbing part in case of the tribals is shockingly high drop out rate of 62.5 per cent.

As per the national university of educational planning and administration survey for the year 2005/2006, it is reported that there are 32,000 schools in the country without a single student in these schools. While, on the other hand, there are 23,000 other schools without having a single teacher in these schools. There are other 30,000 schools having average student strength of 100 to 500 students manned by a single teacher. And budgetary allocation for the 11th Five Year Plan for handling all this mess is 18.2 per cent i.e. Rs. 269 thousand crores of rupees!

Impact of reservation in education can also be judged from post-graduate scholarship benefits availed by SC/ST under various five year plans. Number of beneficiaries availing post-metric scholarship during first year plan were 37,077 SCs and 8,494 STs which gradually recorded consistent upward rise with number of beneficiaries during Ninth Plan (1997/2002) in case of SCs at 21 lacs in number and Rs. 457.29 crores in amount and STs at 5.31 lacs in number and Rs. 176.56 crores in amount. Impact of reservation in higher education, institutes of international fame like IIT/IIM, specific impact on caste bases social inequalities, impact of hostel facilities, impact of reservation on girl education etc. could not be drawn upon in absence of such studies/surveys etc.

Employment

Reservation in employment in government and public sector is one of the important provisions under the Indian constitution. A fixed percentage of jobs for scheduled castes and scheduled tribes in proportion to their population is provided in government jobs. Reservational coverage in job quota in central government and public sector employments is 15 per cent in case of scheduled castes, 7.50 per cent in case of scheduled tribes and 27 per cent for other backward classes. Tables 2.1 and 2.2 show comparative position in respect of employment with the central government services only and do not include the corresponding figures relating to employment in the State Governments and Public Sector Undertakings.

Table 2.1: Employment Position :1953 (Central Government Services)

Group	*Total Strength*	*SCs In figure*	*SCs In %*	*STs In figure*	*STs In %*
A Class I services	5,751	20	0.35	6	0.10
B Class II services	8,756	113	1.29	21	0.24
C Clerical posts	5,49.300	24,828	4.52	N.A	—
D Subordinate posts	7,89,027	1,31,504	16.6	N.A	—
Total	13,52,834	1,56,465	11.56	—	—

Source: National Commission for Scheduled Castes Report, 2004.[2]

The above employment statistics as at the beginning of the implementation of reservation reveals the negligible presence of scheduled castes and scheduled tribe communities. The country had a negligible number of 26 officers from the reserved categories; i.e. just 20 belonging to scheduled castes and 6 to scheduled tribes in class I services in whole of the nation in 1953. Their presence in lower level clerical services was also less than 5 per cent, which by itself specifically reveals educational condition of these people. Utterly poor presence of scheduled castes and scheduled tribes in the government sector in absence of reservation reveals their abymissal literacy for being eligible for such jobs besides denial to them for such opportunities due to grave social inequalities.

Position however in respect of subordinated services such as peon work, sweeping, scavenging etc. their presence is as much as 16.66 per cent i.e. more than presently stipulated reservation percentage in respect of scheduled castes. In other words, lower rungs positions were left open exclusively for them in view of the polluting work attached with these jobs.

Table 2.2: Employment Position: 2004 (Central Government Services)

Group	*Total*	*SCs*		*STs*		*OBCs*	
	Strength	*In figure*	*In %*	*In figure*	*In %*	*In figure*	*In %*
A Class I services	80,011	9744	12.2	3,311	4.1	3,090	3.9
B Class II services	1,35,409	19,602	14.5	6,274	4.6	3,123	2.3
C Clerical posts	20,40,970	3,44,865	16.9	1,36,630	6.7	1,06,309	5.2
D Subordinate posts	8,02,116	1,47,212	18.4	53,776	6.7	26,158	3.3
Sub Total (Excluding Sweepers)	30,58,506	5,21,423	17.05	1,99,991	6.54	1,38,680	4.53
Sweepers	91,601	59,320	64.76	5,368	5.86	3,340	3.65
Total	31,50,107	5,80,743	18.44	2,05,359	6.52	1,42,020	4.51

Source: National Commission for Scheduled Castes Report, 2004.[3]

Implementation of reservation in these services enhanced the strength of SC/ST officers to 12,834 in 2004. One cannot deny the fact that this miracle of 500 times increase of scheduled castes and scheduled tribes in government class I services during the sixty years would not have taken place but for the constitutional provisions implemented after independence. Moreover, these are all higher cadre services directly connected with the state governance. Presence of SCs and STs in these services is a real empowerment of those deprived of such opportunities in past and kept deliberately away from such sharing of power.

The above figures also reveal that representation of scheduled castes and scheduled tribes in class I services in the government is 12.2 per cent and 4.1 per cent respectively aggregating to 16.3 per cent. Stipulated percent of reservation in Central Government Services is 15 per cent for SC and 7.50 per cent for ST i.e. total 22.5 per cent. Thus, there is a marked shortfall of 6.2 per cent in the required representation of SC/ST in these services.

Representation in Class III and Class IV services

There is a substantial rise in number of employees in clerical cadre during post-independence era all around. Since reservation was very much implemented in these services right from beginning, sizeable strength of SC/ST candidates could get in these services over a period of time which is very well reflected in Tables 2.1 and 2.2. They were just less than 25,000 in 1953. With implementation of reservation, their number sizeably rose to approximately 3.50 lacs SCs, 1.40 lacs STs and over one lac OBCs which is by itself a big achievement.

Induction of such large number of SC/ST people in government jobs has multiplying impact in the upward social mobility of backwards. Reservation not only uplifts them educationally and economically, but also culturally which is the strongest factor leading towards establishing social equalities being one of the twin goals behind the provisions of reservation.

As regard Group D services, i.e. class IV employment in central government services was 1.32 lacs in 1953 which rose to 2.06 lacs in 2004. It is pertinent to note that though the number grew phenomenally, percentage representation particularly of scheduled castes therein remained *status quo* at 18 per cent in these services. The reason is that a big chunk of people under these services are engaged in manual scavenging and similar other cleaning work which none other than lowest placed SC people would perform. In other words, there was already an unwritten reservation in these lowest cadre posts even before constitutional intervention. More than two-thirds of the total manpower in the sweepers' category i.e. in unclean occupations comes from the lowest among the scheduled castes. This substantiates Dr. Ambedkar's economic theorem of voluntary unemployment i.e. an upper caste person even in his jobless position would prefer to remain unemployed rather than accepting employment in a lower rung position since such work is socially perceived as demeaning.

In short, the reservation has been bunched at the bottom and the very top of the spectrum remains still unfilled and the range of posts exempt from reservation quota have remained high. Dismal picture at the higher spectrum, it is less due to lack of qualifications and more to administrative indifferences/ hostility. Marc Galanter states[4], "Between 1963 and 1966, when quota-based promotion was virtually abandoned, not a single SC/ST candidate was promoted on the basis of departmental exams or ad hoc selections."

Table 2.3: SC/ST Representation in Civil Services

Group	*IAS*		*IPS*		*IFS*		*Total*	
	In figure	*In %*	*In figure*	*In %*	*In figure*	*In %*	*In figure*	*In %*
Scheduled castes	548	10.60	405	12.40	295	11.50	1,251	10.98
Scheduled tribes	261	4.72	229	6.93	179	7.00	669	5.88
Others	4,710	84.68	2,664	80.67	2,083	81.50	9,457	83.14
Total	5519		3,301		2,557		11,377	

Source: 10th Five Year Plan 2002/2007 Volume I, Sectoral Policies and Programmes, Planning Commission, Government of India[5].

Indian Civil services comprise of bureaucrats managing the overall upper administration of the country. Representation of backward class communities in these services means real sharing of governance power.

Representation of scheduled castes in Civil Services is about 11 per cent as against stipulated percentage of 15 per cent. While the same in case of scheduled tribe is approximately 6 per cent against required percentage of 7.50 per cent. It means all the reserved posts for these categories are not filled in. Representation of unreserved category still remains at about 85 per cent notwithstanding the hue and cry that half of the seats in the Government are earmarked for the reserved category people.

In this regard, observations made in Supreme Court Case *Indra Sahney vs Union of India* (1992) are worth notable;

"The adequacy of representation in administration is further to be determined on the basis of representation at all levels or in all posts in the administration. It is not only a question of numerical strength in the administration as a whole. It may happen that at the higher level, there may be more representation for a class than at a lower level in terms of population ratio. This mostly happens with all the advanced classes. In that case, it cannot be said that the class in question is not represented adequately merely because the total representation is not numerically in proportion to the population ratio. On the other hand, it may happen, as it does so far as the representation of the backward classes is concerned at the lower rungs, they may be represented adequately or more than adequately. Yet at the higher rungs, their presence may be next to nil. In such cases, again, it cannot be said that the class is represented adequately. **To satisfy the test of adequacy, therefore, what is necessary is an effective representation or effective voice in the administration** and **so much the numerical presence.** It is instructive to note in this connection that Article 16(4) speaks of '**Adequate**' and **not proportionate representation**. The practical question therefore is of the manner in which the adequate representation should be secured.

Backlog of Vacancies Under Reservation

Data in respect of backlog in various Government services are not available. As can be seen from the above tables, there is a backlog of 13,000 vacancies in class I and II services and about 500 in Civil services alone. If added to this, similar backlog prevailing in all twenty five State Governments, various Central and State Government owned public undertakings, financial institutions like nationalized banks etc. backlog is likely to be of order over a lac in number.

Huge backlog of SC/ST vacancies in Government jobs on the one hand and vast army of unemployed SC/ST on the other hand, are contradicting each other. There were days when argument that 'Candidates are not available' and now the contention put forth is 'Candidates are not suitable' which is difficult to digest at least in case of non-technical generalized posts. Major chunk of backlog is in respect of ST candidates which is yet a matter of more concern. Implementation of reservation for OBC category has of late commenced. Comparative data relating to OBCs are not available, hence the above observation are only in respect of the scheduled castes and the scheduled tribes.

Similarly, on education front, as per University Grants Commission Report, out of total teaching staff of 3.42 lacs persons in the Country's 256 Universities and 11,000 Colleges, representation of academicians belonging to scheduled castes and scheduled tribes is just 2 per cent with a clear backlog of 75,000 positions to be filled from these reserved categories.[6]

However, the picture is not totally abysmal. The position has been gradually improving which can be seen from the 1953 and the present position. Civil services in the country are the most prestigious services and the ultimate dream of any career conscious youngster. The nation's entire bureaucracy who manages the execution of the decisions taken at the respective highest houses of the peoples' representatives and other surrounding administration of the nation comes through the mechanism of civil services. Since these services are also subject to observing the reservation provisions, ever increasing representation of SC/ST/OBC in these services gives an idea regarding implementation of reservation at the highest level of power and decision-making.

As regards employment in unorganized, private and rural sector, data showing employment representation of the reserved categories viz. scheduled castes, scheduled tribes and other backward classes are not available and hence remains out of comment or comparison. But it is supposed to be very microscopically negligible in view of the typical social structure of the Indian society.

Manual Scavenging where 100 per cent Reservation Prevails Since Centuries

Manual scavenging is rooted in caste as surely as caste is rooted in the nation's psyche. Government of India, Ministry of Social Justice and Empowerment admitted in the year 2002/03[7] the existence of about 6.76 lacs poor scavengers who manually lift the human excretions. (*Front Line* 29 December, 2006)[8] The country has shameful presence of 92 lacs dry latrines spread across 21 States and Union Territories, which requires manual cleaning by the scavengers. **Employment of Manual Scavengers and Construction of Dry Latrine (Prohibition) Act** came into operation long back from the year **1993**, with an object of totally removing inhuman work of manual scavenging from the country. The Act also stipulates vigorous imprisonment upto a year and a fine of Rs. 2,000 or both on those employing manual scavengers for cleaning work of dry latrines. Few voluntary organizations surveyed the actual position recently and filed a petition in the Supreme Court. It took three years that too after strong admonishments from the apex court for the States to respond. Surprisingly, most of them filed an affidavit that no dry latrine exists in their state and therefore no manual scavenger exists. Every body would admit that this is next to impossible. The core issue here is not of identifying the correct position but the attitude and perception to such an inhuman work, which needs to be banned forthwith. The attitude and perception is also reflected from another fact that after passing of the Act way back in 1993, it took another decade for some states to adopt it. Some states refused to adopt the law saying that they don't have any manual scavengers, despite evidence to the contrary; while some states adopted it only after Supreme Court intervention.

The work of these scavengers are carrying out is really horrible. They clean gutters, septic tanks and deep manholes. Septic tanks by itself are health hazards. Sewage and storm water often get mixed and effluents flow into the rivers. Open gutters are yet another menace, making the whole of this population working therein vulnerable to malaria, dengue, gastroenteritis, hepatitis and many other diseases.

Indian Railways is yet another big employer of manual scavengers. Position of scavengers engaged with the Indian Railways is still worst, since the coaches have open discharge system leaving the railway tracks horribly soiled. The Railways which boasts to be the most professionally and profitably managed organization submitted its inability before the Supreme Court to complete a system which would allow waste to be washed away with jets of water which would obviate manual scavenging. *'New Internationalist'* an UK based magazine in its publication of July 2005 notes on Chennai Railway Station as under:[9]

'It has a spot for laptops to download mail, mobile phone chargers, chocolate mousse and chow mein next to hot dossa. Yet, a few meters away, sweeper women clean chit in the most primitive manner possible, lifting it out of railway track with a stick, broom and piece of tin. Why does this unacceptable, utterly obscene dichotomy exist? Because hardly any one wants to change'.

Similarly Indian Army also continues engaging manual scavengers for such cleaning work instead of switching over to some modern alternative. Lacs of institutions of local and self Government authorities too pull on with the same manual scavenging never thinking even on humanitarian considerations and still have manual scavengers on their rolls and continue to employ them perhaps which reflects the extent of institutionalization of the practice and of course the stigmatic mind set.

Displacements of Scheduled Tribes

Of late, the governmental policies also tend to result in dispossession and displacement of the tribals. Scheduled tribe population is traditionally concentrated in India's dense forests, many of fast flowing rivers and on top of the richest mineral resources. Once characterized as closeness of these people with the nature's bountiness which also provided them the means of subsistence and survival has become the target in the name of economic and industrial development. The result is that these poor tribals have to make a way for commercial forestry, large dams, industrial township, SEZ and mines etc.

F.M.Foster in his preface to the famous Novel *'Untouchable'* authored by Mulkraj Anand writes,[10] "The sweeper is worse off than a slave, for the slave may change his master and his duties and may become free, but the sweeper is bound forever, born into a state from which he cannot escape and where he is excluded from social intercourse and consolations of his religions." Excreta avoidance is ritualized, the caste Hindu society not surprisingly, found out its solution in the polluted castes.

REFERENCES

1. www.india.seminar
2. National Commission for Scheduled Castes Report 2004.
3. *Ibid.*
4. Marc Galenter, *Competing Equalities*, 1983.
5. 10th Five-year plan 2002/07 Vol. II Sectoral Policies and Programmes Government of India.
6. *Advocacy Internet* Nov/Dec 2005.
7. Government of India Ministry of Social Justice and Empowerment Report 2002/03 on Manual Scavengers.
8. *Front Line* 29 Dec 2006.
9. New Internationalist publication of July 2005.
10. M. Foster in Preface of *'Untouchable'* by Mulkraj Anand.

3

Stigma of Casteism

A question is often raised as to how long shall this reservation continue? Is sixty years' time of having provided reservation not enough for the upliftment of any targeted group? Will a permanent reservation system not create a vested interest in its beneficiaries and simultaneously a feeling of heart burning on the other side? All these questions are obvious. A common answer to all these queries and confusions lies in a counter question i.e.

Has the stigma of casteism disappeared from the Society?

Answer to this can be had from the very society itself. While ascertaining the obtaining position, one will have to keep in mind the objective behind providing reservation support to the scheduled castes, scheduled tribes and subsequent inclusion of other backward classes. It is experienced at large that social inequalities still continue may somewhere be in its chronic form or somewhere else in its moderate form or somewhere in its new designs and modes. But inequalities are prevailing in the society notwithstanding that every body collectively feel a dire need to establish a harmonious society.

This felt need in the minds of framers of the constitution necessitated providing a statutory support to those who were required to be brought at par with others so as to establish social equality. In absence of such support in the past and the continued discriminatory situations in the country with no sign of any marked improvement in the society before independence, state intervention by way of providing some support like reservation was felt necessary. In other words, this support aimed in the direction towards establishing social equalities. Once this objective is achieved, i.e. social equalities are attained to a satisfactory level; reservations has to have an end. So one has to inquire, whether social equalities are established to a desirable level? For this, one has to examine the present situation now in the society after sixty years with regard to existence of caste consciousness, caste stigma, and other forms of social degradations and so on.

Unique Indian Caste System

National Geography is a world known periodical. The Journal carried out an exhaustive study about Indian caste system moving through out the whole nation before about four years. A gist of their detailed report appeared in their Publication of June 2003 is reproduced which speaks out the real position of caste layers, untouchability etc.

"To be born a Hindu in India is to enter the caste system, one of the world's longest surviving forms of social stratification. Embedded in Indian culture for the past 1,500 years, the caste system follows a basic precept: All men are created unequal. The ranks in Hindu society come from a legend in which the main groupings, or *varnas,* emerge from a primordial being.

From the mouth come the Brahmans—the priests and teachers. From the arms come the Kshatriyas; the rulers and soldiers. From the thighs come the Vaisyas; merchants and traders. From the feet come the Shudras; labourers. Each *varna* in turn contains hundreds of hereditary castes and sub-castes with their own packing orders.

A fifth group describe the people who are *'achhuta'*, or untouchable, the primordial being does not claim them. Untouchables are outcastes people considered too impure, too polluted, to rank as unworthy beings. Prejudice defines their lives, particularly in the rural areas, where nearly three-quarters of India's people live. Untouchables are shunned, insulted, banned from temples and higher caste homes, made to eat and drink from separate utensils in public places and in extreme but not uncommon cases, are raped, burned, lynched, and gunned down!"

Untouchability: A Shame on Humanity

The ancient belief system that created the Untouchables overpowers modern law. While India's constitution forbids caste discrimination and specifically abolishes untouchability. Hinduism, the religion of 80 percent of India's population, governs daily life with its hierarchies and rigid social codes. Under its strictures, an Untouchable parent gives birth to an Untouchable child, condemned as unclean from the first breath.

Untouchables perform society's "**unclean work**" that involves physical contact with blood, excrement, and other bodily "defilements" as defined by Hindu law. Untouchables cremate the dead, clean latrines, cut umbilical cords, remove dead animals from the roads, tan hides, and sweep gutters. These jobs, and the status of untouchability, are passed down for generations. Even the vast numbers of Untouchables who work at "clean" jobs, mostly low-paying farm work for landlords, are also considered impure. In an outwardly free society, Untouchables are trapped at the bottom of a system that can't function without discrimination.

Many people would point out that the crudest and the most overt forms of discrimination have largely disappeared, as a result of sporadic reform movements before and after India's independence in 1947. It's true at least in the public sphere. Untouchables have made progress since the days within living memory when they were beaten if their shadow touched a higher caste person, wore bells to warn of their approach, and carried buckets so their spit wouldn't contaminate the ground. Untouchables couldn't enter schools or sit on a bench near a higher caste person.

But for all the laws and regulations on the books, the hard heart of caste remains un-moved. There are 160 million Untouchables in India; country that trumpets itself as a model for developing nations: the world's most populous democracy, a modern power outfitted with software industries, communication satellites, and plans for making nuclear energy and even nuclear bombs.

"Below the Dom exists still other castes who are the lowest of the low. Known as *Bhangis,* Pakhis, Sikkaliars, depending on the region. They are the manual scavengers. In villages and cities they cart away faeces from public latrines, clean the toilet holes of private houses, and sweep up animal droppings from streets. Non-flush latrines are banned in most states, but the law is not enforced, and municipalities openly hire scavengers, most of them women, to empty them, usually for less than a dollar a day. Even other Untouchables will not take food or drink from a manual scavenger. "[1]

The Indian social system is structured on the premises of purity and pollution. A person is put in a watertight compartment as per the caste status of the family of his/her birth. The fate of his caste so decided cannot be changed under any circumstances. He is then confined to restrict himself with a view to maintaining purity within his caste circle. There is long ladder of such *jaties* i.e. castes. Further there are various layers even within a caste compartment. The norms relating to purity to pollution will slope from upward castes down to the lower ones. Each such caste will expect that there are a few other *jaties* i.e. castes below them so as to prove their comparative higher social status.

Renown thinker and writer **Khushwant Singh** observes, "The one thing that gives lies to the Hindus otherwise justified claim that theirs is the most tolerant of all religions is its caste system which puts *Harijans,* the lowest in the scale, out of social reckoning. Over the centuries, this vicious form of apartheid has insinuated itself so deeply into the vitals of our social consciousness that escape from its shackles by converting to another faith has provided futile. Buddhism does not recognize the caste system yet caste discrimination exists among Buddhists. Islam professes to be a casteless fraternity and yet *Harijan* converts to Islam continue to be treated as Periah. The Sikh Gurus preach against caste yet Sikhs themselves admit the existence of Sikh *Harijans* with Gurudwaras of their own.

Inter marriages between the lowest castes of Buddhists, Muslims and Sikhs and higher castes are almost unknown.[2]

Dr. Ambedkar said in Constituent Assembly, "I am of the opinion that in believing that we are a nation, we are cherishing a great delusion. How can people divided into several thousands of castes be a nation? The castes are anti-national. In the first place, they bring about separation in social life. They are anti-national also because they generate jealousy and antipathy between caste and caste. We must overcome these difficulties, if we wish to become a nation in reality.[3]

Caste consciousness is so rampant and deeply rooted that it is seen in every walk of Indian Social Life. Dr. I.G. Patel world renown Economist and former Governor of Reserve Bank of India once confessed his own experience of casteism. He has while recalling his old memories admitted that when he used to visit any Brahmin's house in his small village of Gujarat, he was offered tea in a different glass because of his caste background i.e., which is considered lower than Brahmin in social order. This was the experience of a Patel, a caste which not only ranks at the upper ladder of the social hierarchy, but also the fact that the casteism did not spare even a world renown personality for whom the whole nation can take proud!

V.T. Rajshekhar, in his book *'Merit My Foot'* writes, "If one has to see man's inhumanity to man in its most naked form, he must come to India, the original home of racism and inequality."[4]

Dr. I.P. Desai Member of Rane Commission for OBC notes,[5] . . . A scholar student with a consistent good academic record in all his earlier examinations, upon repeatedly failing in his first M.B.B.S. changed his surname and appeared in the examination and to every body's surprise got through in the examination and yet more surprisingly, the same boy scored highest marks in Surgery paper of the Final M.B.B.S Examination! There are many instances of harassment to the medical students in their study simply on account of caste hatred imbibed in educated people associated with noble profession like medical.

Is Caste System Decaying?

It was envisaged that impact of modern education and industrialization will give a way in gradual decay of consciousness around the caste system. There are many people who thought and still think that the caste system will wither away with modernization, urbanization and westernization or say in its modern context liberalization, privatization and globalization. Many sociologists and theoreticians consider caste as an anachronistic feudal institution of the past relic of irrational behaviour and hoped that the all-round economic growth would bring an end to it. After the independence and adoption of democratic ruling system with adult franchise many expected that the nation will become free of the evil of casteism. However, the fact remains that the caste belied all these expectations. Caste continues to operate as effectively as in the past. Urbanization and industrialization have brought changes only in some norms of external social behaviour including notions connected with social protocols and of course observance of hardcore untouchability.

The exploitative caste system is backed by legal, religious and cultural sanctions, which enable the ruling classes and castes to continue their dominance and maintain the *status quo* in their favour. As this rigid caste system has continued for centuries, the Shudras and Ati Shutras who are theoretically expected to labour and produce surplus and serve the privileged upper castes, remain deprived of educational benefits, economic opportunities and political power. All this resulted into perpetuating their low position in the hierarchy and consequently their social and economic miseries. It is further ridiculous that the punishment rules framed under the Hindu Shastras were also not logical and uniformly even and justful for one and all. The punishment prescribed for Shudras and women were disproportionately higher than those for the upper caste errants. Though formal authority of the caste over its own members has diminished considerably after independence, the fact remains that hold of the upper castes as a whole has not weakened.

Though Political Freedom Obtained, Social Freedom Yet to be Established

Prof. Satish Deshpande of Delhi University states," Larger part of the society is still heavily invested in caste, because it is trying to climb the steep slope of inherited disadvantage and caste is the only level, it has to reduce the tilt of the playing field. These unequal and opposed parts are also mutually reinforcing in a strange way. It is as if each must weave what the other must unravel.

The first clue to how we got here is in the peculiarity of caste as an institution marked for abolition. Unlike religion or other aspects of traditional culture, there was nothing in caste that was thought to be worth preserving. Modern progressive Indians at least in public desire the annihilation of caste. However, a caste blind state refused to track the differential flow of the benefits of development. Under the cover of this high minded refusal, the upper castes preceded to encash their inherited advantages and monopolise the spheres of urban privileges particularly higher education. At the same time, attempt to mobilise lower caste identities were discredited as 'castiest'

A second clue is in the fact that 1947 was not a revolution, but a transfer of power from British to an Indian elite. What should have been a sharing of power among different social groups turned into a project of 'Nationhood building' controlled by the upper castes.[6]

Casteism Rift Became Stronger During Britishers Rule

The Britishers did not declare good-bye to India in a very happy and usual move. They divided the people on communal lines and ruled so long as they could. The tiny seeds of caste politics sown by them during the last decade of the nineteenth century had fully grown with all its poisonous and thorny branches of big gigantic communal tree by the thirties and forties of the twentieth century. To illustrate it for the first time in the census of 1891, people were enrolled on the basis of caste and caste hierarchy. In 1909, Morley Minto recognized special representation of the depressed classes, which encouraged the social movement for the formation of caste associations with an objective to demonstrate backwardness of the caste and press for preferential treatment. Communal representation was conceded by the government in favour of Muslims, Sikhs, Anglo-Indians, Indian Christians, depressed classes and ab-origines under the Government of India Act 1919. It was conceded to Muslims under the Government of India Act, 1909 and the famous 'Lucknow Pact' concluded between Congress and Muslims. This policy of British Government persued prior to 1919 led the formulations of concessions in favour of different communities.[7]

Nicholas B. Dirks, Professor of Anthropology and History and Vice President, Arts and Sciences of Columbia University, New York, during his recent visit to India has also affirmed British tactics strengthening castes stating that " caste prejudice got worse under the Colonial rule rather than better. And the reason I make that argument is that if you look at historical record, certain kinds of caste disputes became even more virulent in the 19th century under British Rule".[8]

Aloysius in his book *Nationalism without Nation*[9] has sharply pointed out the colonialists' unwillingness to address casteism. He stated that pragmatically they built upon it. Their administrative system almost exclusively appointing upper castes Brahmins to decision-making and value enforcing positions became the means by which the entire country was brought within the uniform sway of the ascriptive ideology of the old order. Worst, the British Administration by upholding caste segregation conferred a modern secular legitimacy to the sacral order. This in turn impeded social change for long hundred and fifty years. Aloysius further says, " The impact of colonialism resulted in hindrance to the social progress, economic diversification and emergence of culture-based politics and reverting back to an environment of pan Indian Brahminical, feudal consolidation. The colonial period was a hindrance to sharpening battle against caste.

The British colonists were loath to take on the caste system. The book *'Cross roads'* published by Vikas Adhyayan Kendra; Mumbai states that *dalits* in Bombay-Karnataka lived like slaves and serfs. It states that the British controlled Government did nothing for example for the education of untouchables. It reports that in 1850, a *dalit* boy was refused an entry to a public school and when he petitioned against the refusal, the Government's decision indicated that it believed that to interfere with the prejudice of the ages for the sake of one or few individuals would do great damage to the cause of education.[10]

Britishers' efforts not only in exposing caste backgrounds of the people, but also questioning at prevailing social treatments with an ulterior motive of creating a hatred towards each other be judged from the questionnaire prepared for the 1911 Census. The said questionnaire pointedly included whether the caste or group receives Mantra from a Brahmin or other recognized Hindu Guru, served by good Brahmins as family priests, is allowed an access to the interior of ordinary Hindu Temples, does he cause pollution by touch, buries its deads like most of other upper caste Hindus etc.

Inclusion of such questions in the questionnaire prepared to enumerate the castes and tribes for the Census purpose, is nothing but an attempt by the British rule to make the people more and more conscious about their caste, social status etc. No doubt it also enumerates synopsis of bitter caste gradations and the pitiable condition of the people put at the bottom level of the social order known as Shudras or untouchables.

Hinduism advocates inequalities in principle as well as practice. There was a host system in professing caste occupations. Under this system, a barber will carry out hair cutting services to the whole village without any charges. The other communities will in turn compensate with food grains and whatever they produce in that village economy. Such hosts will be additionally gratified during festivals, marriage occasions of the respective families and so on. Same will be the case for other service providers i.e. blacksmiths, weavers, scavengers, etc.

Caste Identity Goes All Along

This has undergone a change. This host system is replaced by contract system. i.e. barber will provide hair cutting service recovering his price for the respective service as per the prevailing rate. Is he recognized as a business community or a shopkeeper or a self-employed entrepreneur or still a low caste barber only? The fact is that he is still known or identified as a low caste barber only and not as a businessman irrespective of his income status, higher middle class standard of living and so on. Of course, he will be getting social protocol being called respectfully in the time of modern mannerism and social protocol. The position will also not change irrespective of his status as a self-employed barber, salaried barber, daily wager barber, or a contract based barber.

Occupational transformation that has taken place in all the social layers has hardly changed their social status. A person belonging to the Valmiki, a community considered lowest in the caste hierarchy, continues to be identified with his caste even after joining a government job. A latrine cleaning person would be seen in the society as per his occupation only. Degree of respecting or regarding a person in Indian ethos is never with human values or human dignity but with the work he is professing. Similarly, if he is a leather tanning businessman or sanitary mart owner, but belonging to a lower caste, the people's perception will be based on the caste, he is belonging to and not with his achievements in his business or entrepreneurship qualities he has developed or moral values he is observing in his business. All these hardly matter once his caste is known. Similarly, position will not change in case of a sweeper, whether he is a Government employee sweeper, private sweeper, a house keeping contractor of sweeping in the new regime of privatization and so on. He will in any status be known and identified as a 'Shudra' only while it does not matter with whatever name, or abbreviations or designation he might be addressed as per the modern day courtesy protocol.

Sachar Committee on study of the condition of Indian Muslim in its recently published report has stated that one of the **Muslim communities 'Arzals'** believed to be converted from the Hindu untouchables before few hundreds of years, still continue to be identified as untouchables and suffer from social exclusion because of stigma of caste attached to their traditional occupations.[11]

Justice Venkat Ramaiyah in the matter of *State of U.P.* vs. *Pradip Tandan*[12] gave two minor reasons for taking ' classes' to mean 'castes'. For one thing, it is caste that is pervasive as well as durable in India. He quoted the 'Backward Class Commission Report' to the effect that "The Brahmin taking to tailoring does not become a tailor by caste. A Brahmin may be a seller of shoes and yet his status is not lowered thereby." Surely, the answer to the opposite question tells us as much about India today, when a person who was born into a caste that has been enumerated a scheduled caste becomes a journalist or an IT professional or a film star or a cricket player all above a caste; is he looked upon as someone from a caste or as a journalist/IT professional/film star/Cricket Star?

Social Linkages Play an Important Role in Employment

Upper castes have an edge over others in the recruitment market because of their early entry in the service sector. Figures also substantiate this fact that representation of higher castes was 97 per cent in Government class I/II services and 94 per cent in class III services in 1953. Despite well laid down criteria for recruitment, social linkages play an important role in a caste-ridden society. The upper caste candidate has an advantage of dissemination of information and culture. Caste belongingness has a clear presence in the Indian society, which proves advantageous to the upper castes. This is the reason why there is a dominance of upper castes in the public sector employment even after independence notwithstanding the application of reservation provisions during all these years.

The contrast is more striking between the poor of the upper caste and lower caste. A poor Brahmin has more contacts among elites in administration which distribute divisible and indivisible benefits and has greater say in recruitment of personnel than does the poor lower caste fellow may be a peasantry OBC caste like Koli or an SC/ST, because public as well as private sector administration is dominated by the upper and middle caste bureaucrats. As a result, the poor Brahmin has more opportunities to improve his life chances than a poor person from a lower caste with the help of his better linkage in modern sectors like education, mass media and government administration.

Shadows of Manu Smruti

In ancient days, public administration by local rulers had high influence of religion and old scriptures. The Hindu caste system has its own 'instruction manual' known as 'Manu Smruti'. Summarily, Manu Smruti is a typical code of conduct instruction manual which are irrational and inhuman as well. These rules are positively biased towards upper castes and negatively discriminating against lower castes in every respect.

The laws of Manu, compiled at least 2,000 years ago by Brahman priests, prescribes what to eat, whom to marry, how to earn money, when to fight, how to keep clean, whom to avoid. "**Manu is engraved inside every Hindu**," as confessed by Uma Shankar Tripathy, a Varanasi based Brahman priest.[13]

Manu also instructs that to touch a corpse after final death ceremonies brings great contamination. So it falls to untouchable castes, such as the Dom, to cremate the dead. And like that the Smruti encodes various rituals to be performed, various other social interaction rules to be differently followed as per the graded status of the respective caste. The Smruti also sets out punishment in case of molesting, raping, beating, injuring etc. The so framed rules again are lopsided as per caste based hierarchical placement of the erring person.

If one goes through the set rules and punishments there against, he would hardly believe the very existence of Manu Smruti in today's context, the foundation of all inhuman treatment protocol for the Shudras i.e. Lower castes and the women. These punishment protocols were so horrible that a doubt today can obviously be not out of place as to; Whether; are the kind of oppression and differentiation that these verses imply actually prevailed in practice in ancient times, What is the authenticity of Manu Smruti itself which was compiled over seven to eight hundred years and finally what is the evidence that this text was in fact being lived out in practice?

Instances of atrocities, discriminations and untouchability etc. are seen every day in media or even around wherever we live. A few out of huge number of such incidents are narrated in Chapter 4 "**Untouchability in new idioms and phrases**" to substantiate the present realities with regard to prevailing social discrimination.

If this is the bitter reality as regards social condition even after 700/800 years after Manu Smruti days, one can very well imagine the situation of those holily worshipped Manu Smruti days.

Caste Does Not Spare Modern Professions Too

The caste plays vital role in every walk of life. There is a professional course of chartered accountancy conducted by a very standard and reputed Institute of Chartered Accountants of India. One will say what this has to do with the caste discussion. Education spread amongst the scheduled castes and scheduled tribes in the second generation has gone up to a sizeable level. Many of them in commerce stream of study are keen to make a career as a chartered accountant, which is very tough and challenging as well. The process of this career is such that it would be almost impossible for a lower caste youth to fulfil his dream of being a chartered accountant. Before being eligible for entering into this very prestigious and prospectful professional course, one has to undergo articleship of about three years under some chartered accountant. This articleship provides a very wide, useful and job enriching exposure to the student besides a nominal amount of remuneration. It is experienced that getting an admission as an article for a poor student with backward class background, under a chartered accountant is almost impossible because the caste factor dominates such decisions here too. As against the large number of aspirants, there will be limited number of available admissions in articleship in the firms of the chartered accountants. Hence such limited admissions shall go in the priority such as caste belongingness or caste based recommendations, since it is the sole prerogative of the chartered accountant to consider admissions of articles in his office.

There is large number of scholars belonging to the depressed castes with extra ordinary track record during their commerce graduation. But the sheer caste background stops many of them from such bright career. On the other hand, a student with upper caste background shall have no difficulty for admission to the course. There are no empirical data showing chartered accountants from the backward castes. It must be invisible because of the very entry point hurdle faced by these deprived group chaps.

Similar is the position in the legal profession. Here, though entry as an advocate is not that difficult, caste does play a very important role. Good and all-around exposure is essential in the built up of a person for dealing in the variety of briefs as a successful advocate. A young advocate with lower castes background will not ordinarily get a shelter of a reputed upper caste advocate by all means. Whatever social inequalities and castes consciousness is prevailing in the society at large gets percolated in the compounds of the courts also. Clientele and advocate caste affinity automatically go together barring of course few famous and old established advocates with extra ordinary track record of successful results. Working under the guidance of a successful higher caste advocate makes a good advocate of the juniors. But such an opportunity to a majority of lower caste beginners would be a dream. So their practice normally will be concentrated around routine briefs such as family maintenance matters, bail cases, prohibition etc. Getting good challenging jobs for his self-exposure and having an image in the legal practice market remains far away from him. It is not that all the upper caste senior advocates are heartless having all the times caste hatred. There are exceptions of advocates having raised their strature above all this. They induct in their team such young and fresh backwards and patiently prepare them for good exposure. Gujarat High Court has a similar such senior advocate having extra ordinary career track record.

There are juniors under him belonging to such so called lower caste background and are found coming out of all usual caste ridden complexities normally found in such junior advocates. Such encouraging illustrations found here and there scattered in the society keeps the hopes alive for a harmonious society with a cross section of people working together heart to heart.

Media No Exception to Caste Stigma

Media is considered fourth pillar of the Democracy. The media plays a very prime and crucial role in the opinion formation, which in turn creates bias or sympathy or even the hatred for a particular news matter in the people. Indian media is expanding by leaps and bounds on print as well as electronic front and has been providing huge source of employment to the youth. It is seen that representation of SC/ST in media is very negligible. There are many under graduation and few post-graduation courses in Journalism, mass communications courses, now being taught in various universities. Youth belonging to backward classes do take admissions in these courses with an ambition of making a career in journalism. However, experience reveals that these young aspirants with all determination for hard work and sincerity do not get adequate opportunity in the media world. Community based representation in the Indian media is given in Table 3.1.

Table 3.1: Community-wise Media Representation

Caste Community Group	*% Share in Indian Population*	*% Share in Key Media Personnel*
Top Upper castes	16	85
Intermediary Upper castes	7	3
Hindu OBC	34	4
Muslims	13	4
Christians	4	3
Sikhs	2	1
Scheduled castes	16	NIL
Scheduled tribes	8	NIL

Source: National Census, 2001 and National Election Study 2004 by CSDS[15].

This clearly indicates that India's national media lacks social diversity; it does not reflect India's social profile. *Dalits* and *adivasis* are conspicuous by their presence among the decision makers. Not even a single of the 315 key media personnel belongs to the scheduled castes and scheduled tribes. The proportion of OBC is also abysmally low among the key decision makers in the national media; they are only 4 per cent as compared to their population of around 40 per cent in the country. Muslims' representation though low is at least marginally there as compared to no representation at all in case of *dalits* and *adivasis*. Christian's representation particularly in English media is satisfactory with about 2.3 per cent compared to their population of 4 per cent.

Commenting on total absence of representation of *dalits* and *adivasis* in media, J.P. Shukla, Lucknow based correspondent of the *Hindu* says, "There is no question of any kind of discrimination, because an educated *dalit* prefers his reserved job in government office rather than a hard life as an underpaid stringer." This is not correct. New generation of SC/ ST if tested upon would negate this false assumption. Balanced composition of peoples' representation in the media would help in bridging the society and the media in its right perspective. Therefore, it is expected of media to encourage youth aspirants from this segment. What is required to prepare these fresh lot is initially a patient perseverance by their senior colleagues till they come out with confidence on a right track which is very much essential in a mass communication career. It is possible that they may be found lacking professional mannerism and adequate command over English because of their social background.

English dailies take convent lot, which is again a question in case of poorly educated *dalits* and adivasis youths. Vivek Kumar of JNU says," This is exactly the same as in reserved jobs for backward castes. First it was,' candidate not available,' now it is 'Candidate not suitable' and who decides a candidate's suitability? "The upper caste editor".[16]

Interestingly, whenever any news or decisions relating to reservation breaks, it flares up like a fire in forest with all usual hue and cry and finally the whole anger comes upon the reservation beneficiaries i.e. scheduled castes and scheduled tribes. Caste consciousness and caste prejudices have become an integral part in the Indian society in every walk of life and people working in the media, can be no exception. Hence, it is desirable that Indian media is adequately composed of its caste based social realities.

Media Operates on Double Standards

Vivek Kumar narrates his own interesting experience of caste bias. He says," While he at *'Pioneer'* interviewed the then U.P. Governor Suraj Bhan, a *dalit* by caste having a very respectable place in Indian intellegitia. The Governor was asked questions on the position of *dalits* in society, 48 years after independence. The whole interview was full of deliberations reflecting farsighted vision and rich experience of Suraj Bhan in his long Indian public life. The interview which should have been a page one eight-column coverage, he says was reduced to two columns on page four. Some days later, the paper sent another correspondent to interview Suraj Bhan, the Governor. This time, the interview was without any **'Dalit Angle'** and its insertion in the news paper was right there on front page with eight column space".

Another glaring illustration showing double standard of Indian media is their coverage of two atrocities having taken place in the recent past. One Jesica Lal Murder and another Kheralanji raping and killing of two women. Both the incidences were a big blot on the Indian society and its much talked about civilization. The Delhi based media gave huge publicity to Jessica Lal murder and another Priyadarshini Matto case. The injustice involved in these cases was exposed by the media so effectively that the stories motivated the youth of Delhi to form a powerful movement of protest. The campaign forced the Delhi police reopen the case and sent the accused to Jail thanks to active rather over active role of media.

And how about the role of media, print as well as electronic about brutal killings of two women in Kheralanji? Initially, there was no coverage at all. When the incidence was followed by disturbances in Nagpur and Aurangabad, the media was compelled to give some insertion. Here too, speculations by the Home Minister and the police on the hidden hand behind the *dalit* protests made more headlines than the inhuman brutality of incidence itself. The press photographs echoed a brilliant golden statue of Lord Buddha looking on the flames of the violence, rather than heart throbbing pictures of the Bhotmanges' bodies cut to pieces. Even while the protests were on, there was no detailed interview with *dalit* intellectuals, protesters or leaders except to get their response to the allegations made by policemen with an intention of diverting the core issue.

What a ridiculous and discriminatory approach towards each of these incidences! While both of these were shameful incidences of atrocities on women who is respected by the Indian society nearly as a Goddess, the former drew the media attention in its right earnest, while the later one being an atrocity on *dalit* women was treated so casually without any human sensibility!

Caste Factor in Matrimonials

Marriage organization is considered to be the strongest instrument in breaking the caste barriers. It brings together not only two persons or two families together, but two different societies over a period of time. It was envisaged that with increasing education and spreading upward social mobility, more and more inter-caste marriages would take place which would augment the process of building a harmonious society. Unfortunately, this has not materialized as it should have. Strong and stigmatic caste consideration is the strongest reason for this slow momentum inter-caste marriages in Indian society.

An attempt is made to have a classification with regard to people's perception about inter-caste matrimonial propositions. For this an english daily *Times of India*, Ahmedabad edition is chosen with a view to obtaining an idea about perception prevailing in the minds of cosmopolitan, elite and upper class people. Matrimonial advertisement insertions that appeared in five Sunday editions for the month of February/March 2007 were scrutinized and summarized as under[17].

Table 3.2: Caste Significance in Matrimonial Advertisements

Year 2007	*Total Matrimonial Advertisements*			*Of which No. Where there is no Caste Barrier*		
TOI Dtd.	*Bride*	*Bridegroom*	*Total*	*Bride*	*Bridegroom*	*Total*
18th Feb.	258	338	596	42	49	91
25th Feb.	314	370	684	51	46	97
4th March	233	64	297	33	3	36
11th March	352	312	664	37	33	70
18th March	315	307	622	73	37	110
Total	1,472	1,391	2,863	236 (16%)	168 (12%)	404 (14%)

The classification clearly shows that 86 per cent people living in cosmopolitan environment, with higher economic class do not want to go out of their caste segment in matrimonial. Interestingly, many after giving caste and sub-caste, wrote at the end 'caste no bar' betraying the fact that they believe in their caste and would prefer to get a bride or groom in the same caste.

Barring a few spontaneous cases of inter-caste marriages, it is found in the Indian society that when there is no choice, they are forced to go out of the caste boundary. Many of those not indicating their caste are widows, widowers in their forties, fifties or sixties, willing for a marriage for the second time. It is the circumstances, which are forcing them to seek a partner outside their caste and not a definite attitude rising above caste walls. Perhaps, given a choice, they would also prefer to remain within the age-old caste walls.

International magazine *'New Internationalist'* in its release of July 2005 notes quoting Suman Bureau, a matrimonial agency mainly coordinating India based aspirants in UK, "People are still mentioning the issue of caste and bringing it up when it comes to marriage and generally people don't want to marry into a lower caste. We also find that those who originate from a lower caste prefer to marry someone of the same caste background because they know that they may be victimized because they are of a lower caste."[18]

This speaks how thick is the bond of caste compartalisation and caste preference. It reveals a clear lack of openness for inter-caste integration in matrimonial matters. However, suitability of a matrimonial proposal otherwise in all respects, if forthcoming from a lower caste background would in probability shall have rejection chances since caste consideration would prevail above all in Indian society. More surprisingly, this caste consciousness has not remained restricted in Indian homeland, but has remained magnificently preserved at foreign lands inhabiting the Indian origins.

Indian Society Lacks Moderation of Thinking

Anirudhh Prasad in his book '*Reservation Policies and Practices in India*' states; "The injustice caused by the upper castes people against the depressed in the past is still persisting through unofficial or unsayable implicit reservation. The protective discrimination or say official reservation breed reverse discrimination. The effect of both the official or unofficial reservation is injustice, compromise with the merit and efficiency and societal values. The former i.e. unofficial or unsayable or destructive discrimination is more dangerous because it acts behind the curtain and affects every body except the dominant group.[19]

The most disturbing trend of the Indian society is that Sanskritisation among backwards does not result into moderation of thinking. It only means the following of Brahminical taboo among sanskritised persons. Education does not bring moderation among the upper castes also. Instead of bringing the broad vision in them, education inculcates narrow mindness. The biggest castiest in India are those belonging to the most educated segment of society. **Educational Institutions in India suffer from casteist politics and political life accentuates it.**

REFERENCES

1. *National Geography*, June 2003.
2. *Hindustan Times*, 12 May 1990.
3. 10th Five-year plan 2002/07 Vol. II Sectoral Policies and Programmes Government of India.
4. V.T. Shekhar *Merit on My Foot.*
5. I.P. Desai, *Economic and Political Weekly*, 2 May 1981.
6. Prof. Satish Deshpande, Delhi University, *Times of India*, 3 May 2007.
7. Anirudh Prasad, *Reservation Policy and Practice in India.*
8. Nicholas Bird; *The Hindu* 15 Jan 2007.
9. Aloysius Nationalism without Nation.
10. David Haslam, *Caste Out Caste*, 2004.
11. Sachar Committee Report.
12. Justice Venkat Ramaiyah in the matter of *State of U.P. vs Pradip Tandan.*
13. *National Geography*, June 2003.
14. National Election Study 2004 by CSDS.
15. National Census, 2001 and National Election Study 2004 by CSDS.
16. www.india.seminar Report on Media.
17. *Times of India* dated 18th, 25th February, 4th, 11th and 18th March 2007 Ahmedabad Edition.
18. *New Internationalist* UK of July 2005.
19. Anirudh Prasad, *Reservation Policy and Practice in India'.*

4

Untouchability in New Idioms and Phrases

Incidences of untouchability, harassments and going further to atrocities in one form or the other particularly against the scheduled castes continue unabated in one part or the other unendedly. This includes physical assault, rape, murder, setting fire to houses, confiscation of property, molestation, economic exploitations and so on. Pages and pages of writing will not complete these tragic events that are taking place in the country even after progressive fifty years of independence. Here is a gist of few heart throbbing incidences which speak for themselves the bitter hard realities of caste oppressions and a variety of untouchability practices involving humiliation, subordination and exploitation prevailing in the country which substantiate the case for continuance of reservation for these oppressed classes in the country till such an inhuman psyche is not addressed and removed from the mind set of the Indian Hindu Society.

I. The Kherlanji (Maharashtra) Tragedy

Dalit massacres and mass scale *dalit* atrocities have never been so surprising in India. The Kumher massacre in Rajasthan, Tsundur in Andhra Pradesh, frightening crimes in Gohana and Jhajjar in Haryana and now Kherlanji in Maharashtra all are the painful stories of extreme forms of caste hatreds prevailing in the Hindu upper caste mind set.

Kherlanji tragedy is one of the most gruesome incidents of *dalit* atrocities that took place recently in September 2006, which witnessed brutal killings of four members of a *dalit* family consisting of mother 44, young daughter 18 and two sons 23 and 21. The heinous crime includes stripping the mother and the daughter, parading them all naked, mutilations of genitals of two brothers, gang raping and a series of wicked deeds which one cannot narrate here.

Village Kherlanji of Bhandara District in Vidarbh of Western Maharashtra has a population of about 700 people. Bhaiyalal Bhotmange a scheduled caste farmer with his five acres of irrigated land was comparatively well off in the village. Bhaiyalal's family consists of his wife, a daughter Std. XII scholar student and two sons one of whom was blind. The Bhotmange family was comparatively educationally advanced and economically better than most other upper caste agriculturists in the village. This well off condition of a backward class family was therefore the venom of social hatred and jealousy in the village Kherlanji. Bhaiyalal was already struggling to save his land since last 18 years. He was even unable to get badly required plastering of his house. He was also denied registration of his land in the village land revenue records. In fact 2 acres of his land was already taken away for construction of road in 1996. Now was the demand for remaining 3 acres of land from Powar and Kalar communities belonging to OBC for irrigation canal, which Bhaiyalal was strongly protesting since it was the only left source of bread and butter for the family. The village upper caste communities were also adamant for taking away Bhaiyalal's remaining agricultural land. Hence, quarrels between them was a routine in the village.

On 27 September, 2006, Siddharth one of the supporters of Bhaiyalal and cousin of his wife was beaten. A complaint was also filed in the Police Station and all the 12 culprits were identified. The culprits after coming out of the police custody attacked the house of Bhaiyalal on the same day evening of 29 September, 2006. Bhaiyalal escaped the attacking mob. His wife Surekha and daughter Priyanka were gang raped and then all the four family members viz. wife, daughter and two sons were made naked, taken in common meeting place of the village and then brutally killed to pieces.

What was the offence of these innocent people? It was just their daring before the village upper castes for getting back a portion of their farm, which was grabbed by the landlords.

A matter of further concern as evidenced is the indifferent and caste bias attitude of the administration, medical officer not examining the possibilities of a sexual attack on women victims though their bodies were found naked, Director General of Police avoiding to visit the spot and thereby sending wrong signals to down the police machineries and above all, the local MLA's suspicious and partial role in diluting seriousness of the whole incidence etc.

II. Sambarda, (Gujarat) : 131 days' En Mass Migration by 331 Caste Oppressed

Incidences of atrocities not necessarily have to be physically injurious, crude or blatant. More than not often, they take the form of subtle humiliation and harassment making day-to-day life of the victims quite miserable with lesser barbarities. Such victims don't always file a police complaint out of fear that the victimization would increase rather than get redressed, which in turn points to the fact that police and the elites culprits are in collusion against the oppressed.

Here is a unique incidence of enmass migration of 131 days by 331 lower caste people having been fed up of the local Gadhavis, a caste covered under OBC. The cause after the migration was not for the livelihood i.e. economic as is advocated on and often for deciding criteria for reservation which according to some thinkers should not be caste as according to them, caste oppression and discrimination has completely vanished from the Country. **The Sambarda struggle was a quest for self-respect and human dignity,** when the day in and day out harassments on the poor scheduled castes villagers came to an unbearable limit.

The incidence took place in the year 1989 in the small Village Sambarda District Banas Kantha in North Gujarat. The village is having population of 550 people consisting mainly of two communities i.e. Gadhavis and Vankars, a scheduled caste in the ratio of 45:55. These Gadhavis fall under the category of other backward class (OBCs), but they consider themselves as Kshatriyas, while the other one i.e. Vankars are included in the scheduled castes (SC). The Gadhavis are traditionally court poets and folk singers. The Vankars are traditional weavers. Except one family, none from the Vankars own any agricultural land. While all the Gadhavis own agricultural land except three. Besides, they have other sources of income through services, professional practices etc. The Vankars on the other hand started taking off in their progress after fifties with the help of reservation and other facilities from the government. Most of their forty families are having blue or white-collar jobs. In other words, their crest for education and progress put them to a well off position over a period of time. Traditional relationship before independence between the Gadhavis and the scheduled castes was that of a master-surf. Those were the days when these scheduled castes people were working as bonded labourers in the fields and establishments of Gadhavis, which has since became a past only.

Day-to-Day Humiliation and Harassments to Scheduled Castes

Harassments by Gadhavis to these Vankars in the village was a daily routine. The Vankar women were the worst victims and sufferers of these harassments. The kind of harassments includes, physical molestation, wolf whistles, name calling, overturning of water containers of the women going for the toilet etc. The *dalit* youths in the village were not expected to wear clean or modern clothes, wrist watch, dark glasses etc. A youth passing through the village was not supposed to walk around with his head held high instead of submissively down to the ground. Non obedience of this village protocol could invite physical beating on the poor chap by the Gadhavis! A Vankar guest unaware of these self-imposed Manu Smruti laws of the village was severely beaten up, besides being abused with non-parliamentary words.

The Gadhavis have taken away cattle grazing land known as Gauchar and other wasteland of the village. As a result of this, the scheduled castes were deprived of fodder for their livestock and other developmental activities such as social forestry on the wasteland. Incidentally, B.K. Gadhavi belonging to the very village was a big political heavy weight enjoying at that time Ministerial berth in the Congress led Central Government. This was also a big force behind the muscle power of the young Gadhavis on account of their close social connections with this political gun.

Outburst of Years' Accumulation of Endurance

During all such nuisance and harassments from the Gadhavis, an incidence of beating of a boy Rajnikant on 11 June 1989 took a serious turn. The Vankar families having been fed up of all this, unanimously decided to undertake collective migration. The reasons given in the memorandum submitted by the migrators to the District Collector before final walk out included the caste psyche of Gadhavis, circumstances leading to their migration, power and pelf position of Minister B.K. Gadhavi etc. A police complaint was also filed. The inspector who accepted the complaint was however transferred on the very next day. Finally the *dalits* declared that they're-planning to leave the village for an indefinite time till their harassments come to an end. This was, as usually happens, the outburst of years' harassments of the Gadhavis for no fault. All the efforts were made by the administration, police, politicians as well as leader B.K. Gadhavi himself to dissuade the protest, but the *dalits* were firm to their decision. They moved from the village with all family members including children and their households on 26 June 1989, which was incidentally, a black day of proclamation of emergency in the nation. The procession also consisted of all the female members of the migrating families, which included one woman having full term pregnancy. They all started in a procession towards District Collectorate with a very silent protest all along the way upto Palanpur, the District Headquarters and started staying in a tent on the open land till it was called off after 131 days on 3 November, 1989. These were the days of rainfall. The migrators faced lot of problems during the rainy days. They during heavy rainwater time approached the administration for some shelter, which was flately refused.

A Successful Struggle Against Caste Oppression

There were also all out efforts from Gadhavis, other upper castes, administration and the political touts. But nothing could weaken this long struggle of 131 days carried out in an utmost democratic and disciplined way. The mobilization of *dalits*, support from the other fellow *dalits* and migrants' militant will power to fight out unto the last ultimately brought justice for them after untiring hard struggle with lot many odds in the way. The issue echoed in the State Assembly where a decision of the government agreeing to all the demands of the migrants which *inter alia* includes due justice to them, action against the culprits, alternate residential plots to all the families in the neighbouring Virpur village etc. was declared.

The migrators finally started living in a new village called '**Swaman Nagar'** i.e. a town of self-respect. Yes, It was certainly a victory of self-respect and self-esteem of those who have endured to all such inhuman treatments and humiliations since historic times. But then a question arises; what got infused in them, which motivated them to revolt against a powerful and ever dominant caste, backed by a big political power having a central ministerial position? What did not shaken them to succomb against the multilateral efforts for diffusing their struggle? Which intrisic force worked to withstand them against the hatred and indifferent attitude of the administration working under pressures from the upper castes and their political masters? It was the power of unity and love for the self-esteem which they could inculcate from the education and upward mobility.

How was this possible? This is the impact of reservation which made the oppressed not only more educationally and economically advanced and self-dependent, but also revolting against caste based oppressions and harassments. Reservation made them self-sustained with the help of government jobs, which infused in them courage to agitate against the evils and wrongs.[1]

Dipankar Gupta Communist Member of Parliament has rightly said in his book *'Caste in Question: Identity or hierarchy'*. "To argue that as long as there is prejudice, there should be reservations is simply incorrect. Prejudices can never be fought with policies. Prejudices can be contained when there are proper laws that are intolerant of discrimination. But most significantly, **prejudice is best combated when its victims are strong enough to take the battle up to the victimizers in the courts of law. Unfortunately, prejudice lurks everywhere.** If some people are able to escape prejudicial and discriminating treatment against them, it is because they are strong enough to hit it back."[2]

Untouchability

The power of regime of untouchability is that it transcends the factor of economic well-being in order to derive moral authority from religion and culture. Untouchability is not just an expression of cultural prejudice or preference, but also an inevitably accepted form of exploitation and injustice that violates the fundamental right to life and livelihood of the so-called untouchables. One of the distinguishing features of untouchability is that it requires the continual reproduction of public signs proclaiming the inferiority of those marked as untouchable relative to the rest of the society.

Untouchability continues from time immemorial subjected on Ati Shudras i.e. castes put in the lowest bracket of Indian social hierarchy. These castes include all those engaged in lowest and polluted professions such as cleaning, sweeping, tanning, weaving, etc. castes covered under these Ati Shudra segments are now-a-days known as scheduled castes who were identified as 'Antyaj', i.e. backwards in ancient times. An attempt was made by Mahatma Gandhi to re-name them as *'Harijans'* i.e. people of the God which was not much acceptable to these people. Dr. Ambedkar during his social struggle for upliftment of these oppressed classes gave them a new identification i.e. *'dalit'* a more respectable word to identify these distinguished lots. The use of *dalits* here afterwards means people now known as 'scheduled castes'.

Quite a lot has been said and written about treatment of untouchability with the *'dalits'* of the country by the upper castes of the society. Right from the days of the earstwhile king Siddhraj Jaysinh of keeping sweeping instrument behind him and a pot in the front side, the Indian *dalits* have been subjected to one type of untouchability or the other. The hatred lying in the heart of a layman caste Hindu results in incidences of untouchabilities and atrocities. Untouchability though legally banned is still practised through out the country. Thousands of instances of practice of untouchability can be quoted. However, a few, which have been reported during the recent two years, are stated hereunder with a view to giving an idea about prevalence of this inhuman practice even after sixty years of independence.

Gujarat

- Dhandhuka Branch of State Bank of Saurashtra in Ahmedabad District was headed by a *dalit* Manager. On his visit to nearby village Khasta for the Bank's recovery purpose, he was taken by about ten upper castes loanees at their homes for tea. The problem with the upper caste hosts was how the poor Branch Manager be served with tea. Finally, a common plate was managed from outside for the purpose and was cleverly circulated at all the ten houses for serving tea to the poor branch manager. The tea plate was acting as a pilot before reaching of this untouchable but unavoidable guest to each of the upper caste houses.
- In Village Akru, District Ahmedabad, anaganwadi worker was *dalit*. She was entrusted with polio dosing work. It was found that most of the upper caste ladies did not turn up with their children to avoid touchability with the *dalit* worker.
- In Vejalka District Ahmedabad a *dalit* boy while watching TV at pan shop was so engrossed that he forgot to keep away from touching the shop. The TV

watching cost him so heavily that the shop owner threw calcium pan material on the boy, which injured him severely.

- A ridiculous story is other way round. In Dhandhuka shephered community ladies unknowingly drunk the water from a cart belonging to a *dalit*. Subsequently, upon coming to know about the caste of the cart owner, these ladies went to a temple to purify themselves by taking a footwear in their mouths and then drinking already drunk water by a Bharawad community person.
- In village Kadadra District Ahmedabad, the village of a senior IPS officer belonging to a *dalit* community, there was a clear case of discrimination during Hindu festival of 'Navratri'. The *dalit* ladies were not allowed to participate in Navratri Garbas, a common village dance festival. An upper caste barber also refused the *dalits* for their hair cutting. Upon insistence from the *dalits*, the barber reported that he was in past punished with compulsory shut down of his shop for a week by the village people for having cut hair of a *dalit*! Both these forms of untouchability have come to an end now after agitation by the second generation *dalit* youngsters.
- In village Rania District Kheda, the government health worker came for pouring malaria medicines in the village well. He was required to mix water in the medicine concentrate. He took the required water from a *dalit* house unknowingly which upper castes female members saw. And then, there was virtually a rainfall of abuses on the poor Government employee health worker.
- In village Nadhanpur District Kheda as is quite common, *dalit* women are prohibited from lifting water from the common village well. On 29 July 2002, a *dalit* youth agitated against this system and went to the well with his cord and pot and drew water from the village well. How can this be tolerated by the upper castes of the village? They decided to boycott the entire locality

of *dalit* Community. An upper caste person violating the boycott instructions and keeping relations with any *dalit* person or family was to be fined with Rs. 10,000. The upper caste anger did not subside with this also. These people poured inedible vegetable milk, boiled engine oil etc. in the village well so that the *dalits* cannot use the well water. The matter went upto the police station. There was a compromise later on with the District Collector's intervening role and corrective action.

- In village Kashipura District Surendranagar, the local primary school having been damaged in earth quake disaster during the year 2001 was temporarily shifted in the temple. The problem was of *dalit* students' entry polluting the temple. The school management cleverly kept the untouchable students away from temple entry by granting them special leave till the reshifting of the school to their own building.
- A community known as Dholi is the forerunner of any socio religious function in Hindu society. A social or religious procession shall have the sound of the traditional music instrument Dhol played by a lower caste person. He will be in the foremost front of the procession. However, once the procession reaches the temple, he shall be out. He cannot dream of entering the temple along with the procession for temple *Darshan* or for observing any other religious ceremony. He will be an unfortunate alien spectacular watching from outside the temple Garbh Dwar i.e. central part of the temple housing the idol of God or Goddess.
- In village Dholi District Surendranagar few years ago, there was a death of an old female member in the Valmiki family. This was the only Valmiki house in the village. The problem was carrying the dead body for the cremation. None from the village not only upper castes but other lower caste considering themselves hierarchically above the Valmikis also did not come forward for the last ritual! There was no alternative for

the family, but to keep dead body till arrival of their own caste fellows from the surrounding villages.

It was further an eye opening tragedy that untouchables also observe untouchability with castes ranking lower than theirs'! Replication is a stronger indicator of cultural consensus than complimentality, since it operates within the untouchable subset of castes, where the power of the higher castes does not directly operate.[3]

Tamil Nadu

- K. Rasu a *dalit* Panchayat President in village Chhottathatti, District Shivgangai was humiliated and attacked in public for unfurling the National flag at the Panchayat's official function.

Rajasthan

- There is a village in Alwar District where no *dalit* marriages had taken place so far, during last several years because the upper castes refused to allow any wedding procession to come to the village.

Orissa

- On 3rd April 2001 a *dalit* was tied up with electricity pole and beaten mercilessly for the offence of entering in the Prayer structure during a ritual singing in village Ganda Turum in Bargarh district in Western Orissa. Subsequently, he was taken before the village panchayat, which imposed a fine of Rs. 4,000 on him.
- *Dalit* women from Ghumar village in South Orissa have formed a weavers' co-operative society. The contradiction found in the behaviour of non-*dalit* women buyers from this co-operative society is that they avoid their touch while purchasing sarees from the co-operative society, but don't mind wearing *dalit* made fabric even while performing religious rituals.

- In Village Keredagada of District Kendrapada in Orissa, entry into temples to backwards was forbidden since time immemorial. Upon a Public Interest Litigation (PLI) by one Akhyakumar Malik, the Orissa High Court ordered on 15 December, 2006 to open the doors of the Temple for the backwards and also cautioned the police for maintaining law and order in this regard. The Temple entry was allowed in accordance with the High Court order. Soon after the Court Order was complied with by allowing the temple entry, the Temple Head Worshipper Madan Mohan Panda declared reopening of the temple only after purification of the temple! This was the reality as on the fag end of the year 2006! In Orissa, it is not that Keredagada is the only such village, but there are number of other villages such as Sanghapalli, Ostiya, Balisingpatnam, Sanawada, Gopalpur etc. where temple entry for the untouchables is yet a dream and continues to be denied even today.

Uttar Pradesh

- A judge namely Bharathari Prasad in Allahabad Court belonging to scheduled caste was transferred. The upper caste incumbent judge Shrivastav in his place before taking over the charge in the Court, got the whole office purified with holy Ganga water!
- In Village Chhitipur of Sikandarao, not only the boy Ashok Valmiki passing through nearby temple was severely beaten, but also his grand father, grand mother and younger brothers and sisters were brutally beaten. The Upper castes local people still having not been satisfied of the punishment to the family, attacked the whole Valmiki locality and pushed them out of the village.

Haryana

- In Village Bibipur of Karnal District, upper castes people demolished the temples of Ravidas and Valmiki, which are considered to be the worships of the lower castes. The reason was that these temples were located near other temples of the Gods worshipped by the Upper castes! Gods worshipped by scheduled castes also become *de facto* Untouchable Gods![4]

Countless Forms of Untouchability

Usual instances ranging from moderate to extreme and harsh untouchability i.e. avoiding touching the *dalit*, keeping distance while walking, throwing on of pan masala without physical touch, not allowing eatables in the restaurant, serving tea in a separate plate or if required by some body at his house, then in a steel plate, encroachment in the burial place land meant for these untouchable communities, prohibiting to touch the hand pump while taking water, restriction to the temple entry, separate sitting arrangements for the *dalits* in religious discourses, *dalit* participant to bring his utensils while dining in the common village functions, refusal to accept charity contribution offered by a *dalit*, separate seating arrangements in the government school and endless number of other forms of untouchability are commonly found in Indian society.

Action Aid India Survey on Untouchability

A study undertaken by Action Aid India in the year 2001/2002, of 565 selected villages in 11 states across the country reveals that untouchability is practised in 80 per cent of the Indian villages in one form or the other. It was most extensive in the private and religious spheres and the least present in the public and political places. Though the most blatant and grotesque practices have significantly declined, they have yet not been relegated to the yellowing pages of history. Every other day untouchability related instances make news stories in the media. In one out of ten villages, *dalits* are not allowed to wear new clothes, sunglasses or footwares or to use umbrellas or ride bicycles. Those who violate these norms, face the wrath of the dominant castes. Not only the offending individual, but all members of the community are humiliated and physically assaulted; each *dalit* is denied the right to be an individual and is treated only as a representative of the entire community. The destruction of property and burning of *dalit* inhabitation houses in Gohana in Haryana in August 2005 was similarly precipitated as an offence allegedly committed by one *dalit*, the murder of a Jat man. What should have been perceived as an individual crime to be investigated and prosecuted by the State, was immediately cast as an offence by the entire *dalit* community against the entire Jat community instigating caste based retaliation.

In almost half the villages, *dalit* marriage processions are prohibited on public roads a practice that non-*dalit* castes always take for granted and perform in the most ostentatious manner. *Dalits* are told or made to feel that the village they have lived for generations is not theirs. They are often reminded that the upper castes regard them as worthless. Their contribution to the collective economic and social life of the village is either ignored or appraised negatively. Upper castes reiterate that *dalits* have no claims in the form of village common lands or resources or to its cultural life – festivals and public events. If they are at all allowed now an entry, it is because of the 'broad mindedness' and benevolence of the dominant castes and not as a matter of their right.

It is not surprising that three out of every four villages, *dalits* are not allowed entry in the upper caste homes. One may argue that this proscription is a matter of individual choice and that the State cannot intervene and enforce social interactions in the domain of private life. However, the private realm does not exist in vaccum. Since individual values and practices are shaped by the wider cultural context, state and civil society can and should work to stimulate a rethinking of individual values. Education and re-socialization to inculcate a critical perspective on caste and untouchability is imperative for challenging entrenched norms.

What to talk of the position after fifty years? Amul Dairy of Gujarat till recently headed by personality like Dr. Kurien has an international reputation in milk revolution. Till 1987, milk of scheduled caste suppliers was not accepted by the dairy. What an astonishing illustration of discrimination? Was it because of the nature's gift like milk if passed through the hands of an untouchable also gets polluted?

Representations regarding the caste discrimination in India has now crossed the Indian Boarders. Besides a very strong representation to put the problem of Indian caste discrimination along with the problem of racism in the World Social forum held at Durban in August 2001 and next at Mambai in January 2003, the matter was also submitted before the U.S. House Committee on International Relations on 6th October 2005 by an Indian delegation of SC/ST representatives.

Untouchability in Invisible Shape Prevails at IIT Chennai

Indian Institutes of Technology are the country's internationally acknowledged premier educational institutions. Virus of social discrimination has unfortunately not spared even this highly prestigious institution like IIT, Chennai. It is reported that the majority of core faculty deans are from one particular upper caste. Out of 460 faculty members hardly four belong to SC/ST, which comes to just 0.86 per cent of the strength. It is ridiculous that in a state like Tamil Nadu faculty even for middle level teaching or lower level assisting positions is not available from SC/ST. During the entire tenure of 41 years of this esteemed institution, not even a single student belonging to SC/ST has either got selection as Ph.D. student or having had completed Ph.D.

V. Kuruppan a senior Retired IAS officer filed a PIL in Tamil Nadu High Court quoting IIT director that there is no policy of reservation for SC/ST applicable to IIT, Chennai. This speaks about the attitude of a person occupying the highest position in such institutions of nation's proud. The PIL also includes number of other discriminatory practices at the institutes.

Periyar Dravidar Kazagam (PDK) another social organization in Tamil Nadu has cited among other instances one SC student Sujee Teppal having scored 94 per cent in

Maths, Physics and Chemestry and having also been selected at prestigious BITS Pilani and Ranchi as well was disqualified at IIT Chennai was declared disqualified in preparatory course for *Dalits*. The matter was referred to the institute by National Commission for SC/ST and others with a request to reconsider. However, it was refused.[5]

Discrimination at AIIMS, New Delhi

Badhal a student who had topped in the general category in lab medicine at All India Institute of Medical Sciences, (AIIMS) New Delhi has been recently superceded by the second ranker in the appointment to the coveted post of senior resident at the department of lab medicine. Badhal belongs to scheduled caste. The victimization was probed by a three men committee headed by Sukhdev Thorat, Chairman, University Grants Commission and the discrimination to this post graduate student in a prestigious institution like AIIMS has been proved. Contemporary Vadodara incidence of MS University involving Chandramohan Srimantula's paintings outraged a cross section of voices viz. artists, academics, writers, actors, public intellectuals, lawyers, concerned citizens, there was no one to take Badhal's case which too appeared in *Times of India* and CNN/IBN. It appears that there are people whose victimhood however gravious and morally grounded, does not qualify as a campaign worthy for the rest of the civil society.[6]

Untouchability is Omnipresent

Untouchability in one form or the other is seen everywhere from east to west and from north to south universally through out the country. Persons arguing that caste system has been abolished from the country are perhaps not aware of the ground reality that untouchability still prevails in its modified version. It is true that the caste system is getting loosened from its age-old rigidity. Hereditary occupations as prescribed in the Vernashram are disappearing. Untouchability with regard to eating and drinking together is also gradually disappearing.

However, the fact remains that the caste system does clearly exist all along with stubborn resistance of the dominant caste groups to accept change. All the members of scheduled castes do not experience untouchability of the same degree. For untouchability, economic status of such oppressed becomes irrelevant with regard to treatment they are getting from the higher castes.

Thus, inter sectoral old conventional relationship between such different castes takes altogether a new shape of social hierarchy. In other words, social inequality continues, only its form changes. The so formed social groups and the surrounding socialization, friend circle, tongue, likings, disliking etc. play an important impact on its individual member in ultimately inculcating the feeling of caste apparently look so secular and they all apparently remain invisible in the day-to-day routine. But once their interest conflicts, their feeling of belongingness and feeling of casteism in them to a particular caste or group of caste comes on the surface keeping all earlier described secular virtues and values behind.

Reservation is a compensatory arrangement for the sufferers of this continued, subordinated and highly humiliating treatment from their own brethren! Perhaps putting the provisions of reservations to an end lies in removal of prevalence of these humiliations.

REFERENCES

1. Chandu Maheria/Harshad Desai, *Dalit Assertion for Self Esteem* 1981.
2. www.india.seminar.com.
3. *Dalit Shakti,* Gujarati Monthly of November 2003.
4. *Front Line* 29 December 2006 India's Shame.
5. *Tehelka Weekly,* 16 June 2007.
6. *Economic and Political Weekly,* June 2007.

5

Social Conditions in Rural India

India lives in villages. Seventy two per cent of total Indian population i.e. 74.25 crores people as per Census 2001 is inhabiting in about 6 lacs villages. Thus, real India lives in these rural localities consisting from few hutments to several hundred houses living in caste wise grouped localities with more or less a nomenclature known as village. Inspite of radical transformations, all around and rapid economic development, followed by massive industrialization, substantial changes in agrarian relations, penetration of markets, patterns of consumption, literacy, exposure to media etc. still rural India has preserved its ancient character in so many aspects, one of the foremost being its caste system. A typical rural India reminds one of a small rural economy with agricultural and other allied economic activities, caste-wise inhabitations, existence of caste based occupations and above all observance of untouchability though may not be everywhere visible in all six lacs villages of this vast country.

Position of depressed castes living in these villages is still painful and frustrating. Those categorized as scheduled castes are the most identifiable people out of the whole village composition. *Dalit* localities are invariably found outside the main village shadowed under all curses endowed out of the backwardness led poverty and being branded as permanently polluted people by the rest of the society and so on. Most of them perform work such as skinning animals carcasses, tanning leather, making foot wares, playing in musical bands, butchery of animals, fishing, and above all removal of human excreta with their bare hands, attendance at a cremation grounds and of course as low paid agriculture farm labourers and so on. Various live instances of observance of untouchability in villages are enumerated in Chapter 4 on 'Untouchability in new idioms and phrases'. Violation of this self imposed caste rules even by a scheduled caste individual is treated as crime of the whole *dalit* locality, which becomes a sufficient ground of atrocities and all harassments on the entire inhabitation.

Now, any one acquainted with the rural scene in India would at once recognize that the scheduled castes occupy peculiarly degraded position and are treated, not as persons of caste at all, but as outcastes. Admittedly, even other backward classes (OBC) the co-beneficiaries of reservational benefits on backward considerations also shun on them and treat them as inferior beings. It was because of the special degradation to which they were subjected that the constitution itself had to come forward to make special provision for them.

As regards scheduled tribes, their position is slightly different from that of scheduled castes. Population wise they are half of national level SC population. Majority of them still live in interior forests and monticules and far off locations in small clusters. Tribal population areas are seen with almost total absence of the social and modern day infrastructure, which includes basic education facility at the walk in distance, drinking water, electricity, roads etc. Though millions of amounts are provided in the budgetary allocations year after year, fact remains that these poor tribals are yet to enjoy the real fruits of freedom and our own democratic governance. Barring a few minorities who could avail the benefits of education and subsequently jobs because of provisions of reservation and having settled in the nearby towns or in the city work places, most of these tribals are unable to have full year's even labour work at the places of their domiciles. Therefore, they stay for a monsoon part of the year in their homes and for rest of the year, they migrate to other areas in search of casual labour work with their family consisting of female members and teenaged school going kins. They while working there, stay on the road sides. The whole family including females and children gets engaged in manual labour work. Education even upto a basic level to children of these families wandering here and there is naturally out of question.

Last one, under reservation categories is other backward castes (OBC). Social condition in respect of these other backward classes/castes (OBC) is different from that of the scheduled castes and scheduled tribes. They don't live in segregated inhabitations unlike scheduled castes and scheduled tribes. Their localities are all along with localities of other upper castes. Though they are considered lower in the caste gradations, social treatment with them by the upper castes in day-to-day routine affairs is not that disrespectful and insulting. As they also look like a particularly downtrodden proletariat, sometimes lumpenproletariat, many people suggest to treat them near to scheduled castes. They constitute nearly half of the Indian aggregate population. Economic disparities between well off OBCs and those on the other extreme of economic ladder in the same OBC category is also very wide. Majority of them are also occupation wise field labourers or workers engaged in a large number of so-called unskilled occupations. However, if one examines the difference in the social perception of looking at these two groups, there is a vast noticeable difference. There is no point in attempting to determine the social backwardness of other backward classes by applying the test of nearness to the conditions of the scheduled castes. Such a test would practically nullify the provision for reservation for socially and educationally backward classes other than the scheduled castes and tribes. Therefore, discussion under this chapter covers scheduled castes and scheduled tribes only.

The history reveals that there were sustained and strenuous efforts of many castes to use the Census as the occasion to raise themselves socially in the beginning of nineteenth century. That apart, there is always a tendency found in the informal interactions between the people, wherein an attempt is made that his caste is higher than others. A person ranking lower in social order than his predecessor will continue in establishing that there are other castes placed at the lower rung than his caste and his caste is superior to those.

It is altogether a different story that with political movement to extend reservation benefits to other backward castes (OBC), a move started in a reversal way to show their caste a lower one with an ulterior motive to avail reservation benefits. Recent agitations by Gurjar community in Rajasthan already availing reservational benefits as OBC have demanded for their inclusion in the category of scheduled tribes. Such politically motivated movements for snatching benefits of the reservation provisions have nothing to do with the prevailing discriminatory social practices. Wherever may be the positioning of Gurjars in the Government Gazette for the purpose of reservational categorization, Gurjars shall continue to enjoy a dominating social status far above scheduled castes or scheduled tribes. A political decision of certifying a caste as lower for its inclusion under OBC does not change the age old established social status of that caste in the society. Purpose of this narration is that there has always been a tendency of an individual in Indian society to show that he is socially higher than others.

What induces the people in India to make such sustained and strenuous efforts to show their castes as raised one? This caste raising inducement clearly speaks about the deep-rooted gradation based into higher and lower caste structures prevailing in the country. India is a land of homo hierarchies as against individualism characteristic of modern west. Caste counts everywhere. Every one feels proud to recognize himself at a higher step of social ladder than others. Those placed at the bottom of this hierarchy are subjected to inhumane treatment from their higher counter parts.

Rural Caste Composition

The caste discrimination has not ceased with the legal abolition. Over half a century has passed, since caste distinctions lost their formal character: However, the caste has managed to reinvent and reproduce itself in independent India such that the fault lines of caste have not been blurred appreciably in the realm of poverty, occupation or education.

Table 5.1: Rural-Urban Population Break-up

	Census 1991		*NSSO 1999/2000 (in %)*	
	Rural	*Urban*	*Rural*	*Urban*
Scheduled Castes	18.00	12.00	20.50	14.40
Scheduled Tribes	10.10	2.30	10.50	3.40
OBC	—	—	37.60	51.80
Others incl. OBC	71.90	85.70	31.50	51.80

Source: NSSO 55th Round 1999/2000[1].

Thus, a larger proportion of SC/ST population lives in rural areas than in urban and metropolitan areas. As regard the aspect of untouchability, among the three categories under the reserved group i.e. SC/ST/OBC, only scheduled castes are subjected to untouchability. In other words, a one-fifth of the total rural population are profoundedly affected by the likes and psyches of their own fellow citizens of the country through observance of untouchability.

So far poverty is concerned, this infects the whole nation in spite of so many steps done in this direction. But the above figures further reveal that prevalence of poverty is more penetrated between the SC/ST and OBC. It is estimated that half the scheduled caste, a one-third of the scheduled tribe and a quarter of OBC rural population is living below poverty line. As against this, Proportion of Upper caste Hindus living below poverty line is meagre 11.7 per cent, which is much lesser than the similar proportion of people living below poverty line in reserved category communities. The newly elected Uttar Pradesh State government has affirmed inclusion of this 11.7 per cent upper caste poors also in the reservation net.

The income criteria for official poverty lines for the above period were: Rural Rs. 327.56 per person per month and Urban Rs. 454.11 per person per month.

Table 5.2: Demographic Composition of Population

	Rural		*Urban*	
	% Share of BPL Popu.	*% Share of Rural Popu.*	*% Share of BPL Popu.*	*% Share of Urban Popu.*
Scheduled castes	17.90	10.50	5.20	3.40
Scheduled tribes	27.20	20.50	23.50	14.40
OBC	27.60	37.60	38.40	30.40
Upper caste Hindus	9.60	22.00	15.60	36.90
Non-Hindus	17.70	9.40	17.30	14.90
Total	100	100	100	100

Source: NSSO 55th Round 1999/2000[2].

The above figures clearly reveal that social backwardness and poverty go together. Thirty per cent of SC/ST population, which constitutes about a one-third of the total rural population, they form almost half the total BPL rural population. As regard incidence of poverty in respect of OBCs, the position is better. They constitute about 37 per cent of total rural population with lesser corresponding share of rural BPL population since they account for 27.60 per cent of the total rural BPL population. Living standard of the upper caste Hindus denotes marked difference as regard their BPL population compared to their total rural population share.

Position of Education of SC/ST in Rural India

Education in those ancient days having strong 'Vernashram' base was a sheer cry for SC/ST. A serious thought on the education of the SC/ST started since 1850 during colonial days, with enactment of 'The Caste Disabilities Removal Act of 1850' during British Rule and subsequent establishment of schools with government financial support provided opportunities to aspiring *dalit* students for the first time in India. The demand by *dalit* students for admission to schools increased, but the British administration, under pressure from the upper castes, was not enthusiastic about meeting them. Instances of segregation and denial of admission were many and the State was not always keen to intervene in favour of the *dalits.* In order to avoid conflict with the dominant castes, the British Government opened 'special' government schools for the *dalits* in a few places so that they would not come in contact with the non-untouchables. But these attempts attracted upper caste hostility, as they went against the dominant order. For instance, books were snatched away from Cherumar boys as they went to attend the special schools in Calicut, Kerala. In Kheda district of Gujarat, five to six schools were closed down and as a punishment; the crops of the depressed people were burnt, when they attempted to avail of education.

At present, in rural India 70 per cent of *dalit* females are illiterate as are almost half of *dalit* males. Drop-out of *dalit* students is strikingly higher than that of non-*dalit* due to poverty, discrimination etc. that they frequently face in the schools. Out of every 100 *dalit* students enrolled in class I, only four reach class XII. The drop-out rate is higher in rural areas than in urbans. The main reason for the drop-out is not a lack of desire for education. It is poverty and the need to contribute to the family income by either working for wages or looking after siblings and freeing other family members to take up wage work. Ratio of graduate per thousand population is female 4, male 12 in case of scheduled castes, female 3, male 11 in case of scheduled tribes as against females 17 and males 48 in case of upper caste Hindus.

Residential Segregation

The most visible and long standing form of caste discrimination in rural India and also the most taken for granted aspect of untouchability in the public sphere, is the residential segregation of *dalit* households. Caste segregated neighbourhood tend to be the rule rather than exception in Indian villages and dwellings are usually clustered by caste. However, *dalit* neighbourhoods are unique in the sense that they are subjected to specific and very severe sanctions that are not imposed on other castes.

The sarcastic form of locational sanction is the social banishment expressed in palpably physical spatial terms of the settlement beyond the boundaries of the village. This form of outcasting of *dalit* residents is quite common all over the country. While these customs are not always enforced or followed very strictly, their existence is indicative of the deep-seated nature of untouchability. Residential exclusion from the village, while common is not the rule and many villages have *dalit* neighbourhoods located within the village, but these neighborhoods too are subject to severe sanctions. It is interesting but also worrisome, to note that government programmes for *dalit* housing schemes such as 'Indira Awas Yojna' etc. are unable to remove the spatial segregation dictated by upper caste tradition. State practices can set an example by encouraging inter-caste mixing in the spheres such as housing. At present, there are universal residential segregations in villages, which reinforces social distances and cultural taboos. Even in urban areas, white collar *dalits* such as school teachers, other government employees find it difficult to rent or buy an accommodation in non-*dalit* localities. Such segregation is discretely maintained even in government colonies meant for public employees!

The same practices of segregations and prejudices of untouchability are reproduced when the state creates new villages to rehabilitate those displaced by development projects or natural disasters. In Gujarat, for instance, *dalit* communities were given separate localities in the post earth quake rehabilitation, in which the State and NGOs were involved. It was the situation in case of post-Tsunami rehabilitation in Tamil Nadu. Segregation of *dalits* into separate localities also means that they are less likely to receive state services and social infrastructure such as drinking water, electricity and roads.

Dalit Women and Untouchability

The specific forms of discrimination or say untouchability of one or the other form that a *dalit* woman struggles against are produced by the combined weight of caste, class and patriarchy. Social beliefs about pollution, the economic compulsions of being dependent on upper castes for work and livelihood and the vulnerability imposed by gender subordination, fuse to make the life of *dalit* women especially hard. A *dalit* woman faces numerous forms of discrimination and untouchability which includes sexualized form of oppression also.

The lives of *dalit* women are largely circumscribed by their poverty and lack of access to productive resources like land, financial capital or educational qualifications. The majority of *dalit* women works outside the home most often as agricultural labourers to weed crops, pick cotton, saw potatoes etc. Those working off side the agricultural farms include cleaning the cattle sheds, sweeping the countryard, and sometimes cleaning cooking utensils. They are underpaid for the job carried out by them.

Surprisingly, non-*dalit* women are more rigid about maintaining practices of untouchability than non-*dalit* men. This may be because non-*dalit* women internalize the caste ideology that stresses the role of women as upholders of caste purity for the entire household. *Dalit* women working in the houses of upper castes have to enter through the back side door, work in the backyard and leave from there. Working in the fields and homes of non-*dalit* exposes *dalit* women to sexual abuse and violence. The dependence on non-*dalits* prevents *dalit* women from devising work routines that avoid non-*dalit* spaces and the experience of being humiliated every day. Many *dalit* women also perform tasks of scavenging, midwifery and sometimes to an extent of prostitution also.

Poor villagers use foul land on the out skirts of the village for defecating. The grabbing of the commons has left the poor *dalit* women with nowhere to go. They are forced to defecate before sunrise or at night. If they go to the fields, they get abused and shouted at by farmers. While land owning upper castes families have constructed regular flush toilets in their houses, most *dalits* lack the resources to build these, notwithstanding the government grant to promote rural toilet construction. Sexual harassment also takes the more violent form of physical molestation and rape. *Dalit* women face the paradox of being regarded as polluted and untouchable and yet exploited in the most intimate sphere of social relations.

Untouchability Continues Even After Conversion

Even the conversion has not spared the *dalits* from the calamity of untouchability. Many people from the scheduled castes and scheduled tribes categories having been fed up of the curses of untouchability, have since left Hindu religion and shifted their faith in other religions such as Christianity, Sikhhism, Islam, Buddhism etc. Unfortunately, untouchability has not severed its thick bonding with these unfortunate untouchables even upon conversion also. Shadows of untouchability goes with them all along.

There have been separate gurudwaras even today in many villages of Punjab. Untouchability here may not mean complete exclusion from the main gurudwara, but definitely involves discriminatory behaviour on the part of dominant castes particularly Sikh jats, forced to sit in separate lines, and not allowed to participate in cooking and serving the food. There has been no overt opposition to *dalit* castes constructing their own gurudwaras, but the upper castes prefer not to visit these gurudwaras, or to bring Granth Sahib from these gurudwaras for special function at home. Thus, the practice of untouchability continues to survive despite the fact that Sikhism does not officially recognize it.

In Kerala especially mixed caste church congregations have often led to tensions. Over time, the minority group whether the low caste or the high caste generally splits away and builds its own separate church. Bowing to public pressure, churches of various denominations have begun to ordain priests from *dalit* castes, but they often face resistance from the upper caste congregations.

Dalit conversions to other religion from Hinduism have always attracted the ire of Hindu nationalists. Similarly tribal conversions in tribal belt have also invited similar disturbances. Evidence proves that deeper the expression of *dalit* devotion, the stronger the caste Hindu blackash.

Untouchability Lifetime and After

The most widespread and blatant practice of untouchability in the public secular sphere relates to water and cremation/burial grounds; the bare necessities of life and death. Despite being common amenities that are managed and maintained by the local government, access to both drinking water sources and cremation/burial grounds continue to be governed by the notion of caste-based pollution and untouchability. In almost, half the villages surveyed, *dalits* do not have free access to common drinking water facilities. In many of these villages, *dalits* are forbidden to touch the wheel or handle of the well or pumps and must depend on the consent of the upper caste person to draw water and pour into their pots. In several villages, *dalits* are assigned a separate place on the riverbank generally downstream of the place where upper castes bathe and wash or on the edge of the pond meant only for the untouchables.

In almost half of the villages, *dalits* have no access to the village burial/cremation ground maintained out of public funds. A separate place is generally designated for the *dalits* of one or several villages. In other words, segregation is maintained in life as well as in death.

Non-Government Organizations (NGOs) and Untouchability

In the last 30 years, secular Non-Governmental Organizations (NGOs) have emerged as important agents of social change, delivering social services and mobilizing the poor and disadvantaged to secure their rights. One would expect that those whose professional lives are dedicated to the empowerment of the underprivileged would oppose discrimination against them. However, it is all the more shocking to find that in nearby one-third of the villages, NGO supported Self Help Groups (SHG) practise untouchability in their seating arrangements. Thus, even in the routine working of the organizations formed to facilitate collective action by villagers, the division of castes is reproduced and reinforced.

In some villages, NGOs avoid inter-caste interactions altogether by organizing SHGs by locality a *de facto* segregation of *dalits* from Non-*dalits*.

Market Mechanism and Untouchability

All the evidences from the study show that notion of the market, as a social equalizer is a myth; instead of ignoring caste and class and treating individuals as pure economic agents, market relations are based on the exploitation of caste inequalities. *Dalits* receive lower wages and are forced into ill-paid and arduous work because the market is not neutral. By taking advantage of their vulnerability, market relations perpetuate rather than alleviate the crushing economic predicament of poor *dalits*.

In short, the experience of removing untouchability has been slow, halting and uneven in different parts of the country. The continued presence of untouchability in our society is a crime against humanity. The oppression, humiliation and exploitation ingrained in the practice make it completely indefensible.[3]

REFERENCES

1. *NSSO 55th Round* 1999/2000.
2. *Ibid.*
3. Ghanshyam Shah and Others; *Untouchability in Rural India*, pp. 166-68.

6

OBC Reservation

Reservation for other backward classes is one of the most controversial issues under the provisions of reservation. Article 16(4) of the constitution for the reservation as such covers all backward classes i.e. scheduled castes, scheduled tribes and socially and economically backward (SEBC), also known as other backward classes (OBC).

Other backward castes as defined by Kalelkar Commission are those who have 'ideas of ceremonial purity, restriction on inter-caste marriages, taboos on food and drink, social segregation and feeling of caste loyalty and superiority, all of which have contributed to the backwardness of a large number of communities in Indian society.

As stated earlier, there were no specific provisions for OBC reservation at the time of enactment of the constitution. Hence, there is no uniformity in its implementation in the country. Different states on the basis of their own set up commissions for the purpose formed and adopted a policy of OBC reservation in their states on the basis of local conditions coupled with the political considerations. At centre, its implementation commenced after 1990 upon adoption of Mandal Commission Report by the then V.P. Singh Government. It was again halted due to judicial injunctions in September 1990 and other odds and finally got Supreme Court nod of clearance in November 1992 after passing through all odds.

There are several reasons to emphasize that OBCs as a class are envisaged to be different from scheduled castes and scheduled tribes: Lack of clarity as regards OBC reservation and SC/ST reservation often results into obscure and confound public understanding of the preferences for SC and ST.

First, the OBCs are socially and educationally disadvantaged but they do not suffer from the sort and extent of social privations as the SCs and STs such as untouchability, social hatred etc.

Second, Reservation to OBCs are only for employment and education. There is no provision for electoral posts in their case unlike SCs and STs. Had the constitution intended inclusion of similar facilities and concessions, it would have specifically provided reservations for them in Lok Sabha and other electoral positions/offices also.

Third, the wording of the relevant provisions itself shows that the object of the constitution in regard to both these categories i.e. SC/ST and OBC is different.

Fourth, reservations are really about fraternity and not merely about equality of economic status. Therefore, this policy is best applied where crippling poverty accompanied by the historical dispossession of social assets exists. Here lies the difference between the kind of reservation for such socially victimized castes and tribes and the reservation meant for the peasant castes who are covered under OBC reservation. The beneficiaries under this reservation have rural infrastructural or say socially valuable assets plus more importantly political power. Moreover, they have never faced social discrimination of the kind that scheduled castes and scheduled tribes have.

The objects in regard to the SCs and STs was to end the discrimination of centuries and lift them into the mainstream. Therefore, provisions for reservation for them were embodied in the constitution itself wide Article 16(4) details on which are available in Part III at Chapter 12 on 'Constitutional Provisions'. The object in regard to the OBCs is to remove their social and educational handicaps and secure for them adequate representation in government services. Hence no specific article for OBC is carved in the constitution. In stead, the constitution provided for forming a commission wide Article 340 leaving the detailed provision for them i.e. OBCs to be framed at the discretion of the central government on the basis of recommendations being made by such constituted commissions for the purpose. Text of the said Article 340 providing for constitution of commission are as under.

Article 340 : Appointment of a Commission to investigate the conditions of backward classes

'The President may by order appoint a commission consisting of such persons as he thinks fit to investigate the conditions of socially and economically backward classes within the territory of India and the difficulties under which they labour and to make recommendations as to the steps that should be taken by the Union or any states to remove such difficulties and to improve their condition and as to the grants that should be made for the purpose by the Union or any state and the conditions subject to which such grants should be made and the order appointing such commission shall define the procedure to be followed by the Commission.'

Kaka Kalelkar Commission 1953

A Commission under the Chairmanship of famous educationalist Kaka Kalelkar was set up on 29 January 1953. There were other ten members in the Commission representing Members of Parliament and Bihar/Mysore legislative Assemblies. The Commission started functioning from 18 March 1953 and was supposed to submit its report by 31 January 1954, which was extended to 31 March 1955. The commission finally presented its report before the Parliament on 3rd December 1955. The commission considered following criteria for ascertaining OBC status of a particular caste.

1. Social status of the caste in the traditional Hindu caste stratification.
2. Position of education in the majority sections of such caste or class.
3. Status of representation of such caste/class in the government jobs.

4. Their similar representation in trade, commerce and industries.

The Commission listed 2399 as OBC castes, of which it categorized 837 castes/classes as the most backwards. The Commission made several recommendations such as ascertaining the caste-wise OBC population as per 1961 census, reserving 70 per cent seats in technical and professional educational institutions, reserving job quota of 25 per cent in class I, 33.5 per cent in class II and 40 per cent in class III, also making financial provision of Rs. 200 crores for economic upliftment of these OBCs. And creation of a separate ministry and secretariat at centre and all the states for OBC Welfare.

The Commission's some of the above recommendations were dissented by four members. The Government did not accept Commission's report finally on twin objections, One; if the bulk of the country's millions were to be regarded as coming within the category of backward classes, no useful purpose could be served by separate enumeration of such classes. And Second; the caste criterion was seen as a remedy worse than the evil of backwardness itself, it had suggested, citing the proverb 'use thorn to remove a thorn' that the evils of caste could be removed by measures considered in terms of caste.[1]

Mandal Commission

Issue of OBC reservation thereafter came on the fore after a long stint of 23 years after emergency in the country was over in 1977, which brought a major power shift at the center for the first time with Non-Congress political majority. The new Janata Dal Regime led by the then Prime Minister Late Morarji Desai set up a Commission to examine the need of reservation for other backward classes (OBC) under the Chairmanship of. B.P. Mandal ex. Chief Minister of Bihar along with six other members including one seating M.P. R.R. Bhole and another ex. M.P. L.R. Nayak on 11 April 1978. Incidentally, the Chairman B.P. Mandal was the first OBC Chief Minister in the country having headed the state of Bihar in the year 1962. The Commission was supposed to submit its report by 31 December

1979. The Commission after four extensions, finally submitted its report on 31 December 1980. With their note apprehending that OBCs of the Nation have high hopes for positive response to the recommendations of this commission, but is also afraid of its fate similar to that of the Kalelkar Commission.[2]

The Commission listed 3743 castes as OBCs having approximate population of 52 per cent. These castes included cross sections of the society including Minorities such as Muslims, Christians etc. Almost half the portion of entire Muslim population of 8.40 crores was included in the OBCs. Hindu castes, included artisans castes such as barbers, blacksmiths, potters and various populous farmer castes and many nomadic and wandering tribes. The Commission made several recommendations with foremost of all being 27 per cent reservation for these castes/classes, allowing all concessions in line with SCs and STs, fresh calculation of caste wise OBC population, carry forward of unfilled vacancies and surprisingly also reservation of OBCs in the Government assisted private sector. Quantum of OBC population at 52 per cent was based on 1931 Census. Break up of this 52 per cent is appended at Table 18. (Surinder Mallik, SC Mandal Commission Case 1992)[3]

Dwindling Fate of OBC Reservation

OBC reservation has always dwindled under large-scale ups and downs. Soon after the submission of the Report, there was again a political power change at the centre with fall down of Janata Dal Government which initiated Mandal movement. The report did not thereafter see the day light till change in political power once again at centre in 1989. V.P. Singh the new Prime Minister of the newly sworn in National Alliance Government declared acceptance of the Mandal Commission report on 7 August 1990 and started with implementation of reservation of 27 per cent in all Government jobs, which was later on stayed by the Supreme Court's injunction. The implementation of Mandal Commission Recommendations were confronted with huge uproar and protests. Many students in Delhi protested through self-immolations. There was equally a strong political protest on the parliament floor. Amidst all this, Mandal Recommendations particularly reservation in job quota were finally accepted.

The question naturally arises; as to what changes in socio political situation at the national level took place which led to declining to accept Kaka Kalelkar Report in 1953/55 and then acceptance of Mandal Commission Report surprisingly. What compelled in nineties to prevail over to acceptance of Mandal Commission Recommendations? For this, one will have to study the political power shift at the centre in 1977. The Congress which was ruling right from beginning of independence, lost power at the centre in wake of proclamation of emergency in 1975. The new non-congress Government formed Mandal Commission in 1978. Again before, Mandal Commission could submit its recommendations, there was once again a political power change at the centre. The non-Congress coalition Government could not complete its five-year's term. People's verdict went once again in favour of Congress in 1980. There was obviously no development on Mandal implementation thereafter till Congress regime ruled at the centre upto 1990.

Rising Representation of OBCs in Parliament

At the time of Kalelkar Commission in 1953, 54 per cent OBCs were having electorate representation of just 4.39 per cent in Parliament. This started consistently increasing all over more particularly from seventies. There was also a strong impact of the socialist philosophy of Ram Manohar Lohia. Emerging OBC leaders like Chandrapuri in Bihar, E.V. Ramaswami Periyar in South, Punjabrao Deshmukh in North etc. were also instrumental in creating wide spread awareness about the concept of reservation etc. in these communities by this time.

OBC representation rose to 20.87 per cent in 1990. Moreover, majority of OBC MPs were from the coalition in power at the centre, supporting the Prime Minister. This led to acceptance of Mandal Commission Report soon under the new Non-Congress National Alliance.

Majority voice from upper castes, conventional social thinkers and obviously media as regard OBC reservation was in negative, the resentment was more against its basis which was caste. The social opinion makers suggested income criteria as against the caste criteria, which to their opinion would widen the caste disparities perpetuating caste consciousness permanently.[4]

Mandal Implementation in States

As regards implementation of the reservation for OBCs at state level, there was no uniform policy. Few States such as Gujarat, Maharashtra, Tamil Nadu etc. set up their own Commissions in the state, enlisted eligible castes under OBCs and started implementation of OBC reservation in their state services. However there were few other states, which were yet to move in this direction. The Mandal Commission movements started in nineties at the National level eased the implementation of OBC reservation in most of the states, which included Rajasthan, Haryana, Delhi, West Bengal and Madhya Pradesh etc. Maharashtra, also following the Deshmukh Committee Recommendations, implemented it with 10 per cent job reservations for OBCs and another 4 per cent for Nomadic and Denotified tribes in 1984.

In Gujarat, a Commission for OBCs known as Bakshi Commission was formed on 8 August 1972 under the Chairmanship of Retd. High Court Justice Bakshi along with three other members. The Commission enlisted 83 castes as OBCs and recommended 10 per cent reservation in class III and class IV jobs, and 5 per cent in class I and II. The Commission also recommended 10 per cent reservation in admissions in educational institutions with a rider i.e. there will not be a mark difference of more than 5 per cent between the last general category candidate and an OBC candidate. Subsequently, OBC reservation was uniformly raised to 28 per cent in acceptance of one more Rane Commission Recommendations subsequently in 1985, which added fuel to the fire to the anti-Reservation agitations in the State in 1985.

Implementation of OBC reservation started in eighties at States and nineties at the centre was not quiet and smooth. There had already started a strong resentment against prevailing reservation policy itself so far meant for scheduled castes and scheduled tribes. Implementation of OBC reservation brought that resentment on the fore. Gujarat took the lead of anti-reservation agitations soon upon the implementation of OBC reservation under Bakshi Commission in 1985, which soon evoked similar anti-reservation stirs in the surrounding and a few northern states for over three months. Details of these anti-reservation agitations are discussed in Chapter 7 on 'Anti-Reservation Agitations in Gujarat'. The OBC reservation movements took toll of so many Governments such as Madhavsinh Solanki in Gujarat, Jagannath Pahadia in Rajasthan, Ram Naresh Yadav in Uttar Pradesh and Karpuri Thakur in Bihar. Anti-Mandal agitation mainly remained in Delhi University, which was subsequently spread to few other state capitals of Northern States on a moderate scale.

Mandal Agitations 1990

Mandal Recommendations have its far-reaching impacts in whole of the Nation in a big way as they contemplate to share 27 per cent seats in Central Government employment in whole of the nation. Delhi based students initiated the whole agitation against Mandal Commission. In fact, Mandal agitations remained at and around Delhi Campus only except some remote incidents of violence and protests in few northern Indian cities.

Agitation Concentrated at and Around Delhi only

For this, one will have to know about student mix or demography of Delhi Campus. Students of Delhi based University are mostly from the families of government services. Representation of OBC people in Government jobs at Delhi was hardly 2.59 per cent at that time. In other words, most of the students agitating in Delhi University campus were belonging to upper caste Government employees having strong feeling of a big cake going away from their mouth because of additional reservation to the OBCs. The media took a very big initiative in this agitation. It was gathered that out of 300 Delhi based journalist at that time, hardly 1 per cent belonged to OBC and 98 per cent to general categories.

Rajiv Gandhi from the opposition side delivered a provoking political speech of 150 minutes in the Parliament on Mandal debate on 6 September 1990. While he accepted existence of backwardness in country and inequalities in the opportunities, he opposed the implementation of the report teeth and nail. He suggested removing the backwardness and poverty first. Sharad Yadav M.P. strongly supported the move putting forth pro reservation arguments viz. caste discrimination faced by the backward class candidates who are otherwise very good performer in the competitive written examinations, huge public expenditure in high class professional education, the benefits of which largely go to the upper castes etc. The battle of debate and controversies went on inside and outside the Parliament for days together.

Self Immolations

In September 1990, a student Rajiv Goswami from Delhi University poured kerosene over his body and set himself on fire. According to some accounts, Rajiv had initially only intended a mock self-immolation. As soon as he struck a match, his friends were supposed to have doused him with water, waiting for a few photographs to be snapped. These photographs and the attendant press coverage was to be used to draw dramatic media attention to the protests against caste reservations that had been mounting over previous six weeks. But, in the heat of emotion, in the context of an impassioned protest against a Government decision that was seen as taking all future prospects of respectable employment away from young people with upper caste background. Goswami set his body alight without checking to see whether his friends were anywhere nearby, photographs were taken, his burning body could be seen on the front page of every news paper and the cover of every glossy magazine in India over next few days.

But Goswami by that time was in the critical care ward of Safdar-jung Hospital for his life with 50 per cent of his body burnt. This 1990 Mandal Hero could survive in spite of grave injuries till 2005. This was the violent culmination of a protest. His photographs gave way to similar other terrifying images. In quick succession, youths in a series of cities across northern India from Ambala to Lucknow followed Goswami example and set themselves on fire as well. Within the next few months, more than 159 students also blindly followed suit-attempting suicide by self-immolation, 63 succeeded. Another 100 people were killed in police firing and clashes that accompanied the wide spread protests.[5]

Question arises here is what instigated these boys to rush to die? Many of them were so teenaged that they might not know what Mandal Commission is all about. Rajiv's story above clearly signifies that it was more a drama which unfortunately turned out into a mishap leading further in turn induced the blindly following poor youths towards horrible suicidal attempts.

OBC Reservation Endorsed by Supreme Court

After anti-Mandal agitations in Delhi, Chandigadh, Bhopal, and Jaipur, the matter went upto the Supreme Court in September 1990 There was a writ petition filed against the implementation of Mandal Commission Recommendations, which got the court injunctions till further hearing. A matter of noting with concern here is that there was no upper caste advocate of repute ready or willing to defend the plea of OBCs in the Supreme Court. At last, Criminal Specialist Advocate Ram Jethmalani came to their rescue for this civil matter. The matter came up for hearing before the Division Bench of 9 judges. The judges gave judgment on 16 November 1992 with 6 *versus* 3 majority declaring the Mandal Commission implementation as perfectly constitutional. The judgement noted,

"We don't intend to accelerate casteism. But caste system is a bitter reality of our society. We cannot ignore existence of the caste"... And thus, finally the issue of other backward classes (OBC) got legally settled.

Justice Chenappa Reddy remarked, "Social status and economic power are so woven and fused into the caste system in the Indian rural society. Caste is the primary index of social backwardness, so that social backwardness is often readily identifiable with reference to a person's caste. There is an over powering mutuality between poverty and caste on the Indian scene. So pervasive is caste in Indian society because of Hinduism that it is present even in religions that eschew it—Sikhhism, Christianity, and Islam"

The condition of castes, which are, selected for reservation under the rubric " other socially and educationally backward classes" should be akin to that of "scheduled castes and scheduled tribes". Earlier judgements contain admonitions to this effect. Justice Reddy finally declares, "We do not think that these observations were meant to lay down any proposition that the socially backward classes were nearly the same as those of the scheduled castes and tribes".

Mandal Commission Recommendations

Mandal Commission Report is perhaps the most controversial document on the Indian soil. The report was strongly protested from all the corners i.e. society, opinion makers, judiciary and media as well. The report consists of huge volume with lot of data regarding OBC followed by series of recommendations. It is often misunderstood that Mandal means just 27 per cent reservation to OBCs. But that is not all. If one goes through the recommendations made by the Commission under Chapter 13 of its report, it can be seen that Mandal Commission has thoroughly examined the socio-economic conditions of communities put at one of the lowest social order known as other backward communities (OBC) i.e. their social status, economic conditions, conventional occupations, position of education in these communities and so on. Various recommendations made by the Commission are keeping in view the reality pertaining to these poor masses, need for their total development through various measures suggested in the recommendations. These suggestions are need based, feasible and worth implementable for the real upliftment of these masses towards larger cause of attaining social equalities in the country. Coincidentally, the measures recommended are worth considering for that matter while chalking out plannings and strategies of poor masses of the country irrespective of those included in the reservation of any nature.[6]

13.1 It may appear that upliftment of other backward classes is part of larger national problem of the removal of mass poverty. Here the question arises is that of social and educational backwardness and poverty is the direct consequence of these crippling caste based handicaps. As these handicaps are embodied in our social structure, their removal will require far reaching structural changes. No less important will be changes in the perception of the problems of OBCs by the ruling classes of the country.

13.2 One such change in the attitude of the ruling elite pertains to the provision of reservation for the candidates of OBCs. It is generally argued that looking to the large population of OBCs i.e. 52 per cent, recruitment of a few thousand OBCs every year against the reserved vacancies is not going to produce any perceptible impact on their general condition. On the other hand, the induction of a large number proportion of employees against reserved vacancies will considerably impair the quality and efficiency of the government services. It is also stated that the benefits of such reservations will be skimmed off by those sections of OBCs which are already well off and the really backward sections will be left high and dry. Another argument advanced against this approach is that the policy of large-scale reservations will cause great heart burning to those meritorious candidates whose entry into the services will be barred as a result thereof.

Thus, the Mandal Commission was very well aware of the potential controversies, the report is likely to encounter with. The report further states;

13.3 All the above arguments are based on fairly sound footing. But these are also the arguments advanced by the ruling elites, which is based on preserving its privileges.

Therefore, like all such reasoning, it is based on partisan approach. By the same token, while humiliating some immediate areas of concern, it tends to ignore much larger issues of national importance.

13.4 The battle of backwardness is to be fought in the minds of the backward people. In India, the government service has always been looked upon as a symbol of prestige and power. By increasing the representation of OBCs in the government services, we give them an immediate feeling of participation in the governance of this country. When a backward class candidate becomes a collector or a superintendent of police, the material benefits accruing from his position are limited to the members of his family only. But the psychological spin off of this phenomenon is tremendous; the entire community of that backward class candidate feels socially elevated. Even no tangible benefits flow to the community at large, the feeling that now it has its 'own man' in the "corridors of power" acts as a moral booster.

13.5 In a democratic set up, every individual and community has a legitimate right and aspiration to participate in ruling this country. Any situation, which results in, a near-denial of this right to nearly 52 per cent of the country's population needs to be urgently rectified.

13.6 Apprehensions regarding drop in the quality of government services owing to large-scale induction of SC/ST/OBC candidates against the reserved posts may be justified only upto a point. At present, top echelons of all the government services are manned predominantly by open competition candidates and if the performance of our bureaucracy is any indication, it has not exactly covered itself with glory. Candidates selected against the reserved categories owing to their social and cultural handicaps, they may generally shade less competent. But on the other hand, they will have the great advantage of possessing first hand knowledge of the sufferings and problems of backward sections of the society. This is not a small asset for field workers and policy makers even at the highest level.

13.7 It is no doubt true that the major benefits of reservation and other welfare measures for other backward classes (OBC) will be cornered by the more advanced sections of the backward communities. But is not this a universal phenomenon? All reformist remedies have to contend with a slow recovery along the hierarchical gradient; there are no quantum jumps in social reform. Moreover, human nature being what it is a " new class" ultimately does emerge even in classless societies. Reservations will certainly erode the hold of higher castes on the services and enable OBCs in general to have a sense of participation in running the affairs of their country.

13.8 It is certainly true that reservation for OBCs will cause a lot of heart burning to others. But should the mere fact of this heart burning be allowed to operate as a moral veto against social reform? A lot of heart burning was caused to the British when they left India. It burns the hearts of all whites when the black protest against apartheid in South Africa. When the higher castes constituting less than 20 per cent of the country's population subjected the rest in all manners of social justice, it must have caused a lot of heart burning to the lower castes. Of all the spacious arguments advanced against reservation for backward classes, there is none, which beats this one about 'heart burns' in sheer sophistry.

13.9 In fact, the Hindu society has always operated a very rigorous scheme of reservation, which has internalized through caste system. Eklavya lost his thumb and Shambuk his neck for their breach of caste rules of reservation. The present furore against reservation for OBCs is not aimed at the principle itself, but against the new class of beneficiaries, as they are now clamouring for a share of the opportunities, which were all along monopolized by the higher castes.

Recommendations for Educational Concessions

As stated earlier Mandal recommendations do not only ask for a job quota. It has recommended various educational supports for the real and permanent uplift of the OBCs. These recommendations are;

13.10 Our educational system is elitist in character and results in a high degree of wastage. It is least suited to the requirements of an over populated and developing country. It is a legacy of the British rule, which was severely criticized during the independence struggle, and yet it has not undergone any structural changes. Though it is least suited to the needs of the backward classes, yet, they are forced to run in the rat race with others, as no options are available to them.

13.11 Various State Governments are giving a number of educational concessions to other backward class (OBC) students like exemption of tuition fees, free supply of books and clothes, mid-day meals, special hostel facilities, stipends, etc. These concessions are all right as far as they go. What is required perhaps is not so much of provision of additional funds, but for framing of integrated schemes for creating proper environment and incentives for serious and purposeful studies.

13.12 It is well known that most backward class children are irregular and indifferent towards schooling and their drop-out rate is very high. There are two main reasons for this. First; these children are brought up in the climate of extreme social and cultural deprivation and consequently, a proper motivation for schooling is generally lacking. Second; most of these children come from very poor homes and their parents are forced to press them into doing small chores from a very young age.

13.13 Upgrading the cultural environment is a very slow process. Transferring these children to an artificially upgraded environment is beyond the present resources of the country. In view of this, it is recommended that this problem may be tackled on a limited and selective basis on two fronts.

13.14 First, an incentive and time bound programme for adult education should be launched in selected pockets with high concentration of OBC population. This is a basic motivational approach, as only properly motivated parents will take serious interest in educating their children.

Secondly, residential schools should be set up in these areas for backward class students to provide a climate especially conducive to serious studies. All facilities in these schools including lodging and boarding will have to be provided free of cost to attract students from poor and backward homes. Separate Government Hostels for OBC students with the above facilities will be another step in the right direction.

13.15 A beginning of both these fronts will have to be made on a limited scale and selective basis. But the scope of these facilities should be expanded as fast as the resources permit. Adult education programme and residential school be started on a selective basis will operate as growing points of consciousness for the entire community and their multiplier effect is bound to be substantial.

The Commission notes in this regard that whereas several states have extended a number of ad hoc concessions to backward class students, a few serious attempts have been made to integrate these facilities into a comprehensive scheme for a qualitative upgradation of educational environment available to OBC students.

13.16 After all, education is the best catalyst of change and educating the backward classes is the surest way to improve their self-image and raise their social status. As the OBCs cannot afford the high wastage rate of our educational system, it is very important that their education is highly biased in favour of vocational training. After all, reservation in services will absorb only a few small percentage of the educated backward classes and the rest should be suitably equipped with vocational skills to enable them to get a return on having invested several years in education.

13.17 It is also obvious that even if all the above facilities are given to OBC students, they will not be able to compete on an equal footing with others in securing admission to technical and professional institutions. In view of this, it is recommended that seats should be reserved for OBC students in all scientific, technical and professional institutions run by central as well as state governments. The reservation will fall under Article 15(4) of the constitution and the quantum of reservation should be the same as in the Government services i.e. 27 per cent.

13.18 While implementing the provision for reservation, it should also be ensured that the candidates who are admitted against the reserved quota are enabled to derive full benefit of higher studies. It has been generally noticed that these OBC students coming from an impoverished cultural background, are not able to abreast with other students. It is therefore, very essential that special coaching facilities are arranged for all such students in our technical and professional institutions. The concerned authorities should clearly appreciate that their job is not finished once the candidates against reserved quota have been admitted to various institutions. In fact, the real task starts only after that. Unless adequate follow up action is taken to give special coaching assistance to these students, not only these young people will feel frustrated and humiliated, but the country will also be landed with ill-equipped and substandard engineers, doctors and other professionals.

Recommendations for Economic Upliftment

13.19 Vocational communities following hereditary occupations have suffered heavily as a result of industrialization. Mechanical production and introduction of synthetic materials has robbed the village potter, oil crusher, black smith, carpenter, etc., of their traditional means of livelihood and the paperization of these classes is a well known phenomenon in the country-side.

13.20 It has therefore become very much necessary that suitable institutional finance and technical assistance is made available to such members of village vocational communities who want to set up small scale industries of their own. Similarly, assistance should also be provided to those promising OBC candidates who have obtained special vocational training.

13.21 Of course, most State Governments have created various financial and technical agencies for the promotion of small and medium scale industries. But it is well known that only more influential members of the community are able to derive benefits from these agencies. It is therefore very essential that separate financial institutions for providing financial and technical assistance be established for the backward classes.

13.22 Cooperative societies of occupation groups will also help a lot. But due care should be taken that all the office bearers and members of such societies belong to the concerned hereditary occupational groups and outsiders are not allowed to exploit them by infiltrating into such co operatives.

13.23 The share of OBCs in the industrial and business life of the country is negligible which partly explains their extremely low-income levels. It is imperative that all the State Governments suitably encourage to create a separate net work of financial and technical institutions to foster business venturing and industrial enterprising among OBCs

Recommendations for Structural Changes

13.24 Reservations in government employment and educational institutions, as also all possible financial assistance will remain mere palliatives unless the problem of backwardness is tackled from its root bulk of small land holders, tenants, agricultural labourers, impoverished village artisans, unskilled workers etc. belonging to SC/ST/OBCs. Apart from social traditions, the dominance of the top peasantry is exercised through recourse to informal bondage which arises mainly through money lending, leasing out of small bits of land and providing housing sites and dwelling space to poor peasantry. As most of the functionaries of Government are drawn from top of peasantry, the caste and class linkage between the functionaries of Government and the top peasantry remain firm. This also tilts the socio political balance in favour of the top peasantry and helps it in having its dominance over others.

13.25 The net outcome of the above situation is that notwithstanding their numerical preponderance, backward class continues to remain in mental and material bondage of the higher castes and rich peasantry. In fact, there is already sizable volume legislation on the statute books to abolish Zamindari, place ceilings on land holdings and distribute land to the landless. But in actual practice, its implementation has been halting, half-hearted and superficial.

The Commission points out that a few states like Karnataka, Kerala and West Bengal, which have gone about the job more earnestly, have not only succeeded in materially helping the backward classes, but also reaped rich political dividends in the bargain.

13.26 It is the Commission's firm conviction that a radical transformation of the existing production relations is the most important single step that can be taken for the welfare and upliftment of all backward classes. If this is not possible in the industrial sector for various reasons, in the agricultural sector, a change of this nature is both feasible and overdue.

13.27 The Commission, therefore, strongly recommends that all the State Governments should be directed to enact and implement progressive land legislation so as to effect basic structural changes in the existing production relations in the countryside.

13.28 At present, surplus land is being allotted to SCs and STs. A part of the surplus land becoming available in future as a result of the operation of land ceiling laws etc. should also be allotted to OBC landless labourers.

Mandal Commission made all the above recommendations way back in the year 1977/78. But their relevance and need for immediate implementation is warranted even after almost thirty years, which among so many other things reveals that there is very little improvement on the socio-economic front of the backward communities in the country. As stated earlier, this is the most controversial report. It appears that there is a shortsighted belief that Mandal means only and only 27 per cent OBC reservation. But as can be seen from the above recommendations, it has suggested for a total socio-economic revolution of this more than half of Indian population of the country. Recommendations made in the report are farsighted, feasible and substituting the very need for the proposed reservation in the longer run.

REFERENCES

1. Kaka Kalelkar Report in Parliament on 3 December 1955.
2. *Mandal Commission Report.*
3. Surinder Mallik, SC Mandal Commission Case 1992.
4. P. Radhakrishnan *Religion Caste and State.*
5. Dirks 2001 p. 271.
6. Jayanti Manani, *Backwards, Shudras, OBC Andolan* 2004.

7

Anti-Reservation Agitations in Gujarat

While studying dynamics of the reservation system in India, one cannot undermine the historic anti-reservation agitations that took place in Gujarat in the year 1981 and again in 1985. It is interesting to know how the issue of the reservation initially erupted, how newer and newer reservation related issues went on being added and subsequently how the volcano of casteism came on the surface and enfeebled a virtual war on the streets between the upper castes and the lower castes for months together. It claimed lives of about 32 people, deserted the living of thousands and left after it, a sad memory which the victim backwards have not forgotten even after passage of long twenty five years. In a way it was a test check of self-introspection as to whether really caste consciousness has vanished? Has the social integration process strengthened? Does reservation continue carrying a social sympathy as an inevitable solution of correcting past wrongs? Apart from the apparent reasons such as reservation quota in post graduation of medical faculty, what were the inside reasons that led to such a mass scale anti-reservation provocation?

Though reservation provisions include three categories viz. scheduled castes (SC), scheduled tribes (ST) and other backward classes (OBC), anti-reservation agitation did not pose much of disturbances on scheduled tribes, since their population is in limited districts of the State with a very large concentration there and comparatively, much lesser extent of social discrimination in tribal dominated areas since decades. They were it appears left out from the target group of attacks and atrocities also on account of docile temperament of scheduled tribes. Role of other backward classes remained indifferent as discussed in the later part of this chapter. Thus, the main targets of attacks, atrocities and hatred were scheduled castes whose pace of progress was faster, visible and at times enviable thanks to the blessings of reservation. The communities under this group were vocal, responsive and with counter agitative temperament also. Thus, discussion on anti-reservation agitations would center around scheduled castes also known as *'dalits'* through out in this chapter.

1981 Anti-Reservation Agitations and Blood Shades

The agitation was initially launched by the medicos for abolition of reservation in the post graduation in medical studies which was implemented by the government from the year 1978 i.e. just before three years. Initially, the agitation remained concentrated mainly in medical and engineering college campuses at Ahmedabad. But, it gradually started spreading in other parts of the states. Closure of schools and colleges, calls for 'Bandhs' in main cities and subsequently the whole of Gujarat were some of the manifestations. The agitations and protests gradually landed on the streets and roads creating civic disturbances more or less in most part of the State. All this went on for days together.

Textile mill *dalit* workers numbering to about 75,000 observed a lightning strike on 20 and 21 February 1981 in defiance of their unity to the cause. In retaliation, about 1,50,000 upper caste mill workers observed three days' strike on 23, 24 and 25 February 1981. Incidentally the agitation was in respect of reservation in post graduation medical speciality which had nothing to do with these workers of either side. Here was an atavistic throw back with class reverting back to caste. This reveals that the whole society was vertically divided into anti-reservation lobby and pro reservation group.[1]

Grounds of Agitation

The first provocation in launching of 1981 agitation was ignited by introduction of reservation in post graduation medical courses. Since then, more and more other grounds of protests and unrests all around and against reservation went on being added further and further which included; carry forward of backlog seats under reservation; inter changeability of unfilled reserved seats from one reserved category to the other, implementation of roster, promotion, somewhere even fast track promotions, special recruitment drives for filling up the backlog vacancies etc. The protests and demands did not stop here too and it further snowballed to total abolition of reservation—lock, stock and barrel from all educational institutions and at all stages right from the state services and so on.

The government tried to resolve the issue by creating additional seats in post graduation courses equal to the number of reserved seats and immediate abolition of interchangeability and carry forward. The agitation however not only continued, but also gathered further momentum. Government employees, panchayat employees and police association pressed for abolition of the roster and further demanding total scrapping of reservations.

Incidences of Atrocities on Scheduled Castes

Though the agitation was concentrated initially in educational institutions, it was later on spread in the residential localities of major cities in the beginning then in almost all parts of the State including small villages as can be seen from the gist of few out of number of incidences that took place during this three months' old agitation.

It was the time of April/May of 1981, when the whole Gujarat was caught in the flames of caste hatreds and communal violence. Much talked about social harmony, fraternity and brotherhood all remained unseen on this pious land of Mahatma Gandhi.

Jetalpur District Ahmedabad

Village Jetalpur is situated about 12 km. away from Ahmedabad with population of about 3 or 4,000 of whom

500/600 belong to the scheduled castes. One Shakarabhai Premabhai Sonar, a scheduled caste person employed as a watchman in the local gram panchayat was locked up in the gram panchayat office, a public place on 26th December 1980, poured with kerosene and ignited to death by mob of local residents. The allegation against the unfortunate person was that he was shifty character and had been caught in stealing.

The village had a big temple of Swaminarayan with large number of worshippers in the village. Incidentally it was also a year of Bicentenary Celebration of Lord Swaminarayan. The very people keeping deep faith in the Hindu religious philosophy and worshipping the Hindu Gods brutally killed a fellow Hindu worshipping the same faith and religion simply out of caste hatred. What an unfortunate illustration of hypocritic belief and behaviour ?

Detroj; District Ahmedabad

Village Detroj is some 50 km. away now a Tehsil center in Ahmedabad District. The village consists of upper castes Khastriyas, Patels, OBC category Thakors and also scheduled castes viz. Vankars, Rohits etc. Massive attacks on backward castes inhabitations from the local upper castes mob during these anti-reservation agitations which initially started at Ahmedabad and other big cities but subsequently also percolated in the small rural and semi-urban centers like Detroj. The Detroj attack on backwards was with sole motive of their total ousting from the village. The houses were attacked and set to fire; their households were thrown away. Some frightened inmates who had huddled for protection in their houses were rescued from the inferno only on the nick of time. The panic stricken *dalits* moved out *en masse* with whatever belonging they could carry. While on their way to destination Ahmedabad, they were spotted by Kshatriya Sarpanch of the neighbouring village Kukavav who offered them shelter and placed them under protection.

A local scheduled caste lady teacher named Ushaben Bhalchandra who tried to run away from the rear door was caught by the mob and made virtually naked. The story of atrocities thereafter on the poor lady is just inexpressible.

The height was that none of the newspapers took the cognizance of this heinous act even as a two-line news item!

Pij; District Kheda

In another village Pij District Kheda of central Gujarat is having population of 10,000 upper castes Patels and about 500 lower castes population. On 22nd February 1981, the village main light switch was put off at night 10.30 pm. And the whole village was pushed into darkness. A mob in thousand of numbers attacked the *dalit* locality. Some three *pucca* built up houses were broken, few others were put to fire, shops of a Muslim and a Sindhi were also not spared and therefore put to fire. The *dalits* ran away from the village for a quite good time.

Gozaria; District Mehsana

On 16 March 1981, in wake of anti-reservation stir turned into anti-government agitation, at Gozaria a highly Patel dominant village, in a clash between police and the upper caste mob, two persons were killed in the compelled police firing. The whole anger of the village came down heavily on the local *dalit* residents and the upper castes people declared social boycott of the entire *dalit* locality, i.e. no supply of milk, vegetables, no floor milling services and so on.

Uttarsanda; District Kheda

Uttarsanda is yet a similar village on the attack of upper castes during these anti-reservation agitations. The attack erupted from a procession on 22nd February 1981. Fourteen *dalit* houses were completely burnt in the attack. One of the houses belonged to an old *dalit* widow and her blind son who were earning their livelihood through selling peanuts in the railway trains. No body informed the police about the attack and the fire. Local railway station master when approached for telephone assistance, refused to allow to use railway telephone to contact the police for rescue. By the time, fire brigade arrived at the place, houses of these poor people, which they constructed out of years' hard toiled earnings were finished to ashes.

Modus Operandi of Atrocities

Though, most of the districts in the state were more or less affected with the anti-reservation agitations, Kheda, Ahmedabad, and Mehsana were the main epic centres of the anarchies of atrocities. It is interesting to know why the anger against the reservation was with much at a higher score in these three districts.

These three districts were having disproportionately higher rate of education and urbanization of scheduled castes. Incidentally, these three districts were also having highest concentration of scheduled caste population. Therefore, educational and economic progress of scheduled castes was enviously noticeable. As against this, though upward mobility of scheduled castes was higher in Valsad District than Mehsana and Kheda Districts, the scheduled castes of Valsad District were not attacked as scheduled caste population in this district is very small in number and proportion.

Target of attack on scheduled castes was also with a particular pattern i.e. more advanced castes among the scheduled castes were subjected to higher incidences of attacks and atrocities. Colonies, societies, chawls with more progressive Vankars and Rohit communities amongst SCs in these districts were severely attacked than the lesser advanced SCs such as Valmikis etc. engaged in unclean occupations.

One more feature of these wide spread atrocities on scheduled castes was that these three most hard hit districts i.e. Mehsana, Kheda and Ahmedabad are having commonly highest population of Patidars among upper castes. These Patidars also known as Patel community took lead in flaring the anti-reservation movement in the State. One of the reasons as revealed from many people was that there was no Patel representation in the then State Ministry managing political governance.

Role of OBCs During Agitation

It is also experienced in case of reservation based issues or controversies that the society was divided into all upper castes and *dalits*. Other backward classes on such issues either keep away or took the side of the upper sides so as to be treated themselves as upper castes in general social perception. Moreover, among these vast 52 per cent OBC population, many castes have still very low level of education and general economic development. Hence caste consciousness in them is seen with higher gravity in treating *dalits* at lower hierarchical position.

There was a mix response from the other backward communities (OBC). In some areas, influenced by the upper castes, OBCs also co-operated by joining in such attacks on the scheduled castes colonies. On number of incidents, there was also a confrontation of other backward classes with scheduled castes. Main reason for involvement of these OBCs in anti-reservation agitation was poor state of educational development in many of the most backward castes. Subsequently, when they were explained that they were also the potential beneficiaries of reservational provisions, then they either kept away from such agitations or at some other places supported the pro-reservation movements.

Development Dynamics of Scheduled Castes

Why such agitations started eighties afterwards? This needs going back to the development dynamics of the nation as a whole from independence. Fifties i.e. the first post-independence decade opened new vistas of growth and development for all i.e. upper castes as well as lower castes with huge socio-economic development planning on a massive scale in the country. Though it was open to all to take the accruing benefits of these wide openings, the upper castes had an edge with their better level of education in availing these openings.

Though provisions of reservation started being implemented during these two decades, absorption of SC/ST people in the government services remained much at a low level. The reason was their inability to meet even the minimum educational requirements for the government jobs. The crest for education amongst the scheduled castes and scheduled tribes took off during this period, which gradually made them equipped for the Government jobs from seventies onwards. In other words, fifties and sixties were the decades of open and competition free Indian economy. In view of unmatching situation of social equality, the upper castes could avail the benefits of the new openings to the fullest extent not only in the recruitment, but also in consistent promotions which got also reflected in much higher representation of upper castes in the government jobs till seventies.

Seventies opened up new job avenues in nationalized banking and insurance sector, which were hitherto in the private sector. Job absorptions from the reserved categories were highest in the seventies. By the time of beginning of eighties, presence of scheduled castes and scheduled tribes was more or less started being seen in every sector of government/ public sector fields. A picture remarkably brought home in the upper castes that scheduled castes and scheduled tribes are omni-present in the government jobs. All this played a crucial role in the conflicting and envious situations right from the beginning of the eighties.

As stated above with increasing presence in the government and public sector jobs, developmental graph particularly of the scheduled castes was going up consistently at a higher and higher rate. Social condition from the view point of upward mobility, wide spread education acceleration etc. created an atmosphere that scheduled castes are progressing at a jet speed keeping most of the other castes behind them. Though overall picture of these communities was not so. Whatever improvements seen apparently were in respect of a small fraction of the whole lot of scheduled castes. Condition of a larger lot of these people living in slums and rural areas was still far from the desired level.

Social Intolerance

Though there is an accepted truth that there shall always be an inverse relationship between education and social caste stigma, the position in respect of social scenario as seen in Gujarat during this period was not indicative of this universal truth. The survey of those days during eighties reveals that in 90 per cent village temples and upper caste houses, scheduled castes entry was still denied. Sixty four per cent villages were having separate drinking arrangement for these communities. Forty seven per cent village panchayats were observing untouchability of one type or the other.

Various studies in those days in respect of scheduled castes at national level position revealed few more features in respect of scheduled castes of Gujarat. Rate of education spread in scheduled castes of Gujarat was second highest next to that of Kerala. If this is viewed together with the rate of urbanization of these communities, it was found highest in the whole of the nation. Incidentally, position of the ratio of scheduled castes job seekers is seen, Gujarat was third highest in the Nation after Maharashtra and Kerala. All this put together led in building up a negative bias in the minds of upper castes in Gujarat for the scheduled castes.

More and more families of scheduled castes were mobilizing upwardly with the help of reservation in education and jobs. This was also reflected in enhancement of their general standard of living such as their shifting in better housing localities, admissions of their children in good educational institutions and so on. The upper castes felt that the very people who were hierarchically much below them were now attaining equilibrium with them. During informal meetings for launching anti-reservation agitation all these social changes in the reserved category people were presented in a very inflammatory and probating way.

1985 Anti-Reservation Agitations

The main cause triggering the 1985 anti-reservation agitation was the hike in OBC reservation from 10 per cent to 28 per cent in the State. This time also the lauder voice was from the medical and engineering colleges. The initial agitation of engineering and medical students was intensified in collusion with State Parents Federation and collectively a call was given for boycott of examination in whole of the State. The agitation manifested mainly in the form of violent incidents. The worst affected was the education field. The leaders of the agitation coming from the elite class of the society were able to organize and mobilize the upper class students, organizations of government employees and other sections of the society. A hammering through false misrepresentation started against the entire reservation system stressing that unemployment and cause of non-admissions of upper caste students in medical and other prestigious educational faculties is reservation only. All this collectively created a feeling of hatred in the minds of upper classes. All this ignited in spreading strong feeling among the upper classes that gradually backward classes would dominate everywhere over the society and the former will lose their long retained hold over every thing. This was enough for the upper classes for supporting anti-reservation agitations, although facts showed that in no field, the reservation quota was fully utilized.

The anti-reservation which continued for over hundred days, destabilized the normal civic life in the state with repeated call offs, rallies, disrupting educational functioning imposition of curfew and so on. There were direct clashes between pro-reservation and anti-reservation groups. There were also incidents of individual attacks involving stabbing, beating, property damaging and so on. Economic activities came almost to a halt. In such situations of chaos and anarchies, as usually happens, anti-social elements also took over the command on the situation which further worsened the civic life and law and order in the society. Personal accounts or social, personal, financial rivalry are also settled which all go unnoticed in the name of general disturbances.

More and more agitational programmes by upper castes also gave a way to rally of scheduled castes and scheduled tribes was arranged in support of reservation from whole of Gujarat on 26 August 1985, a day following resignation of the

State Chief Minister Madhavsinh Solanki after prolonged agitations and worsened condition of law and order in the State. It is still remembered as the largest crowd ever gathered at the State Capital so far.

Grounds for 1985 Anti-Reservation Agitations

The apparent ground for 1985 agitation was mainly hike in reservation quota for OBCs as stated above from 10 per cent to 28 per cent. Besides, various progressive steps taken by the ruling government also created resentment in the upper castes minds which developed a feeling that the government is over actively functioning for safeguarding interests of the backwards to the detriment of interest of the upper castes. Similarly, a series of other actions of the government viz. the Land Ceiling Act, 20 point economic programme, favourable economic schemes and policies for the upliftment of the poor and backward classes, mid day meal programme etc. were never acceptable to the elite classes.

Besides, the job quota in employment, government undertook a series of economic upliftment measures such as allocation of unused cattle grazing village land, allotment of residential plots to the scheduled castes, scheduled tribes people from the village common land and enactment of Minimum Wages Act enhancing the wage expenditure on the shoulders of the upper castes beneficiaries of which were lower castes factory workers.

Changing Political Power Scenario in Gujarat

Since the beginning of the eighties, there was a major shift in the political structure of Gujarat with shrinking political importance and control of the elite classes. Especially, those communities, which were traditionally in power since the inception of the state started losing their hold on the political scene. This created a sense of deprivation and feeling of disaffection towards the government. Thus, politically and economically vested interests were apprehensive of the government and its policies and therefore, they joined hands with the agitators. To make the agitation successful, they created a feeling of hatred towards scheduled castes and Muslims.

The State Government withdrew implementation of additional reservation for OBC declared by them before two months fearing the mounting tensions in the state and also in view of the Prime Minister's hint at the possibility of undertaking a fresh review in the matter of OBC reservation in totality. The Union Government also on 17 May 1985 asked all the States to maintain *status quo* as regard to reservation of OBC till a consesus.

Thus there was no cause for continuing the agitation since enhancement in OBC reservation quota was withdrawn by the state government. Despite the same, the agitation was not called off. The anti-reservation agitation was turned now into anti-government stir with the demand for the removal of the Chief Minister. The elite class constituting 25 per cent of the population was vocal, resourceful, and in a position to launch a high-pitched agitation even without the support of the remaining 75 per cent population. The mo*dality* of the agitators was subtle, yet demonstratably effective so as to attract statewide attention. The upper castes also dominated press and other media. Besides, this influenced and dominated State Bar, Employees' Trade Organizations, Panchayats, semi-Government Organizations, which all influenced in converting the anti-reservation agitation into an anti-government movement.

Partial Role of Media During Agitations

The role of the press during this agitation was by no means a minor one in keeping the agitation alive and in accentuating the communal riot situation. The hospitality of the newspaper columns was thrown open to sustain the caste communal hatred and reports and the articles intended to grow disaffection against the state. Anger of media was also provoked on account of attack on one of the Gujarati Daily *'Gujarat Samachar'* causing heavy damage to the press. Exaggerated and extensive accounts of violence, partial coverage of the communal incidents and incitements against the government and the backward classes were the dominant theme of the press. Even in reporting communal violence, special care was taken by the newspapers for publishing the news in such a manner that a section of the society got provoked against the other. The reports were couched in such a manner that their bird view reading would be sufficient to incite an average person who may not be possessing secular bias. Even rumors were carried by the newspapers in inciting the communal hatred. Many of the officers in the government and police were also not free from the communal and caste bias feeling. There were wrong reporting in the media and newspapers against the backwards. Question of news of backward class sufferings was out of place as media was totally controlled by the upper castes and their role in those days was clearly caste prejudised. Even the media failed to the extent of its pious duty of giving unbiased and truthful news to the people.

A fact finding Team of The Editors' Guild of India[2] gathered that there was bias and partial reporting by Gujarat media on several occasions during these agitations a few of which were such as attack on Gomtipur Post Office on 29 January 1981, attack on Jain temple on 2 February 1981. In Gomtipur and attack on marriage party at Khambhatwala hall, Gita Mandir all allegedly by *dalits*, none of which actually took place at all. All such news either false or fabricated in the local print media heightened the caste war further in the state.

The Guilt noted with pain, "However, there is no denying to the fact that in the heated atmosphere, every body lost his balance. The *dalits* were the aggrieved parties and their grouse is understandable, but some of the Gujarati paper could have exercised greater restraint and in this way not given a handle to mischief-mongers to play havoc with public order and decency.

In short, there was a marked economic development in the State. Upper castes too have taken maximum benefit of these new post-independence opportunities. But their minds were still full of old conventional caste based values, perceptions and beliefs. They found emergence of a neo middle caste carved out of untouchables whom they were treating so inhumanly before some time. Their old mindset was not ready to accept new equalizing situation of scheduled castes with their old established social status. All this added fuel to the fire. They apprehended that more and more development of these backward communities means destabilization of the present social order wherein they are enjoying a very high ranked social status.

What was the reality as regards the position of the scheduled castes as a whole? A well developed and progressed section of scheduled castes was definitely emerged before the society. This was however only a small section of the entire downtrodden lot. What was expected of the upper castes was thinking about those who are still left out from the race of the progress which still crave for the development and badly needing the statutory support of reservation.

As marked by Rajni Kothari the leading Sociologist in the State, 'the fact is that there is a gross misreading of the situation. Gujarat is a highly conservative society, intolerant of progress of the lower classes with the highest incidence of untouchability according to the carefully carried out ranking of the Indian States. Social conventions have a tendency of outlasting major transformations in the economy and polity except that in each successive phase, they become more defensive and convoluted and hence more brittle and bizarre.'

Gujarat has always remained a peaceful and progressive state with more or less satisfactory level of social harmony except a few incidences of communal riots The graph of economic progress have also recorded consistently upward trend. The above agitations followed by wide scale attacks by the upper castes on the scheduled castes are big blots on Gandhi's Gujarat. The historical memories of anti reservation agitations have put it in the category of a conservative, intolerant and caste conscious state.

REFERENCES

1. *Aanamat Ni Andhi;* Chandu Maheria 1981.
2. Editors' Guilt of India; *Fact Finding Team's report.*

PART II

Debates on Reservation

Reservations were originally perceived as a national campaign of establishing social equalities by correcting past wrongs. This includes educational and economic upliftment of the pitiful and socially discarded people living in miserable conditions. Of late, this feeling of harnessing the society gradually believed sabotaging with a penchant and nefarious suspicion that it is working against the interests of majority upper castes. New and new points of debate emerged against this policy such as merit, basis of considering reservation, creamy layer, reservation in private sector, self finance educational institutions etc. There are lot of misunderstandings prevailing on these terms such that; reservations are anti-meritarian, reservations are hogged away by creamy layer of the reserved categories, reservation in private sector means dooming of private sector and so on. Various arguments commonly advocated are presented with realities there against and are all discussed in this part.

8

Merit

Most of the debate on reservation circumferences now-a-days around merit. It is believed by majority of the people that reservation means total dilution of merit, reservation means induction of people without observing any norms of merit and so on.

Merit, according to Noble Prize Winner Amartya Sen in his book *'Meritocracy and Economic Inequality'*[1] is a dependent idea and it's meaning depends on how a society defines a desirable act. An act of merit in one society may not be the same in another. The difficulty is that there is no natural order of '**merit**' independent of our social system.

Merit literarily means specific ability, talent and skill. Academic record is one of the first hand criteria of measuring one's merit. Unfortunately in our country, all criteria measuring a person's merit are centered on his performance in the examination. i.e. number of marks he has obtained in an examination becomes the sole criterion to decide how meritorious or otherwise a person is. Merit also includes a person's inner strengths of withstanding against the odd, his sensibilities to the hard realities, and firm conviction for set out goal. If one possesses these virtues, his merit definitely ranks higher than one with simple paper performance. A person struggling from childhood because of his social background, poverty and want of even the basic facilities may score less in the examination, but his well determined struggle for career achievements inspite of the odd has to be taken into consideration while coming to a conclusion about his aggregate merit.

Merit cannot thrive in a purely intellectual atmosphere. It needs another type of nutrition that is, a favourable emotional environment. Reservation will bog the administration in a variety of emotional complexes. The inward issue of inferiority of the backward classes, however muffled by defiant postures, will seek compensation in power politics to the detriment of efficiency.

Examination Marks Cannot Be Sole Merit Criterion

Let us examine therefore what contributes to getting higher marks by a student. The use of single criterion to judge the general ability of a person is misleading. There can be various kinds of merit in day-to-day living; Ability to cultivate or rear animals, or chicken, the ability to mend shoes or weave clothes or build a house or for that matter the ability to cook food or to do a housemaid's work. Similarly the ability to play or shoot an arrow or climb a tree or paint a picture or sing can require tremendous skill. Judging therefore merit through the spectacles of examination marks shall be inadequate and unjustifiable. Coming back to the criteria of percentage or marks, let us examine what are the prerequisites of getting good marks in the examination.

Factors Contributing to Higher Percentage of Marks in Examination/Competition

1. Adequate and balanced diet.
2. Basic reading and study facilities in the house.
3. Education of parents and surrounding environment for study.
4. Availability of means to acquire knowledge.
5. Availability of admission in quality educational institutes.
6. Capacity to afford donation, higher fees etc. in such institutes.
7. Affordability for tuition fees in Science Stream private coaching arrangements.

One will obviously argue that these are not the backwardness specific constraints. Are all these things available to a poor drown trodden student? No... Absolutely No. One may argue that same will be the condition of an upper caste poor student. Yes, definitely, none can deny it. But poverty and backwardness are hand in gloves position in our country. By and large an SC/ST average student barring of course a few exceptions are poor. But reverse will not be 100 per cent fact. i.e. poverty prevalence rate amongst the downtroddens is far very far higher than those in the upper castes as can be seen from Table 5.2 under Chapter 5 'Social Conditions in Rural India'. When one is examining the context of merit with regard to the aspect of reservation, it can be seen that all the above prerequisites are beyond the reach of a lower class poor. All above prerequisites entail lot of financial burden, which a poor backward family cannot afford.

Study Environment of an Average SC/ST/OBC Student

As is known, social backwardness brings in all probabilities with it economic backwardness also. Hence, most of the families belonging to scheduled castes, scheduled tribes and few other backward classes live in over crowded slums where available environment to a student of the family shall have the following realities:

1. A big number of SC/ST population inhabitate in overly crowding slums lacking even the basic facilities such as sanitation, health, clean drinking water, in a small slum housing a big family of 7/8 people. What to think about reading space and other so-called study infrastructure for these poor chaps?
2. The whole locality consists of poor labourer class with all the family members including female and school going age members struggling to meet the two ends of the family. What to talk of study environment, surrounding motivation after school hours?

3. Most of them pursue their studies in the government/ panchayat/municipality schools. Quality of education in these schools is very well to the knowledge of one and all. These schools are perhaps lacking in things such as adequacy of staff, maintanance of class rooms, basic facilities etc. all because of poor budgetary allocation and absence of sensibility towards the poor mass who are studying in such schools. Unfortunately, most of the teaching staff in these schools though hailing from backward backgrounds are seen having lost their social sensibilities and are found failing to their moral social duties in caring these students. Reasons of their neglecting attitude may be job securities in the government set up, and near absence of required basic infrastructure in these schools. All this results in very weak preparations of these students making them so handicap to withstand in today's fierce competition.
4. As stated earlier, as most of these people are working in an unorganized labour market, they are exploited economically with very poor compensation to their hard labour. Thus, aggregate family income does not suffice even to their subsistence. Their thinking about balanced diet i.e. milk, eggs, good green vegetables etc. is out of question.
5. These families are also often addicted to the vices such as drinking of liquor even out of their low income at the cost of the betterment of their children. This adds to the plight of the overall condition of the poor family.

It has to be admitted that majority of the Indian slum dwellings are full with these communities. By and large an upper caste family with the same economic condition, will not prefer to stay in these slums unless compelled by multiplicity of combined circumstances. He is likely to have brighter alternatives for settling in better housing localities considering his social connections etc.

Does Reservation Means Dilution to Merit?

So far evaluation of merit on the basis of marks is concerned particularly in connection with *inter se* comparison of the reserved category candidates with general category student; three points have to be borne in mind;

First, difference of cut off point marks between the reserved category candidates and that of a general category candidate has substantially been reduced. Category-wise difference may be in a varying size. Cut off point marks between scheduled castes and general category candidate is very thin some times even neck to neck. The difference between other backward class and the general category has also come much closer over a period of time. Things are however not encouraging if the similar position is compared in case of scheduled tribe with the general category candidate. In other words, considering very marginal or some times no difference in cut off point marks, aspect of merit in case of scheduled castes hardly gets hampered.

Second, development of skill or efficiency in the candidate after his entry in the institution has also bearing on the quality, environment of the institutions. A candidate getting an admission in the educational institution like IIM, IIT, Bajaj or Birla will have a far better exposure for his overall development as compared to some traditionally managed local educational institutions. Thus, whatever may be initial merit gap in case of reserved category candidate can be abridged in course of time with the help of institutional initiative.

Third, development and strengthening or sharpening of merit also depends upon encouragement and motivation of the superiors viz. teachers in educational institutions or the boss in the office. If they are sympathetic, and sensible towards such reserved category candidates particularly keeping in mind about the background and environment these students are hailing from, they get a very congenial boost for their growth and development. It is experienced that such positive minded superiors have brought miraculous results. There is a need for such commitment for creating a healthy society. The reality is that barring a few such committed people, there are such people in the country having taken such task as a life mission. What is yearning is adding more and more such devoted people from the society looking to the quantum of such commitment. The merit evaluation in case of reserved category candidates could be possibly measured with such potentiality considerations.

Examination Marks as Merit Criteria

Securing marks is not the sure proof of higher proficiency, efficiency or excellence. These are matters of acquired ability by studious application of mind, skills in performance by the candidate concerned whether a general candidate or a reserved candidate. It is a matter of application of the mind, constant assiduity to improve skills, capabilities and excellence in the subject or the field of action chosen by the candidate.

Radhakrishnan Commission Report[2] notes that our examination system is wrong, insufficient, subjective and unreliable. This has been further substantiated by so many educationalists in the country. Non-acceptance of limitations of the marks system for measuring the performance of a student is nothing but dishonesty.

Dr. Ambedkar's example is worth citing. In his matriculation examination, he secured only 37.5 per cent of marks, the minimum for passing being 35 per cent. If his potentialities were to be judged by the said marks, the country would have not gained the benefit of his talent for all the times to come.... "

(Dr. Babasaheb Ambedkar, Life and Mission by Dhananjay Keer)[3].

On that behalf, it is a common knowledge that marks would be secured in diverse modes. It is no indicia that particular percentage of the marks secured is an index of the proficiency, efficiency and excellence. They are awarded in internal examination on the basis of caste, creed, colour, religion etc.

In India, english is the biggest divide between '**Commoners**' and '**Elites**'. It's continued predominance precludes any possibility of this gap being bridged. Higher education, government jobs, professions and business enterprises all necessitate a sound knowledge of english language which is limited to only those who can afford expensive education in select public schools. English, not only wards off 90/95 per cent of our population from better opportunities, but also fritters away energies and talent of lakhs of our children who could not acquire efficiency in its use and in the process, infuse in them a sense of inferiority.

Availability of excellent educational and allied facility disguises with the 'Myth of Meritocracy'. Therefore, the social scientists have rejected the narrow definition of merit in terms of intelligence, which is a measure of just one portion of total spectrum of human mental abilities, associated with knowledge, rather than the limited ability of reasoning.

Why is that we believe that someone who has skills to memorize and regurgitate the answers in an examination have merit? But even to memorize certain prerequisites such as nutrition, environment and at least basic facilities are required.

Lacunae of Merit Identification

Indian Institutes of Technology (IIT) are supposed to be the best and highest centers for technological education. The test for entry to these prestigious institutions is held only in english language, qualifying in which is a matter of proud. The successful few are regarded as cream of technological competence. But a study of the background of these students brings to fore some very revealing facts, e.g. almost all the students come from major urban centers, from reputed schools, from affluent families and also from the so called forward castes excepting statutorily reserved category seats. About 80 per cent were boys i.e. the ratio of girls is very low. An analysis of this open competition shows that prerequisites to entry in the IITs are residence in metropolis, fluency in english language, affluent parents, and belongingness to upper castes. The more of these, one possesses, the better are the chances of being successful. In fact, these are the accepted merits in today's India. It clearly brings home the extreme narrow base of merit and what miniscule population can be called meritorious. Only 20 per cent of the Indian population inhabits in urban areas, only

4 to 5 per cent live in the metropolitan areas. Again only a small fraction of the entire children's population is fortunate to receive a public school education. A very thin percent of the population comes under the bracket of affluent parents. And finally more than 85 per cent population is outside the so-called forward castes! Fifty per cent of population is females. All these taken together, hardly one percent of the population sits pretty at the top of the mountain that is 'merit', enjoying the benefit of most lucrative education and jobs and most attractive facilities and luxuries generations after generations.

Another example is The Jawaharlal Nehru University of Delhi. JNU is considered as an Institution teeming with merit and is also a recognized launching board for entry in elite club of prestigious Indian Administrative Services (IAS). The admissions here are based on written and oral tests. A few years ago i.e. till 1983, out of 100 points set for admission, 20 points were awarded to compensate various kinds of backwardness; 9 points for caste backwardness, 7 for economic backwardness and 4 for regional deprivation. But there was opposition from elite quarters and resorting to the logic of admissions purely on the basis of merit. This provision was rescinded by the University despite strong opposition from the students in 1983. A qualitative difference between the backgrounds of those who joined before 1983 and those admitted after 1983 is clearly discernible. Because of these points to offset backwardness, students from poor families from backward states such as Bihar, Orissa, and Uttar Pradesh were admitted in a substantial number, whereas now public school products of metropolitan cities have become more numerous.[4]

Merit is Always Context Specific

One needs to remember that the criteria for assessing merit are very arbitrary and often not related to the job or expectation. So if we have a better system of assessing skill and attitude other than rote learning and examination based system, many of those currently considered as without merit will get in. Most US Universities, when they seek references specifically ask whether the marks are a true reflection of the candidate's ability and if not, whether there were any reasons why the candidate could not perform well despite being a meritorious or talented person. Why don't we do in India, which is observed at handful of universities?

Merit according to Justice Kapadia in Supreme Court Case M. Nagraj and others, 'Merit is context specific. It derives its meaning from particular conditions and purposes. The impact of any affirmative action policy on 'merit' depends on how that policy is designed'[5].

The Sociologists like Bourdieu refers the term merit as "**Cultural Capital**." While some of these are acquired in educational institutions, part of these and how well we learn them depends upon our social background. So, if we come from an illiterate family without a culture of learning or reading, then in general, we don't do as well, because of many reasons such as limited help at home with studies, interaction with peers who are not very knowledgeable, limited knowledge and awareness because of lack of books, newspapers, TV etc. at home and so on. In India, because of past discrimination, those with a lower economic status are mostly those with a low social or caste status. The objective of reservations therefore is to offset social and cultural deprivations resulting from past and present discriminatory behaviour by one section of the population against another.

Justice O. Chenappa Reddy comments, "There is no merit in a system which brings about such consequences, he says, "Is not a child of the scheduled caste, scheduled tribe or other backward classes who has been brought up in an atmosphere of penury, illiteracy and anti-culture who is looked down upon by tradition and society, who has no books and magazines to read at home, no radio to listen, no TV to watch, no one to help him in his home work, who goes to the nearest local board school and college, whose parents are either illiterate or so ignorant and ill-informed that he cannot even hope to seek their advice on any matter of importance, a child who must perforce know what is happening in the world. Has not this child got merit if he with all his disadvantages is able to secure the qualifying 40 per cent or 50 per cent of the marks at a competitive examination where the children of the upper classes who have all the advantages, who go to St. Paul's High School or St. Stephen's College and who has perhaps been specially coached for the examination may secure 70 per cent, 80 or 90 per cent of the marks? Surely, a child who has been able to jump so many hurdles may be expected to do better and better as he progresses in life. "If spring flower, he cannot be, autumn flower he may be, the Judge says, "Why then should he be stopped at the threshold on an alleged meritarian principle?"

Justice Sawant in Indra Sahney Case

"The instances of Vyasa, Valmiki and Kalidas demonstrate that intelligence, perception, character, scholarship and talent are not a monopoly of any section of the society. Given the opportunity, those who are condemned to the lowliest stations in life can rise to the loftiest status in society. One can only guess how much this country has lost for want of opportunities to the vast majority all these centuries. This aspect of the present and the past history has a bearing on the 'merit contention' advanced against reservation.[6]

The assumption that the reservations lead to the appointment or admission of non-meritorious candidates is also not factually correct. In the first instance, there are minimum qualifying marks prescribed for appointment/admission. Secondly, there is a fierce competition among the backward class candidates for the seats in the reserved quota reaching near the cut off limits for seats in the general quota as some surveys made on the subject show."

Recruitment Through Reservation and Merit

It is very conveniently argued that reservation means dilution to the merit norms. Recruitment of reserved category candidate means an utter ignorance of set merit norms. Extract of the editorial appeared in the *Financial Express,* New Delhi dated 31 May, 2004 is quoted here under, which reflects a general incorrect perception about any reservation policy in our country[7].

"It goes against the logic of economic efficiency and is clearly undesirable. To be efficient, it is desirable that enterprises be allowed to hire the best available talent regardless of caste or class the later may belong to, with the suitability of the candidate for the job based on his or her qualifications, experience and potential. Job reservations may be in public sector or now in private sector introduces additional market distortions and leads to sub-optimal outcomes and this is not desirable...."

But in reality, it is not so. For this, one will have to understand the method and norms adhered to in the recruitment process in government, public sector institutions adhering to the provisions of reservation.

Recruitment in government or public sector undertaking is announced through wide scale publicity by advertisements in national as well as vernacular dailies so that all will generally notice it. This fulfills the most popular principle of personnel management to have choice from the largest possible potential lot. Perhaps, this is not so in most of the other private sector recruitments.

1. There is no relaxation in the minimum basic requirements such as qualifications, experience, skill requirement etc.
   There may be some marginal relaxation to the reserved categories under "The zone of consideration" norms for considering the eligibility criteria.
2. There is no relaxation at all in the physique related requirements.
3. Recruitment process is done through multi-level screenings i.e. preliminary test, IQ/Descriptive examinations, viva voce, group discussions, physical and aptitude tests etc. so as to examine them from multiple aspects for selecting the best in talent as well as aptitude. With the present day unemployment situation, steep competition prevails amongst the reserved category candidates also.

This can be ensured through various ways and means of HRD. e.g. if a post graduation qualification is required, for a particular post, the reservation applicability does not mean doing away, with the lower than post-graduation qualification. Further more, if the job under the recruitment pre supposes an additional background such as computer literacy, law specialization etc. then that is also not expected to be dispensed with. 'In fact, reservation never solicits to fit an unsuitable head for the sake of accommodating one in the name of reservation. What is expected in case of a reserved category candidate is, the positive consideration of his rightful candidature which is likely to jeopardize in the prevailing caste dominant social system'.

In other words, the reservation never stipulates compulsory absorption of a person, whether suitable or not putting aside all the job requirement norms. The whole selection procedure is proven one having enabled induction of best available talent from amongst even the reserved category candidates in the government and public sector so far.

Merit in Armed Forces

Indian army force, which is one of the biggest armed force in the world, has employed 32 per cent personnel belonging to scheduled castes and scheduled tribes in various cadres and ranks. Our Army has got a regiment system, which are named after one caste or another. Objective of naming regiments like this is altogether a different subject. But with all that, the patriotism, discipline and efficient functioning of our army in all emergencies be it on the boarder in Pakistan War of 1950, Chinese aggression 1962, Bangla Desh war 1971 and recently Kargil 1997 or in any crisis of internal disturbances, our army soldiers have risen to the occasion with glorious success without bothering for their own lives.

Representation of SC/ST in Indian army being 32 per cent is much above the adequacy of representation norms stipulated under Article 16(4) of the constitution and various court verdicts. Such a higher proportion of reserved category people was supposed to have violated the much cried about meritarian principle in all probability adversely affecting efficiency of the

Indian Army and what not. But the achievements as enumerated above speak just the otherwise.

What the people concerned with the aspect of merit with regard to scheduled castes and scheduled tribes have to comment in respect of over representation of SC/ST in Indian army? Recruitment of more and more SC/ST and OBC is adding in the total strength of army surpassing the stipulated reservation ceilings does not face any objections or injuctions in the name of much talked about post based roster point reservation, adequate representation or much debated '**merit**'. Perhaps, principle of equal opportunities is not applicable in '**martyrship' for a national cause.**[8]

Reservation not Anti-Meritarian

The relevance and significance of merit is very appropriately mentioned in well-known Supreme Court *Indra Sahney case.* It states that "It cannot also be ignored that the very idea of reservation implies selection of a less meritorious person. At the same time, we recognize that this much cost has to be paid, if the constitutional promise of social justice is to be redeemed.

The judgement further states, "We firmly believe that given an opportunity, members of the reserved categories bound to overcome their initial disadvantages and would compete with and may in some cases, excel over members of open competition. It is undeniable that nature has endowed it upon members of backward classes as much as it has endowed it upon members of other classes and that what is required is an opportunity to prove it. It may not therefore, be said that reservations are anti-meritarian. Merit is there even among the reserved candidates and the small difference that may be allowed at the stage of initial recruitment is bound to disappear in course of time. These members too will compete with and improve their efficiency along with others."

As regard proven merits, there are instances of hundreds of civil services officers belonging to SCs, STs, and OBCs in IAS, IPS, IFS, IRS and various State Cadres. Many of these officers have made a pride name with their outstanding performance. Their excellent and meritorious work is appreciated by one and all at various stages, up to the highest levels.

Were these officers not meritorious? They were... But they could perform that well only upon the opportunity they got.

Recruitment is Always Subject to Human Limitations

As such, there are numerous ways and means to ascertain inherent merit possessed by an aspirant. The most common yardstick in government mechanism is percentage of marks obtained by a person in his higher secondary examination for educational admission. While in case of recruitment, it is grade or class or percentage of marks obtained in graduation. As stated earlier percentage of marks obtained by an upper caste with all the facilities and that by a poor backward class is not comparable. However, since there is no other acceptable alternative available for the *en masse* admissions, this has to be accepted inspite of all its limitations.

Once the person applies for a job, the second yardstick of measuring the merit is the candidate's evaluation in the competitive tests. Such tests are of two types. One taking competitive examinations on the same line with conventional examinations. This will also carry all the drawbacks of our higher secondary examinations system, i.e. comparative availability of the facilities to a candidate belonging to a higher castes and that to a backward caste candidate. Second type of merit evaluation is IQ type evaluation testing the mental ability of a person vis a vis his analytical capability in a given situation. All such comprehensions come in a candidate not through books or examination preparations, but from various factors attributed by his surroundings. Here also situation for an upper caste fellow will have an edge over that of a lower caste fellow.

And last round of merit evaluation in case of recruitment is interfacing, group discussion etc. Here, merit never operates in isolation. Social background of the candidate on one hand and social bearings in the mind of the interviewers invariably play an important role. Persons with rural and interior background will have an inferiority complex. As regard knowledge and information updation also family environment and facilities available shall play in the performance of the candidate. Interviews are conducted by a team of experts. But after all, they are human beings and are drawn from the very society with stagmatic caste considerations. The prevailing Indian social situation the interviewer is living around and built there from his own perceptions and values do effect the selection process. Summing up all, one will come to a conclusion that merit evaluation is subject to so many external factors leaving rare possibility of a bias-proof merit based selection. Simply saying that induction of scheduled castes, scheduled tribes and other backward class people means utter ignorance of merit consideration is not correct.

The method adopted for judging whether a person is competent or otherwise is completely insufficient. In fact, the examinations conducted for the purpose of examining specific 'merit', which is nothing but an art of mugging up books and spewing out that information in the examination are not free of limitations. Even the knowledge of books our education system seems to impart are enclosed capsules of information with no concern for analysis or self understanding. But since the present system of evaluating merit as also competence are based on mugging up bookish knowledge, they indirectly help the upper castes in outclassing all others since they have been more familiar and with better opportunities in higher scoring in such examinations.

Myths of Merit

The Indian Society traditionally is based on vernashram, divided into four categories. i.e. Brahmin, Kshatriya, Vaishya and lastly Shudra. While former three are known as Upper castes, the last one as the backward viz. SC/ST/OBC.

So far general belief regarding '**MERIT**' is concerned. There is an illogical notion that upper castes means merit and lower castes means absence of merit.

Prevailing Indian social system have resulted into creation of dominance of upper castes for centuries. Even today, if one looks at the government sector top positions, higher level judiciary, the whole corporate sector, presence of minority groups, women, *dalits, adivasis* and other backward classes is microscopically negligible as compared to their proportion in the population. As the upper most echelon of the society had been in the top most decision-making and apex administration of the country, can we attribute all the poor and inefficient state of administration, illiteracy, poverty, inefficiency and lack of development in India to the dominance of the upper castes that they lack merit to rule the country? Why is it that we did not develop on many indicators for centuries and for decades after independence in spite of the dominance of the so-called meritorious upper castes in the governance of the nation?

The South Indian states are having higher representation of these reserved category group in Government and private sector. Tamil Nadu has the highest reservation provisions of 69 per cent viz. OBC 50 per cent, SC 18 per cent and ST 1 per cent. Authentic surveys and studies reveal and even the people visiting these states experience that all these states are better performer on most of the development indicators. Higher representation of reserved category in administration in these states has never posed any hindrance either on merit or efficiency count.

Question that arises here is:

- If the Brahmins are so meritorious in the country, why is it that half of the country's population is illiterate? It was their duty to educate the society, in which they have failed.
  Incidentally, The Brahmins represent 5.20 per cent of the country's total population. As against this, they occupy 70.20 per cent employment in the Government/ Non Government. Services as in 1989.[9]
- If the Kshatrias were so meritorious, why did this great nation remain slave of foreign invaders for over a thousand of years! Moghuls, Britishers and many others defeated them and subjugated the nation.

- Similarly, if the Vaishyas were so meritorious, why has the trade and commerce of the country remained in shambles since centuries with our global share never exceeding even 1 per cent?

We must realize that **merit is generally not recognized and rewarded in the society**. In many different ways, **everyone from ordinary people to rich business families are out to protect their privileges and deny basic rights to others** and **merit is usually a casualty in this process**. Further, the characterization of merit in terms of marks, degrees etc. takes away the focus from actual ability, appropriateness, aptitude and competence for a specific task which are actually what you require to do a job well. There is no such thing as a universal or context-neutral merit. Merit is always context specific.

D. Parthsarthi in his Article ' **Towards a Larger Perspective**' in Advocacy Internet of Nov./Dec. 2005 writes on merit as under:[10]

" ... The concept of 'merit ' itself is not properly understood by many. First of all, we should remember that in India, most popular way of assessing merit is through examination, which is not often the best way of doing it. Take our IAS or IPS officers. Many of them have contributed to developing or implementing development programmes which are absolutely useless or inappropriate. A large number of studies have shown that these officers are not actually equipped with the skill to understand the problems or best ways to implement them. If only doctor can treat the patient and software engineers can develop software, how a person who passes theoretical examinations in given subjects can become development and administration expert? Through out the world, there is a trend towards participatory development, wherein it is believed that the poor are better aware of their problem and they should decide the development model to be implemented. However, they cannot pass the UPSC exams and those who can pass have no merit to devise, design and implement development programmes on behalf of the poor!

Efficiency

Another argument against a reservation system is that the people taken under reservations are inefficient as they distort resource allocation and prevent the resources from being used for the optimal productive use. Thus, reservations work against efficiency.

Following is the recent performance ranking of the country on global comparison[11].

- As per the Human Development Index (HDI) 2004, our country is placed at 124th position in the group of 174 countries.
- Only three Indian Universities/Institutions, rank among the top 500 universities/institutions at global level.
- As per UNESCO's Global Monitoring Report-2005, India ranked at 106 in the education reach among 127 countries

Representation of SC/ST/OBC constitutes a small proportion in the governance and polity of India. Is the poor state of affairs as seen above is attributed by the efficiency or inefficiency whatever one may say of that small fraction in the overall governance?

Some Thinkers on 'Merit'

Pratap Bhanu Mehta: Professor Harvard University

Argument based on the claim that reservations are incompatible with merit at best are partially true for a number of reasons. In most of the jobs, merit is a more nebulous category than we suppose and its contours become clear only when we want to exclude someone. Besides, merit based arguments are often made in political bad faith: What is the point of arguing about merit in a context where a whole social structure inhibits the free development of merit?[12]

Prof. A.M. Dharamlingam

Merit cannot be allowed to defeat the principles of democracy and socialism in a welfare state. It must be remembered that Pakistan was created to enable hundred million Muslims to escape from Hindu merit and efficiency. Bangla Desh was in turn created to free it from West Pakistan merit and efficiency. The Germans are acknowledged to be highly meritorious and efficient even by their enemies. The Germans claimed themselves to be the master race to rule the world. The world had to fight Germans in two world wars at terrific costs just to save the Non-Germans from German merit and efficiency. Good government, it is well, is no substitute for self Government, however, inefficient the latter may be. Even so, efficient government by the meritorious minority is no substitute for the self Government of the backward majority. Let us not forget that our freedom movement from 1885 was to free ourselves from British merit and efficiency. The British were talking of us barbarians divided by castes and religions and enveloped in superstition and ignorance and therefore unfit to self-rule. They felt they had divine sanction to subjugate and rule over us. The attitude of some of our high castes is no less different than this"[13] .

Justice O. Chenappa

While we agree that competitive skill is relevant in higher posts, we do not think it is necessary to be apologetic about reservations in posts, higher or lower, so long as the minimum requirements are satisfied. On the other hand, we have to be apologetic that there still exists a need for reservation. Earlier we extracted a passage from Tawney Equality where he bemoaned how degrading it was for humanity to make much of their intellectual and moral superiority to each other.

"One of the superior, elitist approach, is that the question of reservation is invariably viewed as a conflict between the Meritarian principle and Compensatory principle. No, it is not so. The real conflict is between the class of people who have never been in or who have already moved out of the desert of poverty, illiteracy and backwardness and those are entrenched in the oasis of convenient living and those who are still in the desert and want to reach an oasis.[14]

Justice Krishna Aiyer

We select the persons through examinations, but the system of examination is flawed: " Moreover, our examination system makes memory the master of merit and banishes creativity into exile.

I divagate and make these observations only to debunk the exaggerated argument about harijans and girijans being substantiated. We may put aside this angle of vision and approach the problem traditionally because every new idea has resistance to encounter before acceptance, every original thought has been branded a heresy[15].

Prof. Anil Gupta, Chairperson of Entrepreneurship, IIM, Ahmedabad

Construct of merit in many of the merit versus intellect debates is in terms of proficiency in the english language. This is an absolutely gratuitous term of reference, which fails to understand real merit. Gupta further added that in the context of this debate, one needs to take into consideration the fact that 60 to 70 percent of those who win National Innovation foundation Awards are school dropouts.[16]

B.K. Banerji , Director, Financial Resources, Government of U.P.

The protection of merit is manipulative plutocracy of the privileged. Such is the moral and intellectual degeneration of the Indian elite that it feels insecure when reservations threaten this privilege. It raises the bogey of merit being swamped by the multitude because it is not sure of its own competence.[17]

Justice Hegde

"There can be neither stability nor real progress if predominant sections of an awakened Nation live in primitive conditions, confined to unremunerative occupations and having no share in the good thing of life, while power and wealth are confined in the hands of only a few and the same is used for the benefit of the sections of the community to which they belong... Unaided many sections of the people who constitute the majority in this state, cannot compete with the advanced sections of the people who today have a monopoly of education and consequently have predominant representation in the government services as well as in other important walks of life... We have pledged ourselves to establish a welfare state. Social justice is an important ingredient of this concept. That goal cannot be reached, if we over emphasize the "MERIT" theory.

To sum up, **Unless economic assets are largely distributed, education is universally and uniformly available and caste prejudices are non-existent, the claim of selection on merit is a myth** and becomes a process to legitimize preferences of those who control the apparatus of power. Merit is more often the name of opportunity given in a particular social set up, natural endowment constitutes a subsidiary condition. In the Indian context, merit merely reflects a particular social arrangement of group having command over the means of power in society. The principle of equal opportunity in the absence of social rearrangement suits the upper castes. So long as caste sentiments and social differentiation exist, the tests of merit, competition and equal opportunity are eyewash.

REFERENCES

1. Amartya Sen, *Meritocracy and Economic Inequality.*
2. Radhakrishnan Commission Report.
3. Dr. Babasaheb Ambedkar, Life and Mission by Dhananjay Keer.
4. Sunil, Jasvirsingh, *Caste, Merit and Reservations,* 1987. p. 16.

5. Justice Kapadia in Supreme Court Case *M. Nagraj and others.*
6. Justice Sawant in *Indra Sahney Case.*
7. *Financial Express* New Delhi 31 May 2004 on Merit.
8. www.india.seminar *Report on Media.*
9. National Commission for SC/ST Report 1996/97 and 1997/98, p. 22.
10. D. Parthsarthi, *Towards a Larger Perspective.*
11. UNESCO Global Monitoring Report 2005.
12. Pratap Bhanu Mehta, *The Telegraph*, 16 June, 2004.
13. A.M. Dharmlingam, *Caste, Merit and Reservations*, 1987.
14. Justice O. Chenappa; *Vasanth Kumar vs State of Karnataka.*
15. Justice Krishna Aiyer: SC matter in *Akhil Bharatiya Shoshit Karmachari Sangh.*
16. Prof. Anil Gupta, IIMA, *Front Line* 5 May 2006.
17. B.K. Banerji , Director, Financial Resources, Government of UP, *Front Line* 5 May 2006.

9

Base of Reservation: Caste or Economic

Issue of reservation is often confronted with regard to its base i.e. what should be the base for considering reservation? Whether it should be caste/class or economic condition or a combination of the two.

Without a doubt, while some classes, categories and communities in society have enjoyed privileges perhaps for centuries, there have been yet others who have suffered because of social discrimination of one sort or the other, either in recent times or in history.

If one were to grant reservations to all of them, then it would be very difficult to establish a democratic society, where the individual is paramount and where rewards and social worth are judged on the basis of individual accomplishment. A counter argument often put against such assessment of individual worth is that when groups have been downtrodden and exploited for centuries, the scope for consideration on merit must make room for social equality.

Accepting that reservation is essential for creation of a harmonious egalitarian society, next comes the base to be taken for considering entitlement for reservation. With passage of time and experience of the existing reservation policy, changing social considerations under influence of educational advancement, it is advocated that extent of poverty i.e. economic condition should be the base for continuing any type of reservation. A judgment in *Janki Prasad Parimoo vs State of J&K* (1973) rightly focuses its stand on the basis of reservation. It states:

"However in this case, the Court put balance the other way. Mere poverty cannot be the test, it said, because in India, except for a small proposition, the majority people are all poor. To qualify for the assistance that is envisaged by the constitution, the group must be both socially and educationally backward. In India social and educational backwardness is further associated with economic backwardness and it is observed in *Balaji Case* that if poverty be the exclusive test, a very large proportion of population in India would have to be regarded as socially and educationally backward, and if the reservations are made only on the ground of economic considerations, an untenable situation may arise. Even in sectors which are recognized as socially and educationally advanced, there are large pockets of poverty. The task of an investigator is not just to identify the poor, but also to go further and ascertain who, among the poor, are also socially and educationally backward."

Reservation is Not an Anti-Poverty Measure

At first sight, reservations may look like an anti-poverty measure. There is a strong statistical correlation between being a member of a particular caste, tribe or religious community being poor. For this reason, the cultural mark of ascription serves the purpose well, for it is a ready reckoner in determining who are considered to be the beneficiaries of reservations. Reservation should not be construed as an anti-poverty programme, as a stand in for poverty eradication interventions. Programmes that attack poverty should construe independent of reservation because there are poor people in all castes and religious groups. If, in the process, a few well to do families get an undue advantage out of reservational benefits, then so it be. This is a minor matter in the light of the fact that an overwhelming majority of people belonging to a certain group or community are wretchedly poor and what is more, this poverty is the result of grave historic injustices against them.

Scope of constitutional intervention for bringing about just social order has centered on reservation in job quota. But, in fact, it needs to touch upon overall economic development of these communities. This would need in turn to touch the desirable quality of education and training available to these depressed classes across the country. Unfortunately, this vital requirement takes away attention from the major concern i.e. reservation. Reasonable quality of education and training is very much important for these communities to acquire skills and assets that are socially valuable so that they can compete as equals.

Basis as Explained in Indra Sahney Case

Criterion for deciding reservation is discussed at length in famous Supreme Court Case of Indra Sahney, "The reasons for discarding economic criterion as the sole test of backwardness are obvious. If poverty alone were made the test, the poor from all the castes, communities, collectivities and sections would compete for the reserved quota. In such circumstances, the result would be obvious, namely those who belong to socially and educationally advanced sections would capture all the posts in the quota. This would leave the socially and educationally backward classes high and dry, although, they are not at all represented or are inadequately represented in the services. While on the other hand, socially and educationally advanced classes that are adequately or more than adequately represented in the services would snatch away the benefits. This would thus result in defeating the very object of reservations in services under Article 16(4). The provision for reservation in appointment under Article 16(4) is not aimed at economic upliftment or alleviation of poverty. Article 16(4) is specifically designed to give a due share in the State power to those who have remained out of it mainly on account of their social and therefore educational backwardness. The backwardness that is contemplated by Article 16(4) is one, which is both the cause and consequence of non-representation in the administration of the country. Further, backwardness has to be of the whole class and not of some individuals. Economic criterion will thus lead in effect to the virtual deletion of Article 16(4) from the constitution.[1]

Economic Criteria as a Basis for Reservation

Reservation based on castes as is argued enables their elite section to hog away the benefits leaving nothing for those who are the most needy of the reservation benefits.

This is a very common argument against the caste-based reservation. It reminds us of the old usage saying that a mighty shall have a higher proportion in the distribution. Though this is partially correct, it may not be so in each and every application of reservation. For a better understanding, let us divide the prospective beneficiaries broadly into two parts on social basis i.e. upper castes and lower castes, which may further be divided into two sub-sections on economic basis i.e. upper class of upper castes or say elites of the upper castes and other lower class of the lower castes or say poors of the lower castes. Upper and lower class stratification within a caste is based on economic criteria.

Now, as practised at present, reservation covers both the segments of backward communities i.e. elites of the lower castes as well as poor of the same castes. For the purpose here lower castes include all the people of scheduled castes (SC), scheduled tribes (ST) and Socially and Economically backwards castes (OBC) as well. Coming back to the argument that elites of the lower castes eat away the benefits of the reservation, let us examine beneficial impacts of reservation taking economic criteria. Economic criteria will cover all poors upto a stipulated economic limit for being entitled to the reservatioal benefits. Accordingly, job vacancies will be reserved for all the economically poor people irrespective of whether they belong to the upper castes or the lower castes.

Benefits will be Hogged Away by Upper Caste Poors

Let us examine the outcome of application of economic criteria. Now, so far vacancies under the umbrella of reservation are concerned, there will be a competition between the eligible poor candidates of the upper caste with their counterpart poors of the lower castes. What will happen here? In a situation exactly the same merit level, it will so happen that a poor of the upper caste will have far brighter chances to take away benefit. How? Selection process in case of any post in the government job takes place through a series of steps of competition process. Presuming that a reservation category upper caste candidate and his lower category competitor have secured the same level of merit in written examinations, their performance output in the subsequent viva type tests will not be the same for obvious reasons. By all means, the reserved category candidate belonging to the upper caste shall have an edge over his lower caste competitor in so many aspects such as mannerism etiquettes, linguistic commands, knowledge avenues and above all some recommendatory push from his upper caste fellow. All these pre-requisites which are supposed to be possessed by a person for getting through in such selection process comes not from isolation but from the social surrounding a person is endowed with. The poor chap belonging to the lower caste surrounded with his caste complexion, shall be lacking the very much required present day attitudinal sophistication and outer look symbolizing good manners and etiquettes, which will keep him behind his upper caste competitor. The outcome in effect would be that benefit of reservation under the economic criteria would be hogged away by upper caste poor candidate. This will in aggregate, leave poors of the lower castes in the same miseries of social backwardness, economic starvations and educational drop-outs under economic criteria. Reservation in the situations with sole application of economic criteria shall keep the thirsty backwards still starving of water even while standing before the ocean full of water. Cumulative effect of all of this under economic criteria will be that constitutional goal of uplifting socially discarded backward people will remain unfulfilled.

Difficulty in Applying Economic Criteria

It is true that there is a case for considering possibility of economic criteria under this category. However, there are practical problems for partial inclusion or exclusion of any caste for considering entitlement under reservation. It is always possible to have number of poors in an excludable OBC caste and *vice versa*. i.e. existence of well off families in the includable OBC castes. However, a practical way out is chalked out. i.e. concept of 'Creamy Layer' under which families with annual income above the prescribed limit are automatically debarred from the entitlement. Exclusion of better off section out of reserved category though appearing to be a very good idea, but practically its applicability is very difficult. No need to add here unscrupulous ways and means to produce false income certificates by many a people for availing reservation benefits wrongfully.

Problem of particularly scheduled castes is not only economic but it is connected more with social discrimination. Incidents of Kherlanji tragedy and Sambarda harassments and many more have been narrated in Chapter 4 on 'Untouchability in its new idioms and phrases'. Problem in both these glaring incidents was not at all on economic ground. It was the outer shape of an expression of a social hatred. A person belonging to lower castes even with having his educational and economic status at par, with that of an upper caste person continue to be known as a degraded low class person only by all means in the social order being subjected to all usual variety of discriminations.

Poverty Has Caste Differential

A lower caste Koli labourer and a Patidar labourer with the same economic level will not have the same scope of opportunities before them. The Patidar labourer will have lesser difficulties for his economic advancement than that OBC Koli labourer because of the difference in social levelling in both their cases.

Similarly take an example of a poor Brahmin family and that of another poor family belonging to one of the scheduled castes. The former one i.e. Brahmin family will stay amidst the village people who are having better economic condition, some of them may even be quite well off. Inspite of struggling with their poverty, this poor family shall have a benefit of the surrounding of such good locality, he is living in.

There shall be chances of their children's schooling being assisted from the surrounding families. As happens in any poor family whether belonging to upper caste or a lower caste, every body irrespective of child or adult, male or female, one has to endavour to contribute something in meeting the two ends of the family. First; take the example of such upper caste poor family female member. As far as possible, she may not have to go out in search of a laborious and demeaning occupation. If she is educated, she will acquire some white collar job with the help of upper caste recommendations. As regards children in the family, as far as possible, there will always be a tendency not to disturb the children's schooling half the way. He shall also have support from his neighbouring upper caste families, his own caste organizations, Mercantile Mahajans etc. for schooling assistance of his children. Since his children shall not be starved of the basic educational facilities, tomorrow of this upper caste poor family is definitely secured because education is the ultimate master solution of all economic problems.

What will happen in case of the later one's case i.e. poor scheduled caste family? His children shall have an environment what is available in the locality. The family cannot expect economic support from the surroundings unlike upper caste poor as and when required because the neighbouring people too have more or less the same economic level. Hence possibility of help from the nearby is out of question. Similarly it will happen in case of continuation of schooling of his children. These poor chaps will not get external economic support required for completion of their schooling unlike the sources in case of upper caste family. No doubt, he shall get government scholarships. But this does not meet the required educational expenditure on books, notebooks, uniforms, transportation etc. On the contrary, the family's priority will be to have some supplemental economic support from the youngsters of the family juniors by way of some income support notwithstanding the existing labour laws prohibiting child labour. As regards the female family member, she will be equally expected to contribute to the family either by way of early morning waste collection work or other hard toiling labour work or some domestic maid work since she might not have even minimum required education. Leave aside her responsibility of imparting 'Sanskar' to the children.

In short, a poor upper caste person may be deprived of good education for reasons of poverty, but his or her lifestyle radiates a degree of self confidence which a low caste person even from well off background is hard to match.

Income Ceiling to Exclude Creamy Layer has its Own Limitations

There are various court judgments/rulings on misinterpretation or misuse of income ceiling criteria for excluding well offs from availing the reservational benefits. It is observed that income ceiling does not serve the purpose in a country like ours for want of sound evidence system of income testimonials.

Justice Chenappa Reddy in Supreme Court case *Vasant Kumar* (AIR 1985 SC 1495)[2] observed; "No one can possibly claim that the Patels of Gujarat, the Canastas of Bengal, the Reddis and Kamas of Andhra Pradesh are socially backward classes, despite the fact that the majority of them may be poor farmers and agricultural labourers." He further added;

"Are those who produce certificates from an official or a legislature or some authority that their family incomes are less than a certain figure to be so qualified? The rural elite, the upper classes of the rural areas who don't pay any income tax because agricultural income is not taxed? Again, he asked: "**Who will find it difficult or impossible to obtain such certificates?** And answer; of course, is **the truly lower classes who need it the most**."

There are instances of false income certificates and attempt to bypass income limit by deceptive means itself. Thus, in *Jayswal vs Principal*, an applicant to a medical college declined to supply income certificate of his father and instead, he filed his own income certificate on plea that he was separated. As a result, his income was shown below Rs. 3,000 i.e. maximum required income. The Patna High Court rejected his plea and allowed the rejection of his application on the ground of lack of submission of father's income certificate as required.

Mysore High Court caught an instance of camouflaging the income limit of family. In medical colleges, the seats were reserved for those who met occupational test and whose annual income was less than Rs. 1,200. A candidate showed his father's income as Rs. 348.20 i.e. one thirteenth of joint family income, The court counted that income as Rs. 348.20×13 = 4,526.60 and ruled that the family income was in excess of Rs. 3,000 the maximum prescribed by the order. Obviously, the idea of the social status of a member of a joint Hindu family prevailed with the court. There is no clarity as to the size of the joint family and difficulty may also arise in the accurate assessment of income. In *Natraj vs Selection Committee*, **The High Court noted that the machinery for determining income and occupation had been faulty and had given ample scope for manipulations.** We have noted that certificates of backward classes have been issued by tehsildars indiscriminately without proper investigation into the bonafides of the claim."

In short, provisions of income cut off are easy to be circumvented by means of convenient certificates of income obtained from revenue authorities. Agricultural revenue, since not taxable will not reveal correct income. Perhaps only those families whose income is based on recorded salaries either from government sources or public undertakings or large-scale corporates would be easy to be excluded. This means that there will not be just and fair exclusion of all families and only those who may honestly or out of compulsion disclose their income shall be driven out of the reservation benefits. Those others with false income certificate obtained unscrupulously shall succeed in wrongful availing of the reservation benefits at the cost of those really needing the reservation and rather for whom the reservation is really meant for.

Means Test

Means Test is a useful mathematical test for arriving at eligibility criteria particularly in OBC reservation with a view to excluding 'Creamy Layer'. It is an arithmetical averaging formula with a view to arriving at a cut off limit in deciding eligibility while applying economic criteria.

Means test is explained at length in Supreme Court judgment in *Indra Sahney vs Union of India*, "When the means test is analyzed in depth so as to explore its merits and demerits, one would come to an inevitable conclusion that it is not a decisive test, but it will serve as a protective umbrella for many to get into the segregated section by **adopting all kinds of illegal and unethical methods.** Further, this test will be totally unworkable and impracticable in determination of getting somebody in and getting somebody out, from among the same identifiable backward group i.e. SEBC. It will be like a see saw depending upon the fluctuating fortunes or misfortunes. If this means test argument is accepted and put into action by scanning the identified SEBCs by applying a superimposition test, the very object and purpose of reservation intended to the socially and backward class would reach only a *cul-de-sac* and the identified SEBC would be left in a maze. It will be a futile exercise for the courts to find out the reasons in support of the division between and among the groups of SEBCs and make rule therefore for multiple reasons. The reasons indicated above are the tip of an iceberg and any of it is likely to surface at the time when any scanning process and superimposition test are put into practice.[3]

Upward Mobility

The system of reservation has potential to challenge the hegemony and cultural dominance of the upper castes. Reservation has so far paved path for some members of the backward castes to enter the middle class and share power and position with the upper castes. Possibilities of interaction of lower castes and with the upper castes have increased. The backward class elites who entered the middle class have imbibed middle class values and lifestyle and became alienated from their own caste fellows. This gradual process has provided a strong potential to weaken the traditional caste structure.[4]

Reservation makes backward castes persons' upward mobility possible. And once he moves up to the middle class, his social backwardness though not eradicated, is reduced.

Nevertheless, with the class into which he has moved up, his original caste identity will keep him in the minority. This is so, because besides casteism of upper castes, the base of backward castes within the middle class is largely confined to a limited number of castes and further to a small segment within them.

Any system in the social upliftment shall have its own pros and cons and reservation based on castes cannot be an exception there from. But then, one will have to go in the core concept behind the reservation provisions in the constitution. It was mitigation of social inequalities and creating a casteless nation. With implementation of reservation during last fifty years, more and more families hitherto in the lower economic segment and also belonging to the lower castes have with the benefit of reservation through education and jobs are added in the spectrum of middle class of the country. This middle class so far consisted only of the upper caste families. Now it represents families belonging to the scheduled castes, scheduled tribes and other backward castes too. This is nothing but miraculous effect of upward mobility. The process of adding of more and more families of the lower class segment of the lower castes to middle class needs to go on uninterruptedly at least for few years. This transformation process besides bringing economic well being, has facilitated a social integration process between the lower castes and the upper castes middled with living and sharing togather of their cultural values. This would not have been possible without implementation of reservation.

Caste Factor is an Unignorable Reality

It is argued that criteria other than say caste i.e. economic criteria would provide an incentive to caste mitigation efforts. This theoretically appears very excellent, but practically, existence of caste system and all that around caste cannot be ignored viz.

1. Caste disparity, differentiation, and discrimination whatever phrases one may use are after all an outcome

of social system. It is not only inferiority complex of the lower castes, but rather the inhumane treatment they are getting from their upper social castes also matters in social integration process.

2. The need for reservation has to be examined from the viewpoint not of few jobs here and there, but the difficulty encountered by a lower caste chap in getting a due opportunity simply because of the prevailing social inequality.
3. Some social thinkers do talk about the harm of caste system and incorrect caste criteria for entitlment under reservation, but are cleverly silent to what is the way out to eliminate the harms of this inhumane caste system, facing which **the poor victim feels so hapless, worthless and at times even lifeless at every walk of his life.**

What these poor people expect is a non-disrespectful existence in the society. Once he/she gets this, he/she will rather no longer need a supporting stick like reservation. These people too equally love self-respect and cognizance of their existence as a human being

What were the compelling grounds before the framers of constitution, great patriotic visionaries of those post independence days and all those concerned with the national interest to accord top most priorities for a social cause of grave inequalities and in its achievement, need for a reservation policy? It was deep rooted caste discrimination prevailing in the society for over 2000 years. Had it not been there, what was the need at all to earmark a portion in the name of reservation for these unfortunate people? Their presence in the employment of any sort before independence was microscopically negligible. Their socio-economic condition was pathetic. It was after support of reservation only that the marked improvement in the condition of this depressed segment of society is seen.

What was their social condition before fifty years? They did not dare even to come near the upper caste person because of untouchability, inferiority complex and so on. With implementation of reservation coupled with educational growth, a process of gradual social integration has started, sweet fruits of which are seen in the society as a whole. This has gradually started breaking the strong walls of caste compartalisation slowly and steadily. This needs to be further continued. If so, the whole society will be harmoneously one and integrated in next fifty/hundred years. So with reservation, caste compartalisation will gradually disappear from the society rather than getting strengthened as apprehended. The constitution has a humble intention of creating a casteless society in the nation. Once this materializes, there will be no need of taking caste as a base for reservation in the country.

Would Reservation Perpetuate Casteism?

Answering to whether reservation would perpetuate the caste system, late Haroobhai Mehta, famous advocate and social activist states, 'One cannot overlook the purpose of reservations namely mitigating the inequalities accumulated as a result of caste hierarchy dominating on Indian scene. The reservations therefore, are intended to bring the people belonging to backward classes, suffering from accumulated backwardness as a result of caste structure, to the level of the advanced classes. If the reservations were overnight abolished, the result would be to perpetuate backwardness of these classes. We have got to wipe out the inequalities generated in the past centuries on account of caste structure. We just cannot say that people belonging to the backward classes must stay at a lower level forever and treated mechanically, in accordance with principle of equal treatment to all. If an equal degree of advancement is made available to all classes at this stage, the result would be that the gap in the matter of development as between the backward classes and advanced classes will continue to exist for a long period until measures like reservation sets it right to a desired level. Disparities resulted on account of caste structure should be essentially checked in the process of establishing a casteless structure. If therefore, one advocates for continuation of reservation for backward classes, it would not be tantamount to encouraging casteism".

Casteism has Re-emerged in its New Shape

People are found arguing now-a-days that the barriers of casteism have now completely eroded from the country because of education, culturalisation, globalisation and so on. Yes, all these factors have definitely contributed in narrowing down the caste barriers in the society what it was supposed to be before a few decades. But, the roots of the Indian casteism are so deep and long lasting having been nurtured for over a thousand of years, its very existence is undeniable. On the contrary, a new phenomenon of neo casteism is taking a modern shape of late.

Now, more and more number of caste based Voluntary Organizations are coming up. This caste based associations organize number of caste related activities such as honouring their caste dignitaries, community gatherings, mass weddings etc. Such mobilization in the name of caste is not restricted in upper castes and is universally found also in lower castes, linguistic and religious minorities and so on. These caste organizations also provide educational and financial help such as books, fees, and hostel accommodation to the needy members of the caste. Such caste based associations and affiliations get additional weightage and importance during election times. These associations and its politically motivated and connected people utilise such mobilisation sometime in individual or group bargaining also.

The Indian social tendency of caste assimilation has not remained within the country boundaries only, but has accompanied caste Hindus wherever they have settled i.e. on foreign lands also with formation of organizations like Brahmin Society of America, Rajput Association and like-wise Patidar Samaj in America to name a few.

This develops a natural tendency to help their caste fellows for jobs and other obligations. All such obligatory assistance will inculcate in the person a feeling of caste belongingness and reciprocation for the caste fellows. This is the outcome of awakened caste consciousness. There is nothing wrong in organizing such associations. Point, worth notable here is emerging conscious efforts seen in the Indian society to keep the caste factor alive and perpetual in whatever new names and shapes.[5]

Accumulated Caste Ridden Backwardness Needs External Support

Caste distinction cannot be obliterated overnight by a stroke of pen directing the removal of caste labels. On account of long period of unabated unequal treatment, these oppressed classes became victims of accumulated backwardness forcibly transmitted from generation to generation. Now suppose, if all the admissions are to be governed solely on merit without any reservation whatsoever, it would only mean that people belonging to the advanced classes who have acquired a higher accessibility to merit and efficiency will monopolise the appointments and admissions. While those belonging to lower castes will, on account of their accumulated backwardness, not stand even a remote chance in competition with the upper classes. It seems that the unequal position obtaining today would in that case be perpetuated until next few decades of compensatory discrimination can undo the damage caused by unequal treatment through the centuries.

Thus, if one is oblivious of the evil consequences of caste ridden society of India, he cannot but conclude that the social and educational backwardness attached to the people of certain castes being a clear result of birth in a particular community has got to be remedied by suitable measures. No amount of economic spurts can help them tear the cocoon of social and economic backwardness so as to effectively compete in free market for jobs and admissions. The surest way therefore to help them rise up to the level of upper castes is to provide for reservation, until such a time as the said classes are emancipated from the ill effects of accumulated backwardness imposed on them through centuries.

Caste: A Root Cause of the Whole Problem

Reservation for scheduled castes, scheduled tribes and other backward classes, all the three have one common feature for consideration of the support by means of statutory provisions like reservation etc. i.e. People under all the three categories were deprived of required opportunities for their socio-economic development.

Reason for the backwardness of scheduled castes and scheduled tribes are mainly attributed to the total social discard of these communities. Scheduled castes were additionally subjected to inhuman treatment like untouchability. In other words, they were suffering from the entrenched and cumulative nature of group inequalities. So mere economic measures for their upliftment would be insufficient. They have to be uplifted socially also so that they regain human dignity and respect as well.

In case of scheduled tribes, their position is slightly different. They are not subjected to untouchability. Instead, they were pushed back in the forests by external invaders. They remained totally away from the mainstream socialization, culture, civilization, education etc. required for the development of a human being on social as well economic front. The scheduled tribes also because of their being away from the normal social life, are subjected to complexes and almost near to slavery type treatment by the upper castes. Mere economic upliftment in their case too would not suffice. Therefore, they too need some holistic type support out of constitutionally guaranteed rights beyond economic criteria.

As regards, other backward classes (OBC), the position is again different. They were neither untouchable like scheduled castes, nor were subjected to social cut off as is the case of scheduled tribes. No doubt, they were also sufferers of hierarchical social discrimination endowed out of Vernashram system of Hindu society. Of the four *varnas*, the castes under OBCs come under 'Shudra' i.e. these were considered lower in hierarchical ladder of Indian caste system. Castes under this category were for centuries rendering host type ancillary support services like blacksmith, hair cutting, animal rearing, wood cutting, footwear making, cloth washing etc.

Reservations are expected to create a sense of confidence and self worth among people who through history had been victims of various forms of discrimination. They are meant for those who have socially no valuable assets whatsoever. These communities and others too were not allowed in tradition to develop social skills and assets that would help them advance socially.

This handicap weighs heavily on them even today. Therefore, they need positive discrimination to get that extra push to move up and claim their rightful position in a democratic society. It is rightly said, **"Liberty can be established by law, and equity by dictate, but for fraternity to happen, it requires a substantial realization of citizenship."** Reservations are not meant to replace anti-poverty programme but to instill self-confidence and courage among those who had been historically disprivileged.

Indian Society Whether a Class or a Caste Society

The policy of reservation on caste lines is advocated because there is an absence of a class society. By class, we ordinarily mean rich and poor, while in economic terminology; upper middle, lower class, and lastly in Marxian theorem as Haves and Have-nots. The word 'caste' is self-explanatory needing no more elaboration. For a society which is not basically a class divided, a programme based on class action may have some meaning in abstract, but would be practically unfit to attack the roots of prevalent social discrimination.

There are three characteristics distininguishing a class society from a caste society. First; the consciousness of people in a class society is determined by economic factors alone, whereas in a caste society, the social factors predominate the process of base behaviour. Second; the source of exploitation in a class society is the private ownership of property, in a caste society, social status is the source of domination and exploitation. And third; a class society closes its ranks through bloody revolution; a caste society may change even by reform measures.

Let us examine whether India is a class society or a caste society in context with these three characteristics.

A. Determinant of Consciousness

The actual consciousness of people is formed by the experience they gather around society. Their personal aspirations are conditioned from the perception of reality. The goals of life are determined by the personal appraisal of reality with which they have to interact. Since lower caste people are aware of their lack of opportunity, not because of lack of merit nor because of the constraint of economic resources, but due to 'we, they ' reality, they set their goals of life in the light of their experiences. Their worldview does not get conditioned by the material constraints alone rather from the total life chances in the social context in which they live. When the chances in life are different for a poor person of upper caste from that of a poor man of the lower caste, the identical character of consciousness can never be formed.

The labourers fail to become an interest conscious unit because the identity of interest in Indian society is not governed by economic factor alone. The needs of family arise from various exigencies of life, many of which are accompanied by the social institutions in existence. **Caste being the India's largest insurance for which one does not have to pay any formal premium, one can not look for anything else than the solidarity of caste.** A tested solidarity at child bearing, weddings funeral obsequies and so on, catches consequences on other aspects of life including insurance against unemployment, politics and day-to-day hazards of life. It cannot be a false consciousness for those who face what casteism is. The growing literature on land relations has failed to prove that poor peasants have contradictory relationship with rich peasants though there is economic differentiation. The economic differentiation, either in agriculture or in industry, has not undermined the caste solidarity of Indian people and has failed to generate class antagonism. Therefore, the ascriptive status of an individual is in tact in Indian society.

The rationality of class-consciousness has failed to emerge in a caste society. Life of Indian people moves within the boundary of caste and their consciousness is conditioned by the way, life moves in society. In such a situation of real world experience in Indian condition, an advice to the lower castes to forget about the 'actual psychological consciousness' because it is false in essence and to act on 'the imputed rational consciousness' because it is theoretically like advice of Manu not to bother for the troublesome present actual life for the sake of improving chances in the imaginary life after death. Indian society is not a class society and therefore class action is unsuitable. In such a society, caste action is more appropriate for the creation of a casteless society.

B. Primacy of Economy

Another distinguishing feature between a class society and a caste society is the source of exploitation. In a class society, the domination comes via private property ownership. In a caste society; it is the social status, which is a driving force of control and domination. There are various reasons as to why Indian society is not a class society, if it is examined on the basis of the source of exploitation.

The caste system was invented with the primary purpose of distributing privileges in society. This was consolidated through positive and negative actions of retaining the position of power. The area of education and administration was kept preserved for the upper castes that had the necessary skill of articulation. The stratification of Indian society has, thus, been primarily a system for maintaining power relations and privilege allotment through a fixed hierarchy of castes arranged in the descending order of superior to inferior. Caste organization must therefore be seen as a system of protecting the distribution of power through preserving the scarce social goods like education and administration for those in power and manual work for those without power. The lower castes were kept out of power so that they could be compelled to concentrate on heavy manual work and the surpluses could be siphoned off by power-vested castes through keeping their remuneration depressed. In this sense, caste system became the instrument of deprivation by preserving education and administration, which in turn assured them status, power and wealth.

In modern times, the education and administration are still with the upper castes. The change in the nature of state in terms of governance has not changed the social composition of those having control over the state. The source of exploitation, therefore has not changed sociologically. The genesis of exploitation is still rooted to the social division because the same segment of population commends the ownership of property and authority. The abolition of private property in the means of production, does not by itself, constitute an essential distinction as long as the social system remains what it is. The domination over the means of education and administration, which primarily corresponds with the caste status in society and secondarily with the ownership of the means of production, is equally exploitative as that of the ownership of property and responsible for the stagnation of Indian society. So long as the power of domination over Indian society remains exclusively with the upper castes, the social surface will remain unequal. The primacy of the economy does not explain the character of Indian society and therefore cannot break the caste system in the country.

C. Class Revolution

A class society switches over to a new social order by a sudden revolution. When two classes clash, society reaches a stage of classlessness. This is a political revolution. In a caste society, on the other hand, reform measures may erase the lines dividing castes. There is thus a difference between political revolution and a social revolution. Political revolution may be sudden and violent, whereas social revolutions are generally slow. If political revolution takes place according to the theory of class revolution, chances are that the group, which grabs power at the wake of the political revolution, may not allow power to be transmitted to other section of society. If it so happens, there will be only a replacement of one group of ruling minority by another coming from the same section of society. In such situations, social relations will not change fundamentally and today's deprived sections will continue to remain deprived even tomorrow. In such a situation, the class theory of the dictatorship of the proletariat and the weapon of the 'vanguard class' to attain it, conceptually correspond with the Dwija theory of caste system.

The change in social relations constitutes social revolution, which develops so slowly. A casteless society can only be constructed gradually over a longer period, through radical reforms in many different spheres of social life. Social revolution is a process of social reorganization. The process of social reorganization, therefore is very significant. This requires a period of social change and reform in which the hold of traditional social groups gradually breaks down and new social relations are born. This will be consistent with the democratic system of the country in which equality will be achieved without foregoing liberty of the people. The gradual transformation of social relationships and values is more appropriate for the Indian system.

Nature of Indian Society

The movement of Indian society must be studied in the background of the system of caste, which has survived since time immemorial without any break. Indian society cannot be diagnosed correctly away from the framework of caste system since all aspects of Indian life have been influenced by and centered around this basic feature. The caste system is a characteristic product of the Indian genius, just as feudalism was a typical product of the European genius. We are aware that it would be laughable to understand European society in caste system, similarly, applying feudalism to Indian social system should be treated as a misguided approach.

The caste system is not the outcome of economic system though social status consolidates further when economic factors are included. The caste system has got strengthened because of social subordination, which gave rise to power and privileges to the upper stratum, which in turn imposed economic disabilities on those subjugated. Otherwise there would have been no exception to the low caste person being poor. The division being on the line other than economic, the change in economic status does not change the stigma of caste. This explains why the statue of Sampurnanand was washed with the holy water of Ganga when a wealthy untouchable Jagjivan Ram equally a toll political figure touched it. This incident is a representative sample of the real character of our society. It proves very bluntly that caste system is more complex than an economic phenomenon. **Poverty in Indian context is a consequence and not a determinant of caste hierarchy.** Here lies the dichotomy to understand the caste system in terms of rich and poor. It is therefore, unreal to understand the forms of social divisions purely in economic terms. This attests that the treatment of individuals has to be made on the basis of social group rather than on economic levels.

In short, social equality demands that caste can be the only authenticate criterion for granting preferential treatment. Reservation is a must for changing the composition of society and **India being a society of caste and not of class, the action must base itself on caste lines.**

Restricted Opportunities

The prosperity in the society rests under the frame on the rapid economic development and enlarged human horizons. The development of industry and associated culture in it together with western education, changes social order from below and within the whole process of social change may be summed up as the modernization of society in the image of western civilization. When this happens, the existing social structure gives way to a new social order in which the caste system remains stranded by itself in the streets of industrial society.

According to this line of thinking, a just social order is one which recognizes the individual on the basis of his ability rather than attributes of his birth i.e. caste. Now let us see what is the reality in the Indian context. First of all, "Socio-cultural conditions" for economic development have been the main missing element in the Indian strategy of planning for a new economy and society. The neglect of preparing the social forces of production has resulted in the absence of new incentives and motivation supposedly to be created in a modernized society for effecting transformation of a traditional system into a modern one. By overlooking the need for social rearrangement, a sense of frustration has been created among those submerged in the traditional milieu. The failure however, has been much marked on the front of distribution. Moreover, it can be only a wishful thinking that a large part of population can be absorbed in industries in the country. If this does not happen, a new social order on the basis of an industrial economy is out of question. Similarly **western education has not changed the caste prejudices in India.** Even university students belonging to the high castes and most modernized strata of society, have not got rid of the traditional system.[6]

Social Contingencies Cannot be Ignored

The greatest drawback of the philosophy of free enterprise and modernization, as a cure for caste based inequality, is that it rests on the wrong notion of presuming individuals in Indian society as atomized, pre-social and historic human beings. It pre-supposes that every one in society is equally free to achieve a rational life for himself. It overlooks that a person is born and brought up in a family bounded by fixed social modes and a history behind. Individuals differ in Indian society not only in their physical endowments but also in social conditions. It is for this reason that merit is not an outcome of his personal endowments alone but also of his social location. The factors of social contingency are more predominant than natural endowment when looked at it from the experience of the working of the Indian system. In a situation as that of India, a system of weightage on account of adopting preferential treatment, merit is not absolutely sacrificed rather a weightage is given to those who in absence of social contingency, would have been equally meritorious. Any arrangement to make competition perfect by compensating at the start is not a sure guarantee of making competition equal since there is no mechanism to overcome the social bias. The human point of view is not put in the background by making preferential treatment on caste basis since the discrepancies in society are not random but patterned on group lines. Democratic justice demands that natural endowment and social contingency are perceived in the context of prevailing situation and therefore a traditional society must make deliberate efforts to accommodate allowance for adjustment in social contingency. The theory of equality of opportunity, by ignoring social contingency, views individual and his merit in apparent rather than in real form.

The virtues of the market system are incompatible with the values of egalitarianism. It was a terrible mistake in the past to recognize the individual only through his caste, **it would be a more devastating mistake if individuals are recognized unconnected with their social contingencies,** particularly when society has not made any effective arrangement to demolish it. The social environmental privileges must be recognized and discounted for in an apparent competitive atmosphere of securing education and jobs. Where caste prevails, opportunity and ability are restricted to over-narrowing circles of the people, equal opportunity can further widen the gulf. Groups who have commanded the society for centuries have, in modern times made near monopolistic use of equal opportunity. India's experience is a conclusive proof that resilience in the caste system can accommodate any change in Indian society.

Caste Based Reservation: The Best Possible Secular Remedy

According to A.B. Bardhan, 'There is a feeling that reservation is contributing to the strengthening of casteism, by constantly reminding the people about their caste and how they can use it to their advantage. This is not so. When the upper castes set up their caste organizations, hold community organisations, be in the name of welfare, reformer, political or for any thing else, does this not strengthen casteism? When in elections, not so open and some time even open appeals are made to caste affinities, does it not fuel casteism? And when the landed gentry and vested interests from the upper castes organize caste organisations like 'Ranveer Senas' to terrorize the village poor, to keep the downtrodden in their proper place and if necessary, to teach them a lesson, is it not a manifestation of casteism in its most vicious and ugly form? As against this of course, we also have the casteism of backward castes. Both these forms generate caste hatred among the masses and divide the toilers on the basis of caste." He further adds, " The struggle against casteism is thus a multi-pronged and multi-front struggle concentrating fire at several points, upholding social equality and the dignity of man, extending a helping hand to the weak and deprived and so on. Reservation is actually a secular remedy in a situation of real caste-based inequality. It is secular, since it aims at eliminating the discrimination due to caste. It is democratic, since it aims to lift the lower orders and bring them on a level with the rest.[7]

REFERENCES

1. Justice Chenappa *Indra Sahney Supreme Court Case.*
2. Justice Chenappa Reddy in Supreme Court Case *Vasantkumar.*
3. Ram Samrudh *IRS Reservation Policy.*
4. Ghanshyam Shah, *Caste and Democratic Politics in India.*
5. Action Aid Survey on Untouchability 2001/02.
6. Ghanshyam Shah, *Caste and Democratic Politics in India.*
7. A.B. Bardhan, *Debate on Reservation.*

10

Creamy Layer

Concept of Creamy layer is under lot of controversy now-a-days. It is often argued that as per the experience of the implementation of reservation during last fifty years, the benefits of the reservation are found to have been cornered by the elites among the backwards. Some go to the extent saying that a new class within a backward class has been created. This cannot be denied outright. However, the issue needs to be examined in its right perspective. This will have to be seen in the pretext of nature of discrimination these reserved category communities are facing.

A. Application of Creamy Layer in Case of Scheduled Castes and Scheduled Tribes

Concept of creamy layer for the scheduled castes and scheduled tribes has to be examined based on social discrimination in addition to their educational and economic backwardness. An argument is often put forth that major chunk of the reservation benefits are hogged away by the creamy layer upper segment of the scheduled castes and scheduled tribes. For the sake of examination, let us assume exclusion of this creamy layer of these two categories. Then what will happen? Various statistical tables in this book reveal that in spite of vigorous efforts of all these fifty years for filling the reserved vacancies, the fact remains that there is still a backlog of unfilled positions particularly in higher category services. The farthest bracket or say the person standing exactly on the other extreme from the creamy layer would still need to have adequate qualification, exposure and other eligibility requirements for the modern recruitment system.

Hogging of positions is not a problem only in the reserved category, but it is a phenomena connected with the human tendency. In case of unreserved i.e. general category positions also, the same thing happens. From among the candidates of upper caste elite and upper caste poor, the position would always go in favour of the upper caste elite to the detriment of the upper caste poor. Of course again considering inclusion of such upper caste poor under the economic criteria is altogether a separate issue and is already discussed in Chapter 9 on 'Base of Reservation; Caste or Economic'. And finally, as already narrated above, the caste stigma still being faced by a creamy layer scheduled caste and scheduled tribe person cannot be ignored in toto at least for the time being.

If it is felt by person seating in a high rank judicial position that the chair used by a scheduled caste predecessor judge gets polluted as in the infamous incidence of the year 2000 in Allahabad Court which was washed with holy Ganga water by an upper caste incumbent, the concept of Creamy layer in case of scheduled castes and scheduled tribes has yet to wait at least for few more years for being implemented.

N. Nagraj and others *vs.* Union of India (SCA 61/2002 decided on 19 October 2006)

A recent judgment dated 19 October 2006 in the case of Nagraj *vs.* Govt. of India, has evoked a huge debate in respect of application of creamy layer concept to SC/ST as already made applicable in OBC way back in 1992[1].

The Nagraj verdict operates on the premise that the application of the creamy layer rule to SCs/STs has been one of the "Constitutional Requirements: ever since the Mandal judgement which was delivered 14 years ago. The verdict makes a dubious assertion that two provisions that have been introduced in the constitution Articles 16 (4A) and 16 (4B) 'do not obliterate' the constitutional requirement of excluding the creamy layer of SCs and STs from quota benefits. The Nagraj verdict has disregarded a constitutional impediment to the very notion of filtering out the creamy layer from SCs and STs. While OBCs have been listed under a law enacted in pursuance of the Mandal verdict, SCs and STs have been notified by the President under Articles 341 and 342 of the Constitution, respectively. So, unlike in case of OBCs, any attempt to discriminate between the members of SCs or STs, every eligible member, howsoever socially advanced, is constitutionally entitled to bid for its benefits. The only way any section of these communities can be skimmed off from the ambit of quota is again as provided in the constitution i.e. modification/revision in schedule.

Articles 341 and 342 stipulate that the presidential orders issued under their purview can be amended only by laws passed by Parliament and the scope of such laws is immense. Parliament is empowered "to include in or exclude from" the lists of SCs and STs any caste, race or tribe and further also part of or group within any caste, race or tribe". Thus, the later day creamy layer rule does not seem to have been beyond the contemplation of our founding fathers. Except that they were also categorical that the call would have to be of Parliament. The Constitution makers in their wisdom felt that elected representatives i.e. Member of Parliament would be better equipped than judges to determine whether the time was ripe to exclude the creamy layer from SC and ST beneficiaries.

The nine judge bench which delivered Mandal verdict in 1992, steered clear of SCs and STs while introducing the creamy layer rule took pains to clarify that its direction on creamy layer was confined to other backward classes only and has no relevance in the case of reservation for scheduled castes and scheduled tribes.

The matter after the judgment in Nagraj case, was referred to Attorney General, Milon Banerjee, who opined that the creamy layer principle does not apply to scheduled castes and scheduled tribes. He advised to the group of ministers on the *dalit* affairs headed by Pranab Mukherjee, " The Court's views were *Obiter Dicta*, a Latin term that means "**by the way**" and hence was not a binding part of the decision.

B. Categories Suffering from Economic Inequalities only (OBC)

Social conditions of various castes and communities covered under another reservation category identified as other backward classes (OBC) sometimes also known as Socially and Economically backwards (SEBC) are incorporated in Part I Chapter 1 on 'Reservation; an ever lauding debate' and another Chapter 6 on 'OBC reservation'.

As the scheduled castes and scheduled tribes are '**constitutionalised**' the other backward castes have been '**regionalised**', since development of these communities was left at the discretion of states after an abortive attempt with the first backward class Commission till surfacing Mandal Report in 1990. It is found that in post-independence era, upper castes have become quite more powerful as rural dominant castes and simultaneously large lower segment comprising of artisanal castes stayed poor and powerless. More importantly, urban OBCs remained economically and educationally much closer to scheduled castes than to the upper castes. It is only after Mandal, they began to speak the language of national power sharing.

Concept of creamy layer has to be examined from the view of this, i.e. difference in the social treatment to these OBC categories. Based on this, many a states have devised the income criteria for considering eligibility for reservation benefits under this category. Say if a person's annual family income exceeds a financial cut off ceiling, his family members are treated as 'Creamy Layer' and will not be eligible for any benefit under the reservation.

It is seen that this income criteria has certain inherent practical loopholes for its practicability in letter and spirit. So as to be eligible, a person has to produce his annual income certificate on the basis of which a competent revenue authority issues a creamy layer certificate to him. If he is a salaried person having been employed in a government sector or some large-scale corporate entity, his certificate shall be a perfect evidence of his correct income. However, in most of the other cases, possibilities cannot be ruled out for a false income or incorrect income certificate, since it has got no counter check system or even if such counter checks are available, the present administrative system and the level of efficiency, bottlenecks with which it is functioning, it is almost impossible to ensure strict adherence to income criteria. Therefore, the sum total will be that a person with a correct income certificate will be put to an unjust position amidst the possibility of bunching of false or suppressed income certificates. These certificates are required to be renewed periodically. This too has twin effects. In one way, it is good since it provides scope for its scrutiny against its possible misuse and all wrongs. However, on the other hand, it leads to resorting malpractices also for obtaining a required creamy layer certificate by hook or crook, which is not impossible in the present established systems based solely on the paper submissions before the competent authorities.

As regard, fixation of income criteria in the State of Bihar, The Supreme Court came down heavily in **Ashok Kumar Thakur** *vs.* **State of Bihar and U.P.** for positing the unrealistically high level of income or other conditions so as reduce it to a nullity.

1. The exercise of identifying the layer must be deliberate and not just a mechanical one of going through the motions,
2. It must seek to identify the advanced sections on relevant material, and
3. The list must be reviewed periodically. Once backward, always a backward is not acceptable.

Prof. Sukhdev Thorat, Chairman University Grant Commission on Creamy Layer

He states, "Critics of reservation policies in India have claimed that they are inequitable because they make available valuable educational opportunities mainly to the well to do applicants 'the creamy layer' rather than to more needy members of disadvantaged groups. Thus, it is argued that reservations for scheduled castes and scheduled tribes applicants increase inequalities within these groups and reduce educational opportunities for general entry applicants from other groups who may be worse off than the scheduled castes and the scheduled tribes beneficiaries".

The UGC Chairman replies," I have found no evidence addressing directly whether reservation policies in university admissions have increased overall inequalities, by benefiting well off *dalits* and *adivasis* at the expense of less well-off university applicants from rest of the population. To determine, whether there really are such inequitable redistributive effects, one would have to compare the socio-economic class backgrounds of scheduled castes and scheduled tribes beneficiaries with the class backgrounds of those general-entry applicants displaced from university admissions by reservation policies; but such data do not appear to be available. Evidence available makes it clear that among those admitted to university programmes, scheduled castes and scheduled tribes students tend to come from significantly less privileged socio-economic backgrounds than non-SC/ST students. This suggests that it is quite unlikely that those non-SC/ST applicants who are displaced by reservation policies are less well off than the SC/ST students who benefit from them.

There is no lack of evidence on the redistributive effect of reservation policies within scheduled castes and scheduled tribes groups. There can be no doubt that it is indeed a creamy layer of *dalits* and *adivasis* who constitute the vast majority of beneficiaries of India's reservation policies in university admissions. With few exceptions, only children from the better off *dalits* and *adivasi* families are able to stay in school through a full secondary education and thus even be in a position to apply to a college or university. The fact that higher education represents potential earning foregone and call for expenditure on school supplies, housing and possibly transportation, which are rarely covered by government aid programmes, means that it is mainly the better off students who can afford to spend several post-secondary years in an educational institution… "[2]

As per the study undertaken by Velaskar, there is a small segment of scheduled caste students that perform on par with general-entry students come from well off families and English medium high schools. Patvardhan and Palshikar (1992) state that reservation favours urban and male students and conclude that they disproportionately benefit a small number of sub-castes within the scheduled castes group and particular tribes within the overall scheduled tribes group. They suggest further that the beneficiaries of reserved seats are increasingly second-generation students from the favoured group, whose families have benefited from positive discrimination to become middle to upper middle class; while children from more backward sub-castes and tribes find it difficult to compete. In a study, Rao corroborated the above observations," The schemes of reservation tend to reproduce within the beneficiary class the same kind of clustering the reservation is meant to remedy.... Those among the beneficiaries who already enjoy the greatest advantages obtain disproportionately large share of the benefits. This has led to call for more finely sub-divided categories for reserved seats, so that the least well off sub-castes and tribes would be entitled to their own separate reservation category." [3]

However, positive discrimination policies may indirectly benefit less well off members of the beneficiary groups, in so far as the direct beneficiaries are thereby enabled more effectively and more extensively to hire support and otherwise come to the aid of their less well off kinsfolk and community members. (Reservation and Private Sector by Sukhdev Thorat Page 394)

Accepting that the major chunk of the reservational benefits is hogged by the well-off SC/STs, let us examine as to how can this be addressed to. There are two possibilities. One; Applying some income criteria for exclusion of the elite SC/STs so that the benefit goes for the most backward sub-castes/tribes among the SC/STs and second segregating the most backward castes out of the general SC/ST group. Applying income criteria has to be examined in context with the provisions contained in Articles 341 and 342 which empowers the President to include in or exclude out from the list of scheduled castes and scheduled tribes any caste, race, or tribe or part of a group within any caste, race or tribe, in consultation with the respective state or union territory by public notification. Thus income criteria which leads to exclusion of a part of scheduled castes and scheduled tribes involves constitutional provisions, besides having other practical post-application implications. Second one is carving out a sub-fraction out of the reservation quota for the most backwards.

Classification of Backward and More/Most Backward Classes

A clarification is made in Supreme Court Case as regards whether Article 16(4) permit the classification of 'backward classes' into backward classes and most backward classes.

Such classifications could be done in two ways. While the former puts the backwards into backward and most backward, the later speaks of internal classification of each backward into backward and more backward individuals or families. Both the classifications are to be made on economic or other considerations. Whereas the classification would place some backward classes in their entirety above backward classes, the second will place some sub-sections in each section in the same class. The second classification aims at what has popularly come to be known as weeding out of the so-called 'Creamy Layer' or 'advanced sections' from the backward classes.

A society does not remain static. The industrialization and the urbanization which necessarily follow in the wake, the advance on political, social and economic fronts made particularly after the commencement of the Constitution, the social reform movements of the last several decades, the spread of education and the advantages of the special provisions including reservations secured so far, have all undoubtedly seen at least some individuals and families in the backward classes, however small in number, gaining sufficient means to develop their capacities to compete with others in every field, That is an undeniable fact. Legally therefore, they are not entitled to be any longer called as part of the backward classes, whatever may be their original birthmark. It can further hardly be argued that once a backward class, always a backward class. That would defeat the very purpose of the special provisions made in the Constitution for the advancement of the backward classes and for enabling them to come to the level of and to compete with the forward classes, as equal citizens. On the other hand, to continue to confer upon such advanced sections from the backward classes the special benefits, would amount to treating equals unequally violating the equality provisions of the Constitution. What is more, it will lead to perverting the objectives of the special constitutional provisions since the forwards among the backward classes will thereby be enabled to lap up all the special benefits to the exclusions and at the cost of the rest in those classes, thus keeping the rest in perpetual backwardness.

Reservation Aims at Class Upliftment

The object of the special constitutional provisions is not to uplift a few individuals and families in the backward classes but to ensure the advancement of the backward classes as a whole. Hence taking out the forwards from among the backward classes is not only permissible, but also obligatory under the Constitution. However, it is necessary to add that just as the backwardness of the backward groups cannot be measured in terms of the forwardness of the forward groups, so also the forwardness of the forwards among the backward classes cannot be measured in terms of the forwardness of the backward groups, so also the forwardness of the forwards among the backward classes cannot be measured in terms of the backwardness of the backward sections of the said classes. It has to be judged on the basis of the social capacities gained by them to compete with others, they can hardly be classified as forward. The moment they develop the capacities, they would cease to be backward. It will be contradiction in terms to call them backward and others more or most backwards. There will always be degrees of backwardness as there will be degrees of forwardness, wherever the structure of the society. It is not the degrees of backwardness or forwardness, which justify classification of the society into forward and backward classes. It is the capacity or the lack of it to compete with others on equal terms, which merit such classification. The remedy therefore, does not lie in classifying each backward class internally into backward and more backward, but in taking the forward out of the backward classes altogether. Whether they have acquired the capacity to compete with others or not. They cannot be both[4].

Criteria for Judging Backwardness or Forwardness

The mere fact that some from the backward classes who are more advanced than the rest in that class or score more in competition with the rest of them and thus gain all the advantages of the special provisions such as reservations is no ground for classifying the backwards into backwards and more backwards. The phenomenon is evident among the forward classes too. The more advantaged among the forwards similarly gain unfair advantage over others among the forwards and secure all the prizes. This is an inevitable consequence of the present social and economic structure. The correct criterion for judging the forwardness of the forwards among the backward classes is to measure their capacity not in terms of the capacity of others in their class, but in terms of the capacity of the members of the forward classes, as stated earlier. If they cross the Rubicon of backwardness, they should be taken out from the backward classes and should be made disentitled to the provisions meant for the said classes.

Delhi Transport Corporations *vs.* D.T.C. Mazdoor Congress and others (1991)

Law is a social engineering to remove the existing imbalance and to further the progress, serving the needs of the Socialist Democratic Bharat under the Rule of Law. The prevailing social conditions and actualities of life are to be taken into account in adjudging whether or not the impugned legislation would sub serve the purpose of the society.

Social Justice is a fundamental Right. Economic Empowerment is a Fundamental Right. Moreover, the disadvantaged have a guaranteed right to equality of status and dignity. None of these can be secured until the disadvantaged get into the higher posts.

Not just that, unless the SC/ST/OBCs get hold of the higher posts, the equality would be there only on paper, only in law not in fact.

It is obvious that equality in law precludes discrimination of any kind whereas equality in fact may involve the necessity of differential treatment in order to attain a result, which establishes equilibrium between different situations. To give adequate representation to the *dalits* and tribes in all posts or classes of posts or services, a reality and truism facilities and opportunities as enjoined in Article 38 are required to be provided to them to achieve the equality of representation in real content.

U.P. Experiment of Reservation in Reservation

The U.P. State Government formed a Social Justice Committee of seven members to recommend the possibility of segregation of most *dalits* and other most backward castes with SC and OBC respectively. Based on the recommendations of this Committee, the state government devised segregation of reservation quota through an ordinance in the year 2001 amending Section 2 of the U.P. Public Service (Reservations for SCs/STs and OBCs) Act, 1994; Accordingly, main two reserved categories i.e. scheduled castes and other backward castes (OBC). SCs were sub-divided into two categories *dalits* and most *dalits*. OBCs were divided into three categories i.e. backwards, more backwards and most backwards. Since scheduled tribe population hardly constitute 2% of total population sub division in their respect is not done.[5]

Detailed classification rests as under,

Table 10.1: Break-up of SC and OBC Population in U.P.

Scheduled Castes				
	*Dalits**	*Most Dalits*		*Aggre. SC*
Population share in SC	*Reservation*	*Population share in SC*	*Reservation*	*Reservation*
56%	10%	44%	11%	21%
Other Backward Classes				
	Backward	*More backwards*	*Most backward*	*Aggregate OBC*
Castes	Yadavas	Sonar, Kurmis, Jats, Lodha, Giris, Gurjars, Gosais, Kamboij	Few other. backward castes	—
Reservation	5%	9%	14%	28%

Source: Anirudh Prasad, Reservation Policy and Practice in India.

The whole bifurcation matter was challenged in the court with stay on its application. In the mean time, there was a political power change in the state. The new policy squashed the whole idea restoring the original *status quo* position in respect of the reservation provision in the state.

Justice A.P. Sen suggests twin policy

Justice A.P. Sen in *Vasanth Kumar vs State of Karnataka,* 1985 forcefully pointed out that both because of necessity as well as commitment that had been made in the constitution, the socially and educationally backwards must be helped. But unfortunately, the policy of reservation hitherto formulated by the government for the upliftment of such socially and educationally backward classes of citizens is caste oriented. While the policy should be based on economic criteria, he emphasized two considerations in particular why this should be so. First he said, only if this were done, could caste be removed while making special provisions under Article 15(4) and 16(4). Second, he said, "At present, only the privileged groups within the backward classes reap all the benefits of such reservation with the result that the lowest of the low who are stricken with poverty and are therefore socially and educationally backward remain deprived though these constitutional provisions under the Article 15(4) and 16(4) are meant for their advancement."[6]

Therefore, he said, a two-step process should replace the present caste based criteria. In the first instance, gauge the poverty of the person, second; assess him by some direct measures of social and educational backwardness.

Justice Chenappa Reddy in the same matter i.e. *K.C. Vasanth Kumar vs. State of Karnataka* observed, " **Are non-reserved jobs not cornered by the creamy layer? How does the snatching away establish that there should be no reservation? That a few of the seats and posts reserved for backward classes are snatched away by the more fortunate among them is not to say that reservation is not necessary.** That is bound to happen in a competitive society such as ours. Are not the unreserved seats and posts snatched away in the same way, by the top creamy layer of upper castes of society itself? Seats reserved for the backward classes are taken away by the top layers amongst them on the same principle of merit on which unreserved seats are taken away by the top layers of upper castes of society. How can it be bad if reserved seats and posts are snatched away by the creamy layer of backward classes if such snatching away of unreserved posts by the top creamy layer of the society itself is not bad?[7]

This is a necessary concomitant of the very economic and social system under which we are functioning. The privileged in the whole of society snatch away the unreserved prizes and the privileged among the backward classes snatch away the reserved prizes. This does not render reservation itself bad.

Justice Jeevan Reddy on Creamy Layer in *Indra Sahney Case*:

"The creamy layer should be hived off so that it does not hog the benefits of reservations. But he adds a caveat:

The cut off bar he permits is to be placed so high that hardly any one would be inconvenienced by it. A member of backward class, say a carpenter goes to the Middle East. He would earn quite a high income. But is he for that reason to be excluded from the backward class? The judge asks. Are his children to be deprived of reservations ? The only circumstance in which this may be done is, "If he rises so high economically as to become say a factory owner himself, only in such a circumstance would his social status have risen to justify his being assumed to have moved out of the backward class."[8]

To sum up, time for application of creamy layer in case of scheduled castes and scheduled tribes has not ripe. Grave social inequalities negates the feasibility of its application.

To sum up, there is a point in thinking about selectively applying some criteria which ensures the limited and scarce benefits like reservation go for the benefits of its most deserving section of the reserved categories. This could be done as suggested by Justice Chenappa Reddy Commission on Reservation in the State of Karnataka.[9] The commission's report suggested exclusion of some or all of the following categories of reserved groups from availing any benefit under reservation provisions:

1. Either of the candidate/student's parent is class-I or class-II in the service of government or public sector undertaking. If employed under private sector and draws a salary which is not less than a class II officer.
2. Either of his/her parent is professional i.e. doctor, lawyer, C.A. Income Tax or Financial or Management Consultant, Dental surgeon, Engineer or Architect.
3. Both of his/her parents are graduates.
4. Either of his/her parents are income tax assessee.
5. Either of his/her parent is VAT assessee.
6. Either of his/her parents or both together own more than a 8 hectares of rainfed dry land or its equivalent.

Question however about just, feasible, meaningful and bias-free applicability of these suggested exclusions cannot be so easily ruled out.

REFERENCES

1. Justice *N. Nagraj and others vs. Union of India*: (SCA 61/2002).
2. Prof. Sukhdev Thorat, Chairman UGC; Reservation and Private Sector P 394) .
3. Studies undertaken by Velaskar, Patvardhan and Palshikar (1992).
4. *Divya Bhaskar*, Gujarati Daily 17 December 2006.
5. Anirudh Prasad, *Reservation Policy and Practice in India.*
6. Justice A.P. Sen in *Vasanth Kumar vs State Of Karnataka*, 1985.
7. Justice Chenappa Reddy in K.C. *Vasanth Kumar vs. State of Karnataka.*
8. Justice Jeevan Reddy in *Indra Sahney Case.*
9. Justice Chenappa Reddy Commission on Reservation in the State of Karnataka.

11

Reservation in Various Institutions

A. JUDICIARY

Indian judiciary is one of the most powerful organs of the Indian democracy in imparting justice not only in individual matters but also in matters affecting the whole society at large through interpretation of huge and complex laws prevailing on the land. The judiciary has been assuming more and more importance in view of mounting complexities of various statutes, enhancing awareness regarding assured availability of justice through various ways and means and above all, increasing conflicting situations necessitating correct and unbiased interpretation of various laws including provisions contained in the Constitution. Judiciary is not confined to mere courtrooms, but it includes various commissions, tribunals and other judicial formations at various levels.

The judiciary is kept outside the purview of the implementation of the reservation provisions. Total exclusion of the judiciary from these statutory provisions is apparently not justifiable. Judiciary does not mean only judges seating in the Supreme Courts, state High Courts and few other inquiry commissions appointed under statute, but it also includes rank and files such as lower division judges, judicial magistrates first class, government pleaders, public prosecutors, courts' administrative staff consisting of officers, upper and lower division clerks, peons, bailiffs etc.

Reservation provisions are implemented in judiciary up to first class judicial magistrates' cadre. There is no reservation thereafter on the plea that higher judicial positions cannot afford implementation of reservation and these posts have to be filled on merit only. The reservation in non-judicial administrative posts in judiciary should be subject to applicability of all usual reservation norms. However, reservation to SC/ST non-judicial employees was denied at Maharashtra High Court in the recent court case.

Reservation in Non-Judiciary Posts

Apart from the position of judges, the entire judicial administration consists of huge manpower in various cadres. Representation of reserved category people in total number of non-judicial administrative staff in 18 High Courts of the country is as under[1]

Table 11.1: Employment Position in Non-judiciary Posts

	No.	*Actual*	*Required %*
Scheduled castes	1,191	7.40%	15%
Scheduled tribes	272	1.69%	7.50%
OBC	N.A.	N.A.	27%
General Category	14,634	90.91%	50.50%
Total	**16,097**		

Source: Backward, Shudra, OBC Andolan by Jayanti Manani.

A majority of these posts are of clerical and lower categories which too have remained unfilled after 50 years of implementation of reservation that too under the nose of the law enforcing authorities who are supposed to be the real guards of the Constitution and are supposed to have a higher degree of sensibility towards the spirit behind the constitutional provisions for the social justice.

The Maharashtra High Court had received four petitions filed by 20 persons employed as staff in the state judiciary administration seeking promotion under the reserved category. There were mainly two issues. i.e.

1. Whether the High Court has power to direct the Chief Justice to legislate or frame rules in his capacity as the

rule making authority to provide reservations for SC, ST and OBC in the recruitment and promotions of staff of the High Court, and

2. If a person could approach the Court to seek an enforcement of the reservation policy.

   The Court answered 'No' to both the above.

The Court held that Articles 15(4) and 16(4) were merely '**enabling provisions'.** The judges relied on a Supreme Court ruling of 1968 which stated that Constitution did not confer any right on a petitioner and that there was ' No constitutionally imposed obligation to make a reservation for scheduled castes, scheduled tribes either at the initial stage of recruitment or at the promotion stage. The Supreme Court had also conferred a discretionary power on the state to make a reservation for the backward classes when it felt that they were not being adequately represented in the public sector services.

The administration of law and justice is intimately linked with the philosophy of the judiciary and the social philosophy cannot be entirely separated from the social origins of those who dispense with the justice.

Reservation in Higher Level Judiciary

As observed by the former Chief Justice of Supreme Court P.N. Bhagwati, "Since the judges are drawn from the class of well to do lawyers, they unwittingly develop certain biases." The members of the judiciary have so far been drawn from the very section of the society, which is infected by the ancient prejudices and is dominated by notion of gradations in social life. The internal limitation of class interests of such judges does not allow them full play of their intellectual honesty and integrity in their decisions. Their judgments very often betray a mindset more useful to the governing class than the servile class. Such judges can have little understanding of the living forces operating in the servile classes and would have hardly any sympathy for some real measure designed to raise their dignity and progress. Thus, to have a fair representation of the society in the judiciary needs no emphasize which is equally desirable in the interest of nation.

Late K.R. Narayan; Ex. President of India

The late President, K.R. Narayan rightly mentioned based on his own experience, while granting approval in November 1998 to the appointment of judges in the apex Court[2]

"There is no dearth of availability of competent people now after fifty years from this category. It would be consonant with constitutional principles and the nation's social objectives, if persons belonging to weaker sections of society like SCs and STs who comprise 25 per cent of the population and women are given due consideration.

He added: "Eligible persons from these categories are available and their under representation or non-representation would not be justifiable. Keeping vacancies unfilled is also not desirable given the need for representation of different sections of the society and the volume of work which the Supreme Court is required to handle".

President K.R. Narayan's observations had triggered off a debate which continues to rage. The honourable late President has very rightly stressed that it is a matter of importance that in the Judiciary all major regions and sections of the society are represented to the extent possible consistent with requirements of merit and high standards maintained by the Judiciary.

Parliamentary Committee on SC/ST Welfare

The Parliament appointed a committee headed by Karia Munda M.P. in the year 1999/2000 to examine the need and possibility to implement provisions of reservation in the higher judiciary. The committee carried out an exhaustive study in this regard. A gist of the committee's report is appended below[3]

Eighteen High Courts of the country has a total strength of 481 judges of whom 15 belong to scheduled castes, 5 belonging to ST and 35 from the OBC category. The Supreme Court has now got a reserved category representation with the appointment of its chief justice who belongs to scheduled caste.

"Judiciary is visualized as an arm of the social revolution and is of crucial importance in the administration of justice in any country. The social composition of judiciary inevitably affects and influences its judgments. The judges are not super human beings. However, objective and fair they may try to be in their decisions or interpretation of law on any socio-economic issue, they cannot but be influenced by many considerations. A judge's mind is not a mechanical legal slot machine. His judgment is influenced at least unconsciously by his likes and dislikes, prejudices and predilections, his entire philosophy of life in the atmosphere of the on-going struggles in the country.

As is observed by Supreme Court Justice Desai, "Our judiciary has retained its traditional blindfold on its eyes and thereby ignored the perceived realities." It is naïve to believe that in the present state of affairs in our society, justice is really done to those who are outside the ruling fold. The judiciary should therefore be so composed as to reflect the socio-economic realities of the nation's life. The argument is not that judiciary should follow some sort of proportional representation. "The President's statement about representation of SC/ST/OBC in judiciary is totally in tune with constitutional objectives as well as the declared policy of all the governments and political parties and expresses the deep concern of the then president for justice to the weaker sections and an honest attempt to rectify a fault.

The committee further noted that there is very little disagreement among the people over the falling credibility of our judiciary. According to some case studies, in the selection and appointment of judges of the Supreme Court, some importance has been given to regional allocation and religious background in order to preserve semblance of representative framework. But social background was never a consideration for the composition of the higher judiciary, obviously under the false view its being communal representation. In fact, there is no dearth of evidence of the fact that communal bias has been visible in the judiciary up to the highest level. Communal bias is a necessary consequence of the caste system, we are living under. It is premise, which is recognized even by the criminal procedure code (CPC). There are specific provisions in the criminal procedure code showing the possibility of communal bias in the judiciary. The existence of communal bias in the issue of communal character cannot therefore be ruled out. In such a situation, there is no escape from accepting the principle of equitable representation of all the major social groups in the judiciary also for which there is absolutely no bar in the Constitution.

Judicial pronouncements made so far regarding the rights and interests of the weaker sections of society like scheduled castes and scheduled tribes almost constitute confusing milieu of opinion which settles little and unsettles much. High Courts have generally tended to apply restrictive criteria for the reservation policy for such people. So far the Supreme Court is concerned, there were different phases of attitude towards the constitutional provisions of reservation. There is no doubt that the Supreme Court has shaped the course of our national life. Although there was not much of uniformity in the Apex Court's decisions, it laid down certain rules or laws of reservation which were being followed over a period of more than four decades."

The Committee in conclusion expressed its opinion with regard to the implementation of reservation that the government in practice has however, adopted a policy of 'Running with the hare and hunting with the hounds.'

The parliamentary committee's report has been justifying the reservational aspect in judiciary on more than one account.

Caste Operates in Judicial Appointments Too

As per *Times of India* of 2nd February 1999 of the 19 new High Court judges' appointments made in the Allahabad High Court, 2 were sons of retd. Supreme Court judges, 2 sons of retd. Advocate General, one rtd. High Court's judge's son in law's brother, one junior advocate of the retd. chief justice. i.e. 7 out of ten close relatives of the judiciary VIPs![4]

Reservation in Bihar Judiciary

The High Court of Patna was already reserving 14 per cent of posts for scheduled castes and another 10 per cent for scheduled tribes. In the lower Judiciary. In 1991, The Bihar Government issued an Ordinance reserving 50 per cent of these seats for SC/ST/OBC functionaries. Soon enough, the legislature confirmed the reservation by converting the ordinance into an Act. The Act was challenged.

The Supreme Court struck down the act. The appointments to the lower judiciary are to be made by the governor in consultation with the High Court of the state, the Supreme Court noted. This consultation must be effective. The court ruled that attempt to set apart posts by passing an act was wrong. If necessary, the governor and the high court could have brought about the fair representation for the concerned classes through mutual consultation.

The Supreme Court further added, "Even that may not have been necessary, the Court said, as the High Court, being a high constitutional authority, is itself conscious of its social obligations. It is already and without a formal law directing it to do so, ensuring 24 per cent reservations for SCs and STs. If the governor had to come to the conclusion that another lot must be reserved for OBCs, he could have brought that results about, by persuading the High Court which, as noted is in any case alive to its social obligations."

The Supreme Court judgement is not only overtaking the democratic power of the people in deciding *inter alia* reservation matters, but also clearly indicating in an agitating voice not to interfere in the judicial administration at all.

To sum up, it is the high time to think for due representation of the Indian society as a whole which is historically lopsided in the higher judiciary. The judiciary has already given due weightage to the territorial representation in appointments fairly upto a higher level. Expected merit in such appointments from lower rungs will not be shattered as is also affirmed by the late President who himself was hailing from law community. What is desired is just an experiment of providing an opportunity.

B. PRIVATE SECTOR

Issue of reservation in private sector is not a new thing. In fact the national commission for the scheduled castes and scheduled tribes already recommended for reservation in private sector in its report in 1964, which was again repeated in their report for the year 1971. Mandal Commission also incorporated similar recommendation for reservation in private sector long back in their report in 1978.

The hon'ble President Dr. A.P.J. Abdul Kalam said in his Presidential address on 7 June, 2004 on the floor of the Parliament Joint Session, "The Government is sensitive to the issue of affirmative action including reservation in the private sector." He further added "The Government would initiate a dialogue with political parties, industry and other bodies on how best the private sector can fulfil the aspirations of the scheduled castes and scheduled tribes."[5]

National Human Rights Commission (NHRC) of our country has also in its one of the recently published reports on atrocities on SC/ST in 2004 made detailed remarks about the applicability of reservation in the private sector. Though the remarks contained some apprehensions also about the efficacy of this thought, the fact remains that the issue of reservation in the private sector is lauding as an important issue under positive discrimination now a days.[6]

The Prime Minister of India, Dr. Man Mohan Singh has stated in one of his very important press conferences that "It is the high time for introduction of provisions of reservation in the private sector. The remark of the Prime Minister, who himself is a world class economist hardly needs any reiteration about concern of this entire issue.[7]

Why is Now a Need for Private Sector Reservation

Reservation in vast private sector was so far never warranted, though it did come on the fore for consideration. Constitutional provisions related to reservation also exclusively cover Government and public sector undertakings right from beginning after independence. Then, what lead to expanding reservation related provisions to the private fold also? For this, one will have to refer to the New Economic Reforms also known as liberalization, privatization and globalization (LPG) details of which are discussed in Part IV Chapter 16 on 'New Economic Reforms and Reservation'.

The independent India launched socio-economic development with adoption of five year planning strategy. Huge intake of manpower by way of direct employment, found place at various levels in the government administration as well as newly formed public sector undertakings soon after independence. The Nation's thrust on the priority areas, such as primary education, health etc. gave a big boon to the demand for employments in this entire new arena. The government took direct initiative in promoting and managing public utility services with huge investments through the public sector.

In short, because of huge demand for the employment in the government and public sector, a need for private sector initiative in social cause for the upliftment of the despised communities was never warranted though reservation of job in private sector had come under the policy deliberations long back .Of course, a big chunk of workers belonging to SCs/STs/ OBCs were privately employed, particularly in the composite textile, sugar mill industries etc. where attractive job prospects, handsome remuneration were offered naturally because of the high productivity and profitability of these industries.

In the subsequent era of seventies, economic planning was almost settling down. Educational level in the country also went up quantitatively as well as qualitatively. The private sector also started fostering up. This was rather a take off period of the private sector. Indian textiles industry was at its peak. The country was also registering a worldwide name in non-conventional sectors such as pharmaceuticals, engineering, automobiles and so on. Our share in the global exports also went up, in quantum as well as proportion wise. All this did boost employment generating potential in the private sector.

However, all along this, the government sector still remained the major employer. Nationalization of banks, general insurance etc. during the seventies opened entirely a new job avenue for the reserved category people. Vertical as well as horizontal expansion of these sectors i.e. these newly nationalized financial institutions not only multiplied their functional horizons but also expanded their branch network. All this created huge employment in these public sector institutions. Significant beneficiaries of this transformation process were the candidates from the reserved categories as nationalisation only made their entry possible in these institutions, because of statutory application of reservation provisions.

Nineties was the core privatization phase. During this phase, more and more private sector establishments started pouring in. This resulted in registering lion's share in the employment generation by the private sector. Concept of liberalization, privatization, and globalization (LPG) gave further fillip to the private sector expansion. As against this, the non-government sector i.e. privately owned corporates have been found expanding by leaps and bounds. Increase in number of employees in organized private sector was quite phenomenal. It has gone up from 76.75 lacs as at the beginning of launching of new economic reforms in 1991/92 to 86.45 lacs in 1999/2000 recording a galloping spurt of 9.70 lacs people which is four time of the growth in the government sector during the corresponding period.

Employment generation position on the other hand at the government/public sector came almost to a stagnation level. Because of selective withdrawal of the government in numerous economic activities, increased computerization and disinvestments policy etc. the government, which was through out all these years, a major job provider, started withdrawing from entire spectrum of its activities.

Thus, with gradual dismantling of the public sector and selective withdrawal role of the State, jobs in government and public sector are shrinking and as against that, there is paradigm shift in the job transformation process, which clearly indicates that new employment potential avenues are seen generating in the private sector to a major extent under new economic reforms.

After all, the Constitution aims at addressing the social justice for the historically excluded and socially discriminated section of the society by providing adequate opportunities, which they have been denied since centuries. Reservation provided in the Constitution under Article 16(4) has been restricted to the government and public sector so far.

Maharashtra State Private Sector Reservation Law

Maharashtra State Government made a maiden attempt in introducing reservation in the private sector. As per the powers conferred upon the states under Article 348(3) of the Constitution, Maharashtra Government enacted a legislation in the year 2004 making reservation provisions to be applicable to private sector units, co operative societies and non-government organizations (NGOs) which are either established out of the state funds or are aided by the government funding. Initially, the Act covered all the private sector units in the state. However, upon strong protests from corporate houses and their representative federations, those units where the government funding exceeds 51 per cent of their total stake were brought under the purview of the Act. Certain categories were however exempted from these provisions such as medical super speciality, single post positions and those being filled by deputations or transfers. One more feature of this legislation was the provision of punitive action in case of deliberate violation of the Act or any of its provisions.

Massive Private Sector Expansion

New economic reforms i.e. LPG launched in 1991, now having settled all over in its operations has given rise to fastly expanding job potentialities in various sectors as under.

Large Scale Retail Market

Globally operating corporates are now entering into India's huge retail business by establishment of shopping malls. This has created high hopes and opportunities for the nation's unemployed youth who may not have much of required technical or other job oriented skill or qualification. Such jobs include sales boys/girls, supply chains, logistics, delivery, godown, and retail management etc.

Telecommunications

Similarly, there has been a revolutionary expansion on the telecommunications sector. The Mobile telecommunication is expanding by leaps and bounds. Mobile market, a new technological concept started before 10 years with mobile ownership of about 1.5 crore handsets during first 5 years. At present, there are 9 crores Mobile owners and is likely to be expanded rapidly to double in numbers in next 3 years. There is also a net addition of 5 crores landline subscribers. All this will open vast service market avenues in urban and more than that in rural areas.

Softwares and IT

Indian software companies' growth rate is 50 per cent which is highest in the world. World's top most 500 fortune companies get their 80 per cent of software and developmental work from Indian software companies. Indian requirement alone is 25 lacs software engineers and 50 lacs technicians as against present availability of just 20 per cent. All this will simultaneously also enhance demand for hardware people, skilled hardware technocrats, computer programmers, call center managers, content providers etc. On information technology (IT) front, there will be expansion of 8/10 lacs jobs in next couple of years.

Banking and Insurance

Similar is the likely acceleration in banking and insurance business. 50,000 branches of private sector banks are likely to be opened in next 2 years. ATMs are likely to be doubled in next 3 years. At present, there are 19 insurance companies with 15 per cent business growth. It is estimated that nearly 50 per cent population of the country is still left uninsured. 30 crores in life insurance and 60 crores in healthcare is the potential insurance market in India. Insurance of Intellectual properties, Houses, Books, Valuables etc. will further expand the scope for general insurance in the country. All this will create jobs for marketing and sales agents, surveyors, assessors etc. in several thousand numbers.

Education

In education sector also more and more foreign universities with huge investments and with variety of curriculum are intending to set up their establishments in India. There is also a new trend of establishment of schools and colleges by corporate houses. All this will provide vast job opportunities in the Education sector.[8]

However, in spite of all this, still shortages of institutions providing good manpower for the above demands continue all along.

Private Sector Job Reservation; Justification

To recall Dr. Ambedkar; "Reservations for the scheduled castes and scheduled tribes were meant to bring about fraternity. Fraternity is a collective project quite unlike equality and liberty. The State has to be the prime mover in all attempts to shore up fraternity for, it can neither be established by law or through unmediated market forces."[9]

Given the onus on the state to go fraternity off the ground, it is necessary that the private sector also now takes the responsibility of reservation and affirmative action. Affirmative action includes policies that advocate representation of different communities and groups. In addition, affirmative action also encourages and rewards those companies and institutions that get state funding when they show a satisfactory mix of communities on their employment rolls.

It is a general perception of the private sector people at large that reservation should be restricted to the public/government sector only and the private sector should be kept out of the purview of the provisions of reservation as the responsibility of undertaking such social justice and equality measures rests upon the government only.

Since reservation centers around employment which is now shifting from Government and public sector, thought on reservation will also have to be moulded accordingly. Following new changes in public policy calls for invocation of private sectors' role play in shouldering the social responsibility through various affirmative actions including reservation.

Privatization of Public Sector Enterprises

Policy adopted by the nation way back upon independence regarding role of public sector in numerous economic activities is now on reversal trend.

- Privatization of public sector enterprises viz. BALCO, IPCL etc.
- The government has so far sold 123 public sector undertakings from the year 1990/91 to 31 May 2002 realizing Rs. 30,738 crores and it further intends to raise another Rs. 47,562 crores by selling some more public sector undertakings.
- Equity dilution in the public sector undertakings, so as to bring down government's equity holding through public offers. e.g. ONGC.
- Private sector entries through takeover of the public utility services, hitherto solely owned and managed by public sector. e.g. BSNL a new Company having taken over the Central Government run telephones department. Split of Gujarat Electricity Board (GEB) hitherto a Government of Gujarat undertaking solely managing electricity supply services in the State, now converted into seven public limited companies constituted under the Indian Companies' Act 1956.

All this will further narrow the scope the employment expansion in the government, which will in turn reduce the scope for people from the reserved category in the government sector.

Indian Private Sector and their representative organizations have now started talking about '**Corporate Social Responsibilities**', which is a constructive thought in the direction towards affirmative action for those who are denied social equalities and social justice. Recently published **J.J. Irani Report** on behalf of the Confederation of Indian Industries has also suggested number of recommendations that the private sector can undertake. After having realized about 'corporate social responsibility,' what is needed is now its launching with a firm and whole hearted determination without anticipating for the immediate results at least in few coming years.[10]

The constitution aims at the upliftment of oppressed and backward classes who have remained far behind in the progress. The new as well as the expanding economic avenues as narrated above are going to open ample job opportunities for the youth in the country. This leaves considerable scope for consideration of positive discrimination in all these private sectors for the scheduled castes, scheduled tribes, and other backward classes.

Infrastructural Support Out of Public Exchequer

The entire role of the government got diversified from hitherto being the major operator in the economic activities now to a facilitator. The government has been gradually withdrawing from economic activities and giving simultaneously a free hand support to the private sector viz. providing required infrastructural support and facilities such as rails and roads, power, health, sanitation, human resources development, ports, airports, telecommunications, education, tourism, water, irrigation, entertainment etc. The infrastructural development has assumed a great amount of importance in the economic reform era. Few of the prestigious infrastructure projects so far undertaken by the government in collaboration with the private sector includes, national golden quadrilateral highways, express ways, widening of existing highways, massive telecommunication connectivity. Expansion, electrification, modernization in Indian Railways, ambitious multipurpose water projects like Narmada, river linkages and water greed, establishment/upgradation of international and domestic airports, special economic zone (SEZ) developments etc.

Such investments boost overall momentum by way of economic principles of income velocity, which ultimately benefits the private sector the most in several ways. Infrastructural capital expenditure is an important and inevitable expenditure for any ambitious economic project whether in private or public sector. Had the government not come forward with such initiative, it would have created huge financial burden on the private sector posing a threat on the viability of many private sector projects.

Thus, government spends huge funds for infrastructural development, which facilitates faster private sector development. Therefore, it is the reciprocal duty of the private sector to respond to the expected social obligation by way of providing some job opportunities to reserved category aspirants, which hitherto was directly provided by the government.

Supply of World Class Professional Manpower from Government Educational Institutions

Private/Corporate sector draws best technical and professional manpower from government assisted educational institutions like IITs, IIMs and many other renowned government academic institutions/universities. Such professionals are the backbone of the private sector in bringing high profitability to the private entrepreneur. It is estimated that an amount of approximately Rs. 5.00 lacs per student is incurred out of the public exchequer at these institutions viz, IIT, IIM, etc. Most of the professionals qualified/skilled at these institutions are taking jobs in the private sector corporates like Reliance. Tata, Infosys, Arvind, HCL, HLL, Thapar, Birla etc.

Similarly, the corporate hospitals like Hinduja, Jashlok, Sterling and Appolo etc. are known for their worldwide reputation for quality medical services. Medical acumen and surgical expertise of Indian doctors have brought huge revenue and name as well by way of foreign exchange and medical tourism for the country. The highly skilled and very well experienced doctors attached to these hospitals are the products of the government hospitals connected medical colleges. Crores of rupees are being spent out of public funds for running and maintaining these hospitals and medical educational institutions.

The concept of the private sector reservation is nothing but a sort of reciprocating 'PAY BACK' of the benefits that are available to them out of public money as narrated above.

No Network; No Private Sector Jobs

Indian private sector barring a few corporates has thin representation of the lower category people. The reasons are many such as presence of caste consciousness in private sector, non-transparent nature of recruitment pattern in the private sector etc. Hardly, one sees regular advertisement for jobs in the private sector. This is primarily because employers in these companies generally prefer applicants that are recommended by their own caste fellows. They are reluctant to go to the open market to search for prospective employees. This smacks of a lack of professionalism, which is why their plea of upholding standards sounds hollow to many. Most private sector organizations choose only between those who are network recommendees. This excludes a vast majority of potential applicants from any active job consideration in such organizations.

The scheduled castes and scheduled tribes lack such network connections. Rule of thumb for private sector recruitment is : No network connections, No jobs. This necessitates having provision of affirmative action in the form of reservation in the private sector

Dipankar Gupta Communist MP states as regard network connection, "Different communities and classes have different sets of aspirations. Now the elite among the lower classes have experienced what it is to be among the better off in the public sector, their outlook has undergone a change. Like other well to do classes, their ambition is now to be in the private sector which has all along been rather exclusivist in its recruitment policies. The private sector is not a homogeneous group. There are numerous enterprises big and small that constitute the private sector. The reservationists are aiming their sights at high end jobs in major multinational and other Indian listed companies. The fact is that most of the private sector companies have serious problems regarding their hiring policy. Very few of them have a transparent system of recruitment. In most of the cases, it is the network that counts. This network excludes certain people rather discriminates against them. In other words, regardless of one's caste background, if the network is not supportive of the applicant, then, the chances of making it to the post are extremely limited."[11]

Private Sector Hardly Remains Private

If one looks at the financial composition of any private sector enterprise, it will substantiate the truth that a private enterprise is hardly a privately owned entity. The promoters of such projects contribute a small part of the total cost of the project with rest raised from public equities, term and working capital financing from financial institutions which are funded either by the government or the public at large. No doubt, the private entrepreneurs pay a price for all this. But it is fairly less and quite competitive as compared to prevailing money market terms.

As per the government industrial promotion policy, it provides numerous incentives to boost private sector industrial development initiative starting right from land allotment at much concessional rates or in many cases at throw away prices with all land revenue and title of ownership related statutory clearances. Besides, the government provides various initial financial aiding support by way of capital subsidy to new industry, interest subsidy, power subsidy, price difference subsidy, certain budgetary concessions, area specific income tax exemptions, export promotion incentives, selective customs/ excise reliefs, VAT deferments etc. It is possible that all of these incentives might have been either withdrawn by now or modified subsequently as a policy review. Notwithstanding the same, aggregates of the all above reliefs/concessions etc. accumalate to several thousand crores of rupees out of the public exchequer so far, going for the benefits of the private sector.

Majority of their raw materials come from natural sources such as land, water, forests, mines, minerals etc., which are all publicly owned national properties. They are getting required labour from the society and are further abstained from worries relating to law and order which all are managed out of public resources.

Private Sector Response to Proposed Reservation

The immediate response to the proposed reservation by the private sector is straight in negative. The representative organizations have strongly protested the proposed movement. Their main argument in opposing private sector reservation is generally focused on 'Merit'. They advocate that private sector has to operate amidst highly competitive environment and therefore are required to have best available meritorious employees. Their underlying assumption is that recruitment of people through reservation means people with either poor merit or no merit at all. But it is not so in reality. Reservation does not mean induction of people whether or not they possess all requisites stipulated for the post. Reservation never expects this. Private sector must not relax their norms with regard to qualifications, experience etc. What is solicited is giving them an opportunity with caste free openness and if a reserved category candidate is otherwise suitable, giving him a chance with all sensibility, providing him some additional grooming to come upto the corporate expectations which is desirable keeping his social background.

As regard merit, this is discussed at length under in Chapter 8 on '**Merit and Reservation**'. Merit especially in private sector is very much essential to withstand the competitive market forces, to maintain quality aspect and further to ensure cost effectiveness functioning. Availability of fresh as well as experienced youngsters from reserved categories with industry specific requirement is not difficult. Industry and Corporate houses have also realised the yield of investment in training their staff with in-house on the job and outside theoretical trainings by professional experts. A little more vigorous and extensive training and care to the so recruited reserved category persons will make an useful permanent asset to the institution. What is required is a positive attitude and a considerate will with helping hand to these oppressed masses of the larger Indian society.

It would not be out of place to mention that presence of Indian commerce and industries on the global platform does not exhibit a prideful place in spite of having so-called meritorious manpower at their disposal in absence of reservation. Perhaps the stalwarts in Indian private sector realm have not come out of their social stigma as can also be seen from summarised gist of following opinions.

Jurist, Fali S. Nariman says," The government's plan to reserve jobs for SCs/STs in private sector is good in theory, but extremely difficult to implement and monitor."[12]

Sukhdev Thorat, Professor of Economics, Jawaharlal Nehru University, New Delhi and now **Chairman, University Grants Commission** terms private sector reservation as a remedy against the market discrimination. He says, "If the prevalence of economic discrimination is the justification of the reservation in the public sector, why can it not be the reason for reservation in the private sector? In countries like US, Northern Irelands, Malayasia and Latin America '**affirmative action**' was developed from very beginning, both in the public and the private sector.

Therefore, it is the high time that we introduce reservation in the private sector and provide long withheld justice. Economists have now enough evidence to show that markets don't remain neutral, but do discriminate against the so-called untouchables and other low castes. Some strands in main economics, which forms the theoretical supportive base for affirmative action policies in the west, believe that market discrimination not only brings about "unequal income distribution," but also adversely affects economic growth by bringing imperfection in the labour market, and further by also inducing inter group conflicts. Affirmative action as a remedy for market discrimination is thus justified, on the ground of both equity and growth.

Thorat is of the firm opinion that India must enact an **'Equal Employment Opportunity Act'** in line with US law, so as to provide legal safeguards against discrimination. This could be supplemented by affirmative action in terms of reservation in some categories of jobs and other markets."[13]

Nanik Rupani, President, Indian Merchants' Chamber has strongly opposed extension of reservation in the private sector. While on one hand, he appreciates removal of inequality from the society, unilateral imposition by the government, without any negotiation with the private sector is not fair according to him. He also suggested planning of free industrial trainings for absorption of trained backward class youth in the private sector.[14]

Sunil Kant Munjal, former President, Confederation of Indian Industries," Merit is non-negotiable in the Industry in the private sector." He also pointed out that the Industry was ready to co-operate with the Government to spread social justice. He further says; he can hardly be faulted for describing reservations as at best a "Patchwork" solution. The first step is for the power that be to "upgrade the skills". In other words to enhance "the employability of the backward sections."[15]

P.N. Bhagwati, The Renown Jurist opines, ' Reservation without minimum standards would be against the interests of the country. There would be no incentive among *dalits,* also to improve their educational performance and to compete with others. Also it will prejudicially affect the quality of the administration.'[16]

Ratan Tata, Leading Industrialist has openly favoured introduction of reservation in the private sector. The Tata

Group has written to the central government, "Tata group very well understands their obligations to the society. They support to the Government plea for reservation in the private sector. They are devising a scheme in this regard, for being presented to the government."[17]

To sum up, most of the industrialists or their representing organizations are against the application of reservation in private sector. A general private sector perception is that it is the sole responsibility of the government for bringing about such social justice and correcting the age old social discrimination. Many others admit the need of the reservation in theory, using highly professional jargon such as "**Employability enhancement**" etc. but disowns at the same time their own role in this crucial social cause. Yet there is a section of positive thinkers like Tata etc. who have come out openly supporting the reservation and also its implementation, "Charity should begin from home"

Need for a Safety Net

Prosperity of private sector shall need existence of a society. Private sector cannot operate in isolation. It has therefore but to take the aspirations of the society in to consideration. Can our private sector not create 'A Safety Net' through more jobs for those who have remained deprived of their legitimate right of share from the economy? Therefore, one is forced to argue that these paradigms for the development would become redundant for the drowntroddens if one and all concerned fail to think about this. Do we have some alternative paradigms, for the development of this section of the Indian population, which is structurally located at the different pedestal of the Indian society?

The purpose of the economic growth is the creation of a good society and nothing else. Scriptures say that the *'Artha'*; i.e. economic growth should be pursued in accordance with *'Dharma'* i.e. Social Goodness. We should willingly realign economic interests to secure a good society. *Ability of our private sector lies in finding ways for securing social good without hurting our national economic goals.*

C. SELF-FINANCE EDUCATION INSTITUTES

Growth and development of education in any society or for that reason a nation is the pre requisite in its quest for fighting against all social and economic evils. Lack of education, miserable poverty and economic backwardness all these three are interlinked, i.e. one leads to later and *vice versa*. The vicious circle gets compounded day by day in a geographic proportion. Ultimately, the whole nation comes in the trap of slavery. It is the spread of education only which can break this hard to crack vicious circle. It is education only, which will push away all the hurdles in the way towards economic progress and make the path of social revolution uninterruptedly smooth.

The country has done remarkably well as regards spread of education since independence as can be seen from the following statistics.[18]

Table 11.2: Expansion of University Level Education since Independence

	No. of Universities	*Colleges*	*Students*	*Teachers*
1950/51	32	695	1.74 lacs	NA
2001/02	265	13,150	88.21 lacs	4.27 lacs

Source: Advocacy Internet Nov/Dec 2005.

The country has resources constraint for providing adequate education facility to its 30 crore school going pupils. Hence private initiative in education system was introduced along with various post-economic reform measures which is popularly known as **'Self Finance Education System.'**

The newly introduced self finance education system is basically nothing but extended privatization of education. More and more colleges and self finance education institutions are being floated under this arena. The share of these institutions which was quite negligible in the beginning of nineties, has gone upto now 5,14,356 students in engineering and technical courses and about 20,000 students in medical branches in the year 2005/06.

The system has far reaching adverse implications in relation with social justice to the SCs/STs/OBCs.

Though self finance education system is altogether a separately debatable issue, it has following features so far as the reserved categories are concerned.

- Exorbitantly high fee structure beyond the affordability reach of poor and backward class people.
- No job reservation in the teaching/non-teaching staff employed at these institutions.
- Management quota for discretionary admissions.

Private sector education set up has been in existence in our country right from British days. The present self finance education system is its extended version. Private sector education institutions are normally found at high school and routine college education. They are government aided and hence are supposed to adhere to job reservations, admission transparencies and other statutory norms. The newly formed Self Finance Education Institutions as the name suggests, manage their affairs out of their own resources, without Government aids and hence are out of these reservation and other statutory obligations. As per the recent apex court's orders, self finance education institutes are supposed to observe transparency in students' admissions. The way and speed with which self finance education institutions are coming up, it is likely that in a very near future, the education which is now perceived as a market of 30 crores students will be under the total control of these SFEIs, where:

(1) There will be no reservation at all i.e. in teaching as well as non-teaching posts, which would have otherwise provided job opportunities to several thousands SC/ST/OBC job aspirants.
(2) As said earlier, admissions in these institutions will be beyond the reach of poors of the country.
(3) The management quota at the discretion of the owners of the institutions will invite so many undesirable and

unfair practices, such as admission on the basis of monetary bargaining.

Reservation in Post-Graduation in Medical Specialities

Reservation in post-graduation particularly in medical speciality has been a centre point of various reservation related controversies. Since medical profession is directly connected with one's life, it is often used as a weapon to inflame anger of a common man with argument that reservation in medical speciality produces sub-standard doctors posing a threat to the human life. Absence of the correct position in this regard has emerged as one of the major points of unrest against reservation policy which provoked a wide spread anti-reservation stir in 1985 in Gujarat and few other states in the country as discussed in Part I at Chapter 7 on 'Anti-Reservation Agitations in Gujarat'.

Decision for reservation in post-graduation particularly in medical faculty was taken by the Union Government, Health Department in the year 1974. Actual implementation started from 1977/78. Though reservation in under graduation i.e. M.B.B.S. courses was there from very beginning. There was no reservation in post-graduation courses like MD, MDS, MS, etc. till 1977/78. Out of total strength of 737 post-graduates holding teaching posts in medical faculty, in whole of Gujarat, those belonging to reserved category were just 24 comprising one professor, one associate professor, five assistant professors and remaining 17 in class II tutors' post as in March 1981 in whole of Gujarat. It remains unrecognized as to how such SC/ST doctors after their graduation remained in so thin number in post-graduation. There are after about 800 seats in MBBS in Gujarat, approximately 25 per cent of whom normally are taken in post-graduation every year. Taken all these factors together, there should have been adequate presence of SC/ST/OBC doctors in post-graduation, which was not the case in absence of specific provisions of reservation in this behalf. Implementation of reservation in post-graduation from eighties boosted increasing representation of post-graduate doctors from SC/ST.

Ratio of post-graduate doctors continuing to serve in the Government set up and those settling their own private practice from general category vis a vis reserved category doctors is worth examining. Exact statistical data are not available in this regard. However, a cursory survey does reveal that general category doctors going in practice ratio is many time more than that in respect of the reserved category doctors. Government contributes 95 per cent of medical education expenditure. As against this, very few of these beneficiary post-graduate specialist doctors pay back to the Government through their services for the larger community benefits. Government hospitals cater the health needs of the masses hailing from the poor classes of the society. Thus, larger number of post-graduate doctors from the reserved category in the government service goes in the benefit of the masses who are otherwise unable to afford the treatment charges of such specialists. Of course, compelling reasons for joining Government services by these specialist doctors are many including their social acceptability in the upper caste locality etc. The socio-economic background of these post-graduate specialists from reserved category also inculcate in them a sentiment for better serving of these ailing masses. The specialists in the medical college attached hospitals also contribute in the medical education, examinership etc. Quite a few have been further elevated to posts like dean. Would all this have been possible but for the provision of reservation in the post-graduation specialities?

Reservation in Post-Graduation does not Necessarily Produce Sub-standard Doctors

Reservation is provided in the post-graduate medical specialties in clinical branches such as Surgery, Medicine, Gynecology, Pathology, Radiology and non-clinical branches such as anatomy, pharmacology, Preventive and Social medicine etc. Every student after admission into the post graduate speciality or super speciality is required to undergo the same course of study, same standard and same examination pattern for qualifying the courses for conferment of the degrees in the respective speciality or super specialities or technical subjects.

In post-graduation medical courses, the entrant has to undergo vigorous residency of three years. The residency requires the student to remain 24 hours available to the hospital he is attached to. He will render a full time service besides pursuing his patient's bedside teaching, post-graduation tutorials, presentations under the head of the Unit. The grilling during this residency remains so rigorous that the student gets maximum independent handling of complex live cases. Upon successful completion of three years' practical work in the hospital, submission of dissertation etc., all the students have to appear in the final written examination and viva voce and to get through. All these standards for being qualified are uniform for all the students irrespective whether the student belongs to a reserved category or otherwise. In other words, SC/ST/OBC student has also to pass through all these qualifying standards for being awarded prestigious post graduation and for getting a registration to practise thereafter. This amply clarifies that a graduate medico admitted through the reserved quota is also thoroughly grilled and tested at par as a general category student and therefore he would be equally well equipped surgeon or a physician or pathologist or radiologist. There are hundreds of SC/ST doctors having commendable reputation of being very good specialist in their respective branches working in government hospitals.

A.B. Burdhan says, " Is it true that because of reservation, the level is going down and we are producing bad doctors, engineers etc.? Experience and study have shown that even though the scheduled castes, scheduled tribes, and other backward classes get in with lower marks at the entry point, there is a sufficiently long period of co-habitation and co-education, where all students are equally exposed to the same academic and social atmosphere, the initial level of difference narrows down in general. After the initial entry, every candidate, irrespective of his caste or community, has to go through the same series of tests and examinations. There are no separate examinations oral or written, for the reserved candidates and there are no concession in marks. There is no quota in the number of candidates who are declared successful in the final examination! The final qualification as doctor, engineer, scientist etc. is the same for all, based on merit. **The final product—good, bad or indifferent—carries no caste mark. If there is any dilution here, it is the same for all and is the outcome of the general devaluation of academic life and examination system today.** Speaking of merit; what happens when the passport for entrance to professional institutions is a whacking sum of money, euphemistically termed as 'capitation fees'? Here again, we see that those who are economically and also socially advanced, manage to get in through the back door by paying large sums, after having failed to secure admission on the basis of merit. As to the scheduled castes, scheduled tribe and deprived sections, they cannot avail this facility for obvious reasons"[19].

Supreme Court in Post-Graduate Institute of Medical Education and Research Case

It is the constitutional imperative of the executive to provide opportunities and facilities to the handicapped to acquire the degree in specialties, super specialities or technical posts. Denial thereof is a total denial of right to enjoy equality. It is well settled legal position that fundamental rights are to be interpreted broadly to enable the citizens to enjoy the rights enshrined in Parts III and IV of the Constitution vide *The Ahmedabad Xavier's College Society vs. State of Gujarat*, MANU/SC /0088/ 1974, *Marri Chandra Shekhar Rao vs. Dean, Seth G.S. Medical College*, MANU/ SC /0457/1990 and *Ashok Kumar Gupta vs. State of U.P.*, MANU/ SC/1776/1997.

Reservations in post-graduation specialities or super specialities are detrimental to the high degree of efficiency and violative of Article 14 is obviously incorrect, erroneous, illegal and unconstitutional. Thus, it is held that the reservation in post-graduation speciality or super speciality is valid under Articles 14, 15(4) of the Constitution.

Chief Justice Lahoti in recent Supreme Court case; *P.A. Inamdar and others vs. State of Maharashtra and others* (C.A. 5041 of 2005) decided on 12 Aug. 2005 on unaided professional educational institutions whether minority or non-minority observes;[20]

A. Imposition of state seats in unaided professional institutions are acts constituting serious encroachments on the rights and autonomy of private professional educational institutions.
B. Merely because the resources of the state in providing professional education are limited, private education institutes which intend to provide better education cannot be forced by the State to make admissions available on the basis of reservation policy to less meritorious candidates.
C. A limited reservation not exceeding 15 per cent may be allowed to NRIs depending on management's discretion subject to condition that such seats should be utilized for bonafides NRIs only and for their children or wards and that **within this quota merit should not be given a complete go by.**
D. Unaided Institution can have their own admission system if fair, transparent, non-exploitative and based on merit is adopted in the admission process.
E. Every Institution is free to devise its own fee structure and generate reasonable surplus to meet cost of expansion and augmentation of facilities subject to the limitation that there can be no profiteering and no capitation fee can be charged directly or indirectly or in any other form.

Abolition of state quota and reservation may appear correct in so far as it is constructed as interpretation of law.

1. When the constitutional provision for job quotas are enforced only in the State services and not in the private sector, why the fuss about extending the parallel

provision for educational institutions in the private sector, and

2. As the constitutional mandate for the social and educational advancement of backward classes is for the State to honour it.

In response to the first, it is important to take note of the increasing pressure for going for reservations in private sector a debate on which is going on and the fact that employment and educational reservation are qualitatively different. As education is a *sine qua non* for individual and includes the excluded groups through education are the most important tasks of any human society.

The response to the posture that it is for the State to honour its constitutional mandate is that it is one thing to fault the state where failure relating to the backward classes has been gross and tragic and quite another to legally address the issues of the victims of its wrongs. As the state like the judiciary is a creation of the society, its wrongs should not be allowed to shadow the society and to be turned into failure on two grounds, first because of the state failure and second because of the judicial insistence that the state should withdraw from reaching out to the weak through the private sector education. In this connection, it is important to reaffirm the earlier observation that as education is *sine qua non* of individual and social development reaching the undetached and including excluded through education are the most important tasks of any human society. In this sense, a liberal interpretation of constitutional mandate to the State should necessarily mean that if its foray into the private sector serves the greater good, it is well be within its rights to do so. If the State has failed in its important social task, it is for the judiciary which is expected to be an epitome of humanness and social vision to pull it up and if necessary, to work in other ways to fill in the void and redress the wrongs.

Merit *vs.* Reservation in Educational Admissions

The enunciation of the Bench that reservation to backward classes is contrary to merit and untenable for a number of reasons. Among others, the Mandal judgment by 9 Judge Bench had affirmed that reservation is not anti-meritarian. If reservation is anti-meritarian, it should be more so on employment front. Tamil Nadu has implemented reservation with as high as 69 per cent in State services and education. In spite of this it is one of the relatively most advanced and efficient States in the country. Indian Medical Association has also having been satisfied with the maintenance of public health services predominantly because of a very large fraction in these services from the reserved categories has endorsed continuance of reservation.

When all is said, Reservation has more to do with scarcity of resources and opportunities than merit which in the context of education should be seen as lack of access to the small education cake. When the policy really addresses needs of the really backwards or whether advanced among backwards corner the benefits which they really do not need, is a different issue which the judge is expected to probe.

TJS George Columnist on NRI quota: " Actually the court gave a stick to the political hands to beat it with. Even as the judgment abolished quotas and reservation, it allowed 15 per cent quota for Non-Resident Indians (NRIs) with a tame caution that within this quota, merit should not be given a complete go by. What we can now expect from aforementioned is that a Resident Indian (RI) will first become NRI-RI and spend a few more lacs to acquire the right to play with lives of patients. Never has so much been done by so many to achieve so little for the common good[21].

Admission Racket

Thus, if in judgment that enabled institution can have their own admission, if fair, transparent, and non-exploitative and based on merit is having a big 'IF'. Many of these institutions have not been fair, transparent and non-exploitative in their admissions and their admissions are not really merit based. One of the many incidents relating to admissions in Tamil Nadu should drive home.

On the basis of a written test in a Deemed University in Chennai, called for counselling in one of its colleges. But there was no counselling. Students were shown a Print Card informing that seats in certain branches were available for the amounts shown against them as the capitation fees, which in the case of engineering was any thing between Rs. 2 to Rs. 5 lacs p.a. They were asked to pay then and there, a part of the amount to book the seat and remaining amount within few days. To avoid losing the seat without any guarantee of a seat, many anxious parents rushed to pay entire amount.

When a senior academician not the chancellor or chairman of this Deemed University was contacted to change the admission of a candidate from one branch to another, the response was that the candidate has scored low marks in the written test. We can shift him to the other branch, if you pay Rs. 3 lacs extra for the seat in another branch. When the person asked how these extra amount would change the performance of the candidate in the test, which he had already appeared, the chancellor had no reply.

With different private institutions charging different amount of fee, with no idea of the likely fee hike in the remaining years with poor infrastructure facilities, poor teaching staff and other infirmities, the private education system is a dom of corruption, greed, incompetence, sleeze, unscrupulousness and the institutions hold the parents and students captive using admission uncertainty syndrome. Here it is important to remember that while private institutions have strong lobby network and bargaining power through political clout, money power, all India associations and consortia and all against that, students have nothing to fall back upon them.

The suggestion by the Bench that private institutions can have their own admission and fee structure may not be practical in the absence of standardization and state intervention. The situation is chaotic and disquieting.

Profiteering

While banning capitation fee and profiteering in private institutions, the Bench has also dwelt in these evils; Capitation fee cannot be permitted to be charged and no seat can be permitted to be appropriated by payment of capitation fee. 'Profession' has to be distinguished from business or a mere occupation. While in business and to a certain extent in profession, there is a profit motive. Profession is primarily a service to the society wherein earning is secondary or incidental. A student who gets a professional degree by capitation fee once qualified as a professional is likely to aim more at earning rather than serving and that becomes a bane on the society. The charging of capitation fee by unaided minority and non-minority institutions for professional courses is not permissible. Similarly, profiteering is also not permissible. Despite the legal position, this court cannot put its eyes to two hard realities of commercialization of education and evil practices being adopted by many institutions to earn large amount for their private or selfish end.

TJS George observes, "As far as in 1953, the Supreme Court has declared levying of capitation fee by professional colleges as illegal. Andhra Pradesh and Kerala had put ban on it. Tamil Nadu and Maharashtra followed it. In August 2003, Supreme Court put a complete ban on capitation fee and emphatically said that under no circumstances, should educational institutions be allowed to indulge in profiteering. Yet, profiteering flourishes in professional education more uproaringly than to say in the edible oil adulteration business. This results in two disastrous consequences. First when a rich idiot gets admission into the MBBS just because he has paid Rs. 40 lacs as capitation fees, he emerges as a dom who is likely to destroy more lives than he saves. Those who are not too rich and not too idiotic, will focus on just one thing, how to recover that Rs. 40 lacs and make another Rs. 40 lacs to Rs. 80 lacs for his children's admissions. The second disastrous consequence is that a poor kid simply won't get an admission at all even if he has the most brilliant brain on the land. This naturally is enough what the politician has seized. He says that Supreme Court ruling is a blow on social justice that it does not factor in social realities"[22]

Self Finance Education System will open a flood gate for inflow of such doctors moving out in the society for recovering such lacs of rupees with whatever ways and means. Where will incidence of this burden stabilize? Who will ultimately be penalized for these uneconomic and extravagant costs?

The judgment insists on no capitation fee and no profiteering. K.T. Thomas retired judge who was one of the eleven judges' Bench comments, "How many state Governments will make regulations to ensure that the above twin insistence is implemented; that a proper law is passed to prevent management from collecting capitation fee and also to ensure that standards of merit will not be at stake owing to non-payment of bribe may be camouflaged under any other name.

Here a distinction needs to be made between minorities institutions started several years ago and minorities and non-minorities institutions started now. Most of the institutions under the first category are known for their earnestness in purpose and commitment to the cause of education . They do not work for profit. The website of some of them contains a notice during admission time that "The college does not collect any capitation fee or donations. If any body approaches you on behalf of the college for capitation fee or donation, please bring it to the notice of authorities." While these noble institutions are also caught in the odds of globalization and the related knowledge revolution, their contribution to the society's education system is invaluable.

It is the institutes of the second category, which are a menace driving the education system haywire. The Deemed University mentioned earlier is a case in point. Its website claims that its chancellor began foray into education by starting a school dedicated to his mother. How that school recently spawned so many state of the art buildings and campuses which may now fetch a few hundred crores of rupees is a mystery.

State Failure

No doubt it is the State abducting their responsibilities of expanding higher education. With the few Government aided colleges unable to meet the demand of engineering and medical courses, which first necessitated establishment of unaided private institutions. In the absence of proper policy of establishing unaided private institutions soon turned into piracy and on-going chaotic proliferation of professional institutions particularly engineering and medical colleges. Justice Thomas in his write up earlier drew attention of the mushrooming of self financing private professional colleges inspired by huge wealth accumulated by the professional college racket and to the fact that a lobby developed and succeeded in wrangling government sanctions for starting such colleges in number of states.

Chhatisgarh Enactment Leading to Mushrooming of Private Universities

Privatization of education has created a sort of fierce inter state competition in opening abound avenues to the private sector. The newly formed State 'Chhatisgadh' enacted a state legislation on the line of 'Deemed University' entitled as 'Chhatisgarh State Private University Act'. The Act was so liberal that it enabled rapid coming up of universities across the state resulting that as much as 112 universities in a very short span of time came into existence. Such mushrooming of universities lacked the basic prerequisites of infrastructure and space, which are very essential for any educational institution. The overall situation became so chronic that the Supreme Court had to interfere which declared that the Act was a colourful piece of legislation beyond the legislative competence of the State legislature. In the ensuing chaos, the establishment of all those 112 teaching shops was declared null and void and 30,000 students were left in the lurch, facing an uncertain future. The Supreme Court actually provided a list of addresses of the universities in the judgment and some of them have been located on a single floor of a shopping mall and one in a car garage[23].

Perhaps such cannot be the motive behind privatization of education simply in the name of resource constraint at the exchequer.

REFERENCES

1. Backward, Shudra, OBC Andolan by Jayanti Manani.
2. The late President, K.R. Narayan while granting approval in November 1998 to the appointment of judges in the apex Court
3. The Parliamentary Committee headed by Karia Munda M.P. 1999/2000.
4. *Times of India* of 2nd Feb. 1999.
5. President Dr. A.P.J. Abdul Kalam in his Presidential address on 7 June, 2004 on the floor of the Parliament Joint Session.
6. National Human Rights Commission (NHRC) on report on atrocities on SC/ST in 2004.
7. *Sandesh* Gujarati Daily of 25 October 2004.
8. *Divya Bhaskar* Gujarati Daily; 17 December 2006.
9. *Dr. Ambedkar Writing and Speeches*, Vasant Moon; Vol. 13.
10. J.J. Irani Committee on behalf of the Confederation of Indian Industries Report.
11. Dipankar Gupta Member of Parliament (CPI) *Business Standard* of 16 June 2004.
12. Jurist, Fali S. Nariman, *Financial Express* of 11 June 2004.
13. Prof. Sukhdev Thorat, JNU, New Delhi and Chairman, UGC *Economic Times* 26 March 2004.
14. Nanik Rupani, President, Indian Merchants' Chamber.
15. Sunil Kant Munjal, former President, CII *Financial Express* 22 June 2004.
16. P.N. Bhagwati, The Renown Jurist; *Financial Express* of 11 June 2004.
17. Ratan Tata, Leading Industrialist.
18. Advocacy Internet November/December 2005.
19. A.B. Burdhan : *Debates on Reservation*.
20. Chief Justice Lahoti in Supreme Court case; *P.A. Inamdar and others vs. State of Maharashtra and others*.
21. Sunil, Jasvirsingh; *Caste, Merit and Reservations* 1987.
22. *Ibid*.
23. *Times of India* 7 May 2007 on Chhatisgarh Self-Finance Edu. Act.

PART III

Legal Aspects of Reservation

Reservation as such is statutory provisions embodied in Indian Constitution. These provisions have undergone numerous constitutional amendments subsequently. Central government's important instructions known as Office Memorandums (OMs) on vital issues and various other operational instructions pertaining to reservation during all these sixty years form very important bearing on the entire reservation policy. A few most important of these are covered in this part with some discussions thereon. This includes important reservation related constitutional provisions and amendments, few office memorandums (OMs), some Supreme Court verdicts/cases etc. Reservation is also surrounded with many wrong notions with regard to constitutional provisions, its interpretations, some debatable court verdicts, conceptual ambiguity in administrative instructions etc. And finally an attempt is also made to throw some light on some of such aspects of reservations carrying wrong notions.

12

Constitutional Provisions

India became a republic in 1950. The preamble and directive principles of the Constitution envisage building a social order around the principles of equality, liberty and fraternity. The intervention of the State in social transformation for an egalitarian and secular social order is the core and the spirit of the constitution. Keeping this core spirit at heart various articles have been embodied in the Constitution which *inter alia* covers provisions relating to reservation initially for the scheduled castes and scheduled tribes and later on other backward castes.

The Constitution has defined each of these three categories, enlisted eligible castes /tribes/classes and has also laid down authority and procedure in case of modification if any required therein. Facilities under reservation includes reservation in electoral seats, admission in educational institutions and employment i.e. in recruitment and promotion both in government and public sector services.

Primarily, Indian Constitution is based on premises of equality of all before the law. i.e. it considers every body equal irrespective of whatever status; social, educational, positional one may have. **Article 14** of the Constitution enumerating this important provision of **Equality before Law** states that the state shall not deny to any person equality before law or the equal protection of law within the territory of India'.

The Constitution has defined scheduled castes as under;

Article 341 : Scheduled Castes (SCs)

(2) The President may with respect to any state or union territory and where it is a state, after consultation with

the governor thereof, by public notification specify the castes, races, or tribes or part of or groups within castes, races, or tribes which shall for the purpose of this constitution be deemed to be scheduled castes in relation to that State or union territory as the case may be.

(3) Parliament may by law include in or exclude from the list of scheduled castes specified in a notification issued under clause (1) any caste, race, or tribe or part of a group within any caste, race or tribe, but save as aforesaid a notification issued under the said clause shall not be verified by any consequent notification.

Article 342: Scheduled Tribes (STs)

(1) The President may with respect to any state or union territory and where it is a state, after consultation with the governor thereof, by public notification specify the tribes or tribal communities or parts of groups within tribes or tribal communities which shall for the purpose of this constitution be deemed to be scheduled tribes in relation to that state or union territory as the case may be.

(2) Parliament may by law include in or exclude from the list of scheduled tribes specified in a notification issued under clause (1) any tribe or tribal community or part of a group within any tribe or tribal community, but save as aforesaid a notification issued under the said clause shall not be verified by any consequent notification.

Besides reservation and all other devices of protective discrimination at par with scheduled castes, there are certain additional provisions for the people under scheduled tribe category. This includes provision of '**Scheduled Areas**' under 5th Schedule of the Indian Constitution entailing direct central control over administration of these areas and direct central financial responsibility, extensive executive powers in respect of these scheduled areas to insulate them from the application of inappropriate laws and to fashion protective regulation especially regarding allotment and transfer of land and money lending. The President promulgates these scheduled areas.

Article 340: Formation of Commission for Other Backward Classes (OBCs)

Text of the Article and explanation is available in Part I at Chapter 6 on 'OBC Reservation'.

Reservation in Electorate/Political Seats : Articles 330 and 332

The Constitution has provided for reservation in all electorate positions in Lok Sabha wide Article 330 and in constituent assemblies wide Article 332, so that members belonging to scheduled castes and scheduled tribes can have their share in the political power which is very important in democratic governance. Reservation under these provisions in case of electorate positions were initially allowed for a period of ten years from 1950 with a sub-provision of its extension **under Article 334** in case of felt need by peoples' representatives.

The **reservation for electorate political positions** as provided above were accorded five times periodical extensions of ten years each through constitutional amendment (1) No, 8 dated 5 January 1960 upto 1970, then by (2) No. 23rd dated 5 November 1971 upto 1980, (3) 45th dated 14 April 1980 upto 1990, (4) 62nd dated 25 January 1990 upto 2000, and (5) finally 79th Amendment dated 25 Janaury 2000 upto 25 January 2010.

The above provisions of reservation in Lok Sabha and Legislative Assemblies do not include other backward classes (OBCs).

73rd constitutional Amendment became an organ of realizing real democracy at the grass root level with reservation brought in the institutions of local self governments such as village panchayat, tehsil and district councils, municipalities and so on. This amendment specified categorically reservations down upto village sarpanch as per the roster points for SC/ST/

OBC. The noteworthy aspect of the reservation provisions under this amendment is 33 per cent reservation made for the first time for the women section of the society.

Reservation in Admission to Educational Institutions : Article 15(4) and 15(5)

Educational backwardness of scheduled castes, scheduled tribes and other backward classes had multiplier effects which leads in continuing social backwardness and coupled therewith economic backwardness. Education is also an instrument of social change apart from shaping the nation's overall development. Realizing the urgency for enhancing education spread in these communities, the Constitution has from very beginning provided for reservation in admission to all educational institutions either run or aided by the government.

Article 15: Prohibition on the Grounds only of Religion, Race, Caste, Sex, Place of Birth or Any of Them

(1) The state shall not discriminate against any citizen on the grounds only of religion, race, caste, sex, place of birth or any of them.

(4) Nothing in this article or in clause 2 of Article 29 shall prevent the state from making **any special provision for the advancement of any socially and educationally backward classes of citizens or for the scheduled castes and scheduled tribes.**

Implementation of these constitutional provisions of reservation has contributed in substantial spread of education in these communities.

Reservation Extended to Self Finance Educational Institutions (93rd Constitutional Amendment)

Reservation hitherto were available in educational institutions either run by or aided out of the government funds. With enormous increase in number of self finance educational institutions, reservation in such educational institutions knocked the Supreme Court door recently in the matter of *P.A. Inamdar and Pai Foundation*

The Supreme Court contemplated that as the unaided colleges do not take government funding, they are under no obligation to follow central government quota for socially deprived classes. The Apex Court in its judgment in *P.A. Inamdar and Pai Foundation* gave a right to decide their own admission policies to self finance educational institutions.

The judgment had long consecutive repercussions. With new economic reforms and more and more liberalizing policy, non-availability of reservation in unaided private educational institutions for SC/ST/OBC was reviewed by the government and accordingly 93rd constitutional amendment was passed in the Parliament which nullified the above judgment by making following addition in Article 15.

Article 15(5): Reservation in Self Finance Educational Institutes

'Nothing in this Article or sub clause (G) of Clause (1) of Article 19 shall prevent the state from making any provision, by law, for the advancement of any socially and educationally backward classes of citizens or for the scheduled castes and scheduled tribes in so far as such special provisions relate to their admission to educational institutions including private educational institutions, **whether aided or unaided by the state**, other than the minority educational institutions referred to in clause (1) of Article 30'.

Article 46: Promotion of Educational and Economic interests of SCs, STs and other Weaker Sections

This Article reflects the noblest intention of the framers of Constitution for the total upliftment of all backward classes of the nation. It is pertinent to note that the Constitution has spoken about '**weaker sections**' of the society and not merely scheduled castes, scheduled tribes and other backward classes for promotion of educational and economic interests.

'The State shall promote with special care the educational and economic interests of the weaker sections of the people and in particular of the scheduled castes and scheduled tribes and shall protect them from social injustice and all forms of exploitation.'

This is a very important article, clearly spelling the goal of the Constitution and in its fulfillment, the defined role of the State. The Article categorically states that

- it shall be the duty of the state to protect the weaker sections of the society from prevailing social injustice and all forms of exploitation of this section.
- it shall be the duty of the state to promote with special care their educational and economic interests.
- there has been a specific mention of scheduled castes and scheduled tribes for care to be taken and protection to be given.

Weaker Section Under Article 46 and Backward Classes Under Article 16(4) as Distinguished

Weaker section under Article 46 has a wider expression and it extends to individuals and their weaknesses, which may be due to several causes such as poverty, natural calamity or physical handicap. Individuals belonging to weaker sections under Article 46 may not form a class and they may be weaker as individuals only. Their weakness may not be the result of past social and educational backwardness or discrimination. Weaker section under Article 46 could be a bigger lot which would also include backward classes as defined under Article 16(4). **Article 46 stipulates certain measures for removal of weaknesses of such section, while Article 16(4) provides for reservation for the class known as backward class covered under this Article.**

Justice Hegde has commented in light of the provisions under Article 46, "One of the greatest drawbacks in our social structure is the existence of caste system dividing the society according to status and rank. Whatever might have been the origin of the caste system, it has given rise to various gradations in the society, which in turn, has resulted, into social inequality and discrimination. The caste system and consequent discrimination are not compatible with a democratic society. These social gradations have created economic and educational disparities. The caste system among the Hindus has its repercussions to an extent on other religious groups also. With a view to remove these gradations in our social life and to reshape the society on democratic lines, the Constitution directed the state under Article 46 to promote with special care the educational and economic interests of the weaker sections of the people and in particular of the scheduled castes and scheduled tribes and it is expected that the state shall protect them from social injustices and all forms of exploitations."[1]

Reservation in Employment

The Constitution of India has provided for equality of opportunity in all government and public sector jobs. In other words, there will be no discrimination whatever among the candidates for any job they are applying for.

Article 16 : Equality of Opportunity in Matter of Public Employment

(1) There shall be equality of opportunity to all citizens in matters relating to employment or appointment to any office under the State.
Article 16(1) flows from Article 14. Articles 14 and 16(1) are closely connected as they deal with individual rights of persons. They give a positive command to the State that there shall be equality of opportunity to all the citizens in public employment.

(2) No citizen shall on grounds only of religion, race, caste, sex, descent, place of birth, residence or any of them be ineligible for, or discriminated against in respect of, any employment or office under the State.

(3) Nothing in this article shall prevent Parliament from making any law, prescribing in regard to a class or

classes of employment or appointment to an office under the government or any local or other authority within a State or union territory prior to such employment or appointment.

(4) Nothing in this Article shall prevent the state from **making any provision for the reservation of appointments or posts in favour of any backward class of citizens, which in the opinion of the State is not adequately represented in the services under the State.**

Justice Sawant comments with regard to equality of opportunity, "Article 16(4) is not a poverty alleviation programme. Its aim is not economic upliftment. Its singular aim is to redistribute power to those who have been kept out of the state apparatus and through that redistribution, to end their educational, social and economic backwardness.

Reservation in Recruitment : Article 16(4)

Article 16(4) is the backbone of the entire reservation mechanism enacted under the Constitution. It empowers the state to provide for making any provision for the reservation in the appointment for backward classes, which are not adequately represented, in the state services. Thus Article 16(4) incorporates provisions for backward classes i.e. scheduled castes, scheduled tribes and other backward classes. For Article 16(4), who can be considered to be backward classes is answered in Supreme Court Case popularly known as **Indra Sahney *vs.* Union of India.**

"Backward class of citizens can be legally considered by adopting constitutionally permissible methodology of identification irrespective of their race, religion or caste. Although the work should normally be left to be undertaken by the state as the courts are ill-equipped for such exercise due to lack of data, necessary expertise and relevant material but with the development of role of courts from mere 'superintend and supervise' to legitimate constitutional affirmative action, this court is not only duty bound, but constitutionally obliged to lay down principles of guidance for those who are entrusted with this responsibility, with a sense of duty towards the country as the occasion demands never more than now, but with remotest intention to interfere with legislative or executive process with a view to giving better protection to the weak and outnumbered to minorities and unpopular individuals that are inadequately represented in the political process".[2]

Reservation in Promotion

Reservation in promotion has been constantly dwindling between judicial and political battle. It was last restored consequent upon 85th Constitutional Amendment in the year 2002.

The scheduled castes and the scheduled tribes have been enjoying the facility of reservation in promotion since 1955. The Supreme Court in its judgment dated 16.11.1992 in the case of *Indra Sahney vs. Union of India* however, observed that reservation of appointments or posts under Article 16(4) of the Constitution is confined to initial appointment and cannot extend to reservation in the matter of promotion.

The said Supreme Court decision was reviewed by the government. It was felt that the ruling of the Supreme Court would adversely affect the interests of the scheduled castes and scheduled tribes. Since the representation of the scheduled castes and the scheduled tribes in services in the states have not reached the required level, it is felt necessary to continue the existing dispensation of providing reservation in promotion in case of the scheduled castes and scheduled tribes. As its commitment to protect the interests of the scheduled castes and scheduled tribes, the government decided to restore the existing policy of reservation in promotion for the scheduled castes and scheduled tribes.

Accordingly, Article 16(4) of the Constitution was amended by inserting a new clause (4A) in the said Article to provide for reservation in promotion for the scheduled castes and the scheduled tribes.

Other Reservation Related Constitutional Provisions/ Amendments

Consequential Seniority

The government servants belonging to scheduled castes and scheduled tribes had been enjoying the benefit of consequential seniority on their promotion on the basis of rule of reservation. The judgments of the Supreme Court in the case of *Union of India vs. Virpal Singh Chauhan* (1995) 6 SCC 684 and *Ajit Singh Januja (No. 1) vs. State of Punjab* AIR 1996 SC 1189 which led to the issue of the OM dated 30 January 1997, have adversely affected the interests of the government servants belonging to the scheduled castes and the scheduled tribes category in the matter of seniority on promotion to the next higher grade. This has led to considerable anxiety and representations were also received from various quarters including Members of Parliament to protect the interests of the Government servants belonging to the scheduled castes and scheduled tribes.

The government reviewed the position in the light of views received from various quarters and in order to protect the interests of the government servants belonging to the scheduled castes and scheduled tribes, it was decided to negate the effect of OM dated 30 January 1997 immediately. There was also review of seniority aspect of the government officers/ officers and it was felt at the senior government level to grant of consequential benefits to such government employees/ officers. This led to amendment to Article 16(4A) of the Constitution in the case of promotion by virtue of rule of reservation. Accordingly, it was decided by the Cabinet to give retrospective effect to the proposed Constitutional Amendment to Article 16(4A) with effect from the date of coming into force of **Article 16(4A),** itself. i.e. **from 17th day of June 1995** through **85th Constitutional Amendment 2002 revising Article 16(4A):**

"Nothing in this Article shall prevent the State from making any provision for reservation in matters of promotion, with consequential seniority, to any class or classes of posts in the services under the state in favour of the scheduled castes and the scheduled tribes which in the opinion of the state are not adequately represented in the services under the State"

Constitutional Bench in the matter of **M. Nagraj** states, "We are of the opinion that the 'Catch Up' rule and 'Consequential Seniority' are judicially evolved concepts to control the extent of reservation. The scope of these concepts is in service jurisprudence. These concepts cannot be elevated to the status of an axiom like secularism, constitutional modernity etc. It cannot be said that by insertion of the concepts of 'Consequential Seniority', the structure of Article 16(1) stands destroyed or abrogated.

Backlog Vacancies not to be Included in 50 per cent Ceiling: Article 16 (4B)

The vacancies reserved for the scheduled castes and scheduled tribes, which could not be filled up by direct recruitment on account of non-availability of the candidates belonging to the respective categories were treated as backlog vacancies. These vacancies were treated as a distinct group and were excluded from the ceiling of 50 per cent reservation. The Supreme Court in its judgment in *Indra Sahney case* held that the 50 per cent ceiling includes such backlog vacancies too. Government implemented this 50 per cent verdict through its OM dated 29 August 1997.

81st Constitutional Amendment was passed in the year 2000 for overcoming the restricting 50 per cent cap in reservation. This Article enables the State to make provision to fill up the backlog of reserved vacancies by launching special drive.

Article 4 (B)

'Nothing in this Article shall prevent the state from considering any unfilled vacancies of a year which are reserved for being filled up in that year in accordance with any provision for reservation made under clause (4) or clause (4A) as a separate class of vacancies to be filled up in any succeeding year or years and such class of vacancies shall not be considered together with the vacancies of the year in which they are being filled up for determining the ceiling of 50 per cent reservation on total number of that year".

The Supreme Court observed in *Ashok Kumar Gupta vs. State of U.P.*, "Article 16(4) aims at providing 'adequate representation' to SC/ST/OBCs in government services. Unless these groups get reservation in the higher posts, they will not be adequately represented".

Justice Fazal Ali in Supreme Court Matter of N.M. Thomas

"As to what would be a suitable reservation within permissible limits will depend upon the facts and circumstances of each case and no hard and fast rule can be laid down, nor can this matter be reduced to a mathematical formula so as to be adhered to in all cases," he said, "Decided cases of this Court have no doubt laid down that the percentage of reservation should not exceed 50 per cent. This is, however, a rule of caution and does not exhaust all categories. Suppose for instance, a state has a large number of backward classes of citizens which constitute 80 per cent of the population and the government, in order to give them proper representation, reserves 80 per cent of the jobs for them, can it be said that the percentage of reservation is bad and violates the permissible limit of Clause 16(4)? The answer must necessarily be in the negative. The dominant object of this provision is to take steps to make inadequate representation adequate." So, 80 per cent, it could be![3]

When a person gets recruited in a service, he assumes all the duties that goes with the service and he acquires a right to all the incidents of that service. Getting to the higher positions is one of the rights he acquires by virtue of joining that service. In a word, promotion is a facet of recruitment. Reservation in promotion has been evolved as a facet of equality where the appropriate government is of the opinion that the *dalits* and tribes are not adequately represented in the class or classes of posts in diverse cadres, grades, category of posts or classes of posts."

Every citizen or group of people has a right to share in the governance of the state. The Supreme Court holds, " The *dalits* and tribes are equally being citizens have a right to share in the governance of the state. The right to seek equality of opportunity to an office or a post under the state is a guaranteed fundamental right to all the citizens under Article 16(1)"

Other Miscellaneous Constitutional Provisions

Article 17 Abolition of Untouchability

'Untouchability' is abolished and its practices in any form is forbidden. The enforcement of any disability arising out of untouchability shall be an offence punishable in accordance with law.

Article 29 : Protection of Interests of Minorities

(1) Any section of the citizens residing in the territory of India or any part thereof having a distinct language, script or culture of its own shall have the right to conserve the same.

(2) No citizen shall be denied admission into any educational institution maintained by the state or receiving aid out of state funds on grounds only of religion, race, caste, language or any of them.

Article 335 : Maintenance of Efficiency in Administration

The claims of the members of the scheduled castes and scheduled tribes shall be taken into consideration, consistently with the maintenance of efficiency of administration, in the making of appointments to services and posts in connection with the affairs of the Union or of a State.

Justice A.C. Gupta states on Article 335, "The Article does not create any right in the members of the scheduled castes and the scheduled tribes, which they might claim in the matter of appointments to services and posts; one has to look elsewhere, Article 16(4) for instance, to find out the claims conceded to them. Article 335 says that their such claims shall be considered consistently with administrative efficiency. This is a provision, which does not enlarge but qualify such claims as they may have as members of the scheduled castes and scheduled tribes".

Comments on maintenance of efficiency in Administration are available in Part III at Chapter 14 on 'Some wrong notions about reservation'.

Relaxation in Qualifying Marks and Standard of Evaluation: 82nd Constitutional Amendment

The scheduled castes and scheduled tribes had been enjoying the facility of relaxation of qualifying marks and standards of evaluation in matters of reservation in promotion. The Supreme Court in its Judgment dated 1 October 1996 in the case of *S. Vinod Kumar vs. Union Of India* held that such relaxations in matters of reservation in promotion were not permissible under Article 16(4) of the Constitution in view of the command contained in Article 335 of the Constitution. The Apex Court also held the same view as laid down by the nine judge Constitution Bench of the Supreme Court in the *case of Indra Sahney* judgment, which held such relaxations in promotion as being not permissible under Article 16(4) in view of the command contained in Article 335 of the Constitution. Government implemented the verdict of these judgments vide its OM dated 22 July 1997. To obviate the effect of these judgments, the Parliament passed **82nd Constitutional Amendment** in the year 2000 adding following to Article 335.

Amendment to Article 335

'Provided that nothing in this Article shall prevent in making of any provision in favour of the members of the scheduled castes and scheduled tribes for relaxations in qualifying marks in any examination or lowering the standards of evaluation, for reservation in matters of promotion to any class or classes of services or posts in connection with the affairs of the Union or of a State'.

Reservation Under 9th Schedule of Constitution

The Indian Constitution was initially having in all 365 Articles and eight Schedules at the time of its inception in 1950. Ninth Schedule was a subsequent addition through the first Constitutional Amendment on 18th June 1951 by inserting clause (B) to Article 31.

Enactments brought under the roof of 9th Schedule to the Constitution gives an immunity to these acts from legal challenges on the ground that they violate the fundamental right enshrined in Part III of the Constitution. The relevant provision of Article 31 (B) reads as under;

Article : 31B : Validation of Certain Acts and Regulations

Without prejudice to the generality of the provisions contained in Article 31(A), none of the acts, and regulations specified in the ninth Schedule nor any of the provisions thereof shall be deemed to be void or ever to have been void, on the ground that such act, regulation or provision is inconsistent with or takes away or abridges any of the rights conferred by, any provisions of this part and notwithstanding any judgment, decree or order of any court or tribunal to the contrary, each of the said acts and regulations shall subject to the power of any competent legislature to repeal or amend it, continue in force.

The Supreme Court while delivering judgment in *Indra Sahney and others vs. Union of India* on 16 November 1992 gave directives of adhering to the reservation provisions under Article 16(4) well within 50 per cent limit, which the central government and most of the states complied with. The State of Tamil Nadu was an exception to this with reservation there at 69 per cent much exceeding stipulated ceiling of 50 per cent. The only rescue to the Tamil Nadu decision was bringing the said reservation provision under the purview of the 9th Schedule. The Parliament passed 76th Amendment in 1994 putting the Tamil Nadu State reservation provision free from all judicial and legal challenges permanently. Details of series of developments ultimately leading to putting 69 per cent reservation in the State under 9th Schedule are available in Part IV in Chapter 18 on 'Politics of Reservation'.

Can All Provisions of Reservation Be Brought Under Schedule IX?

It is very commonly found now-a-days, that progressive legislation of any kind conceived by the government are imperiled by litigations. Provisions relating to reservation are subjected to such impediments in a very routine fashion. Social laws like reservation have to go beyond mere gauging of the legal interpretation, which is lacking in the present Indian judicial system. Therefore, the time warrants for considering putting all reservation related laws and provisions under the ambit of 9th Schedule.

Can the same thought not be extended for the total shelter to the entire reservation provisions? 9th Schedule already contains 284 such other enactments brought through numerous Constitutional Amendments as and when a need for their inclusion in 9th Schedule was warranted.

Implementation of Reservation

Effective and wholehearted Execution of any policy or decision and particularly that concerned with socially discharged subjects is very important. So far evaluation of implementation of reservation policy is concerned, it can be said that the fruits of the reservation policy are clearly visible since seventies onwards.

More and more legislations for addressing problems connected with downtroddens are emerging at center as well as various states governments. It appears that there are enough number of laws and provisions for safeguarding the interests of the scheduled castes, scheduled tribes etc. What is badly required now is the sincere and whole hearted enforcement of all these available statutes. The present state of affairs in this regard leaves much to be done as can be seen from sample survey in respect of following few out of number of laws enacted for the welfare of SC/ST in this regard.

Prevention of Atrocities (POA) Act 1989

This is a very effective enactment in checking incidence of atrocities on scheduled castes and scheduled tribes. It is very much distressing that implementation of Prevention of Atrocities (POA) Act 1989 is so half heartedly and ill-willfully done that conviction rate to culprits under this Act is hardly 3 per cent which in reality is next to impossible. Had this Act been sincerely and religiously implemented, occurrence of atrocities on these poor people would have slashed down drastically in apprehension of possible convictions.

Employment of Manual Scavengers and Construction of Dry Latrine (Prohibition) Act 1993

This is also similar by an another act effective in checking the inhuman work of manual scavenging of non-flushing toilets. However, the most distressing thing is that not a single person is reportedly convicted and/or fined in whole of the nation during all these fifteen years of its implementation under this statute though the act carries vigorous punishment such as imprisonment. This is the most glaring instance of how central government responded to a serious issue with a populist mindset without displaying a commitment and sincerity.

Reservation in Non-aided Educational Institutions

Similarly, recent 93rd Constitutional Amendment of 2005 regarding reservation in self-finance educational institutional aided as well as unaided was made effective w.e.f. 20 January 2006. The enforcement of the said Act was subject to further notifications to be made by the respective states. However, this was not done in majority of the states. This resulted in the non-implementation of reservation in self financed medical colleges in number of states well in time before conclusion of administration process. But for this notification not being made well in time, quite a good number of SC/ST candidates are deprived of their chances of becoming doctors.

Accumulations of Backlog

Casual implementation of reservation provisions, rigid and negative interpretation of administrative directives and absence of deterrent provisions in case of breach in implementation of various reservation related provisions by the responsible authorities have resulted into accumulation of backlogs of vacancies to be filled from the reserved categories. Barring a few vacancies not getting candidates as per the job specifications required for a large number of lower category services is somewhat unbelievable. Because of such callous attitude, backlogs are further mounting up year by year. This also refers to the contents in Part I at Chapter 2 on 'Reservation Aspirations and Achievements'.

Central Government Office Memorandum (OMs)

Reservation is one of the most complicated administrative issues now-a-days in the country with huge number of court judgments, multiplicities of governmental instructions, interpretational aspects and so on. Some Supreme Court cases like Indra Sahney and host of few other judgments drastically altered the years old laid down policies and practices pertaining to reservation. Out of all this, five government office memorandums issued by the central government all in the year 1997, needs mention. These OMs includes fresh instructions relating to recognition of seniority in case of promotion to SC/ST employee, redrafting of rosters, withdrawal of certain concessions so far given to the SC/ST, calculation of backlog etc. These OMs were;

1. *No Seniority on Promotion ; DoPT OM No. 20011/1/96 Estt.(D) dated 30 January 1997*

As a general rule, seniority upon promotion in the higher cadre shall be on the basis of date of promotion in that cadre hence seniority in respect of a promotee SC/ST category employee would also be accordingly as per the merit order of the promotion.

The above OM changed this general rule. With this OM, an SC/ST employee on promotion will not carry with him his seniority as on the date of the said promotion. A general category promotee candidate getting subsequent promotion at a later date will automatically be senior to his earlier promoted SC/ST fellow employee on the ground that he was senior in the earlier cadre than his SC/ST colleague.

The OM was issued pursuant to the Supreme Court Judgment dated 10 October 1995 in *Union of India and others vs. Virpal Singh Chauhan.* However, the concept of seniority was again restored in another court matter of *Jagdishlal and others vs. State of Haryana and others* by Supreme Court on 7 May 1997.

The parliament subsequently passed 85th Constitutional Amendment reinstating the seniority as per the earlier norms by inserting Article 16(4A) in the Constitution.

2. ***Change in Roster System ; DoPT OM No. 36012/2/96 Estt. (Res) dated 02 July 1997***

This OM changed the system of the maintenance of rosters in government both for direct recruitment as well as promotion. This was consequent to the Supreme Court Judgement in the case of *R.K. Sabharwal* which stressed on adequacy of the available positions for the reserved category candidates in that particular cadre. Thus, rosters which were hitherto maintained on the basis of **vacancy based** are now drastically changed to **post based**. Moreover, in the earlier roster maintenance system, roster points for reserved categories were in the beginning, which are now put at the end though there were no specific instructions for such a shift in the said Judgment.

3. ***Withdrawal of Concessions; DoPT OM No 36012/23/96 Estt (Res) dated 22 July 1997***

In accordance with the constitutional provisions and increase in backlog of posts/vacancies reserved for the scheduled castes and scheduled tribes, the Government of India had accorded certain relaxations and concessions to these category candidates in direct recruitment and promotions as well. This OM which was issued in implementation of the Supreme Court judgment in case of *Indra Sahney* and *S. Vinod Kumar* curtailed many of such concessions.

4. *No Reservation in Promotion; DoPT OM No. 36012/08/95 Estt (Res) dated 13 July 1997*

Reservation in promotion was introduced subsequent to 77th Amendment in the Constitution. Accordingly a new section was added in the existing Article 16(4) which embodies provision of reservation for scheduled castes and scheduled tribes and other backward classes. As per the added Article i.e. 16(4A) reservation was provided in the promotion for these categories. Under this OM reservation in promotion was withdrawn.

This OM almost brought a halt on promotion processes going on in the country creating lot of uncertainties and unbalances in the government administration till it was once again nullified with 85th Constitutional Amendment in the year 2002 reinstating reservation in promotion on *status quo* basis.

5. *Backlog Vacancies; DoPT OM No. 36012/05/97 Estt (Res) dated 29 August 1997*

The government often undertakes special recruitment drive with a view to filling up the backlog of vacancies reserved for the scheduled castes, scheduled tribes etc. as these vacancies remained unfilled through the normal process of recruitment. There is a 50 per cent ceiling to which reserved seats can be filled. So far the backlog filling up of SC/ST vacancies were not considered under the purview of this 50 per cent ceiling. With this OM now, a flat ceiling of 50 per cent is imposed irrespective of the backlog of such vacancies.[4]

All these OMs came into effect simultaneously during 1997. Its cumulative effect was so thunderous that they were almost tantamounting to fresh redrafting of reservation provisions. A few of these were in response to Supreme Court Indra Sahney case judgment of 1992. Sudden implementation of all these OMs altogether soon brought a sort of halt in the recruitment and promotion of SC/ST through reservation till three of these five were reversed through constitutional amendments.

Reservation on Change in Religion

Necessity for having reservation has its roots in the caste based disparities in the country. These disparities were having religious sanctions from ancient times. Thus, the concept of reservation is ultimately connected with the religion. If one goes in the details as to why the caste disparities in spite of fastly increasing education and globalization and culturization are not getting that weakened as they should have been. The reason is blind faiths of the Hindu society in the old religious scriptures which have prescribed graded caste system, may it be in actual preaching or in the religious stories. There would have been no need of reservation to this an extent and for a long time, if the feelings of caste stratification would have gradually disappeared from the minds and hearts of the caste Hindu society. So the religion has a definite relevance on the concept and provisions of reservation.

Reservation in case of scheduled castes is connected with the religious barriers i.e. scheduled caste person belonging to Hindu and Sikh and now Budhha religion only is eligible for the benefits and privileges available under the purview of provisions of reservation applicable to the members of scheduled caste. In other words, the moment, he/she ceases to be a Hindu, Sikh or Buddhist he/she no more remains a scheduled caste member. Idea behind this must be that the reservation to scheduled castes is embodied in the Constitution considering the caste discrimination prevailing in the Hindu society which deprives from availing equal opportunities in the jobs and education. Other religions don't profess in principle untouchability or caste disparities. Therefore the person shifting his religious faith from Hindu religion, is presumed leaving behind him the discriminatory caste stigma which he was facing in the old religious faith i.e. Hinduism. It is altogether a different story that caste shadow does not spare person even after his religious conversion. He continues to be branded as lower caste person in the pretext of one or the other identity. It is just like that famous Hutch advertisement logo,"

Wherever you go, Our network follows." Thus, for considering eligibility under reservation in case of scheduled caste, his religious attachment is the pre-condition. With awakening and politicization of the concept of reservation, the converted *dalit* Christians and now, some backward Muslim castes have also knocked the doors of the Supreme Court requesting for their inclusion in the scheduled caste category on the ground that they continue facing the discriminatory caste practices even after religious conversions. The Government of India, Ministry of Minority Affairs constituted a commission on 29 October 2004 i.e. National Commission for Religious and Linguistic Minorities (NCRLM) under the chairmanship of Retd. Justice Rangnath Mishra and four other members to examine considering inclusion of such *Dalit* converts to other religious faiths for the purpose of benefits of reservations as are available to Scheduled Castes.

The Commission (NCRLM) has recommended for such inclusion. Few writs in this regard are sending with Supreme Court and State High Courts.

Recently tabled Sachar Committee Report is also on the forefront of the debates centering around reservation. The Committee has recommended reservation for one section of the Muslims under the category of scheduled castes (SC) and for another section under other backward class (OBC) notwithstanding that 50 per cent of existing Muslim people are already covered under OBC reservation[5].

As regards reservation in case of scheduled tribes, the provisions are different. In case of reservation for the scheduled tribes, religion is not a yardstick for reservation eligibility i.e. in case a tribal converts to any other religion, the person continues enjoying all the privileges of reservation hither to he was enjoying as a scheduled tribe member. The consideration behind this must a contention that scheduled tribes even while remaining in Hindu faith, do not suffer from untouchability or similar other kind of caste hatred. Secondly, it is believed that a scheduled tribe does not have a specific religion. Here too a demand is voicing from a section of the society that the reservation to scheduled tribe should also be in line with the provisions meant for the scheduled castes and a tribal upon conversion should be debarred from benefits of reservation meant for the scheduled tribes.

Whether Reservations are Mandatory or only Enabling Provisions

It is often argued that provisions under Constitution's Article 14(4) and 16(4) indicate enabling provisions construing thereby that they are not statutorily a must. This is premised on the wording in the Article i.e. the state **may**. Instead, it is argued that they have become mandatory provisions. The twin objectives of Articles 15 and 16 were to provide adequate protection to the disadvantaged on the one hand and through special measures, raise their capabilities so that they would on their own compete with the rest. The duty to provide adequate protection became the duty to give preferential treatment.

Basic principle underlying Article 14 is that the law must operate equally on all persons under like circumstances. Along with this, the Constitution has also at various subsequent provisions laid down to take special care of the scheduled castes, scheduled tribes and other backward classes and also to provide for reservation for them. These two provisions one stipulating equality before the law and the other giving a preferential treatment by way of reservation to a fraction of the people is not contradicting each other since this requires to abridge the gap between the advanced section of the society and those having suffered inequalities so far. In short, equality from the point of view of reservation, is not violated by mere conferment of discretionary power. It is violated by arbitrary exercise by those on whom it is conferred.

REFERENCES

1. Anirudh Prasad, *Reservation Policy and Practice in India.*
2. Surrender Malik, Supreme Court Mandal Commission Case 1992.
3. Justice Fazal Ali in Supreme Court Matter Of N. M. Thomas.
4. National Commission for SC/ST Special Report dated 22.1.1998.
5. Justice Rajinder Sachar Committee Report 2006.

13

Judicial Activism and Reservation

The issue of reservation is one of the most focused subjects of judicial activism as it involves constitutional interpretations in deciding any subjudiced matter relating to reservation.

'Judicial Activism' is a term used by political scholars to describe a tendency by judges to consider outcomes, attitudinal preferences and other policy issues in interpreting existing laws. It is also used pejoratively to denote judges who are perceived to endorse a particular agenda. Judicial activism may occur in many ways. The most debated cases involve courts exercising judicial review to strike down as unconstitutional views that constitutional interpretation abound ranging from strict constructionism to the living construction and therefore judicial decision issues have increasingly come in the periphery of judicial activism. Followings are few occasions giving cause to judicial activism;

- Overturning legislation passed by elected legislatures using an interpretation of the Constitution not clearly mentioned or implied by the constitutional text.
- Ruling against the text or intent of a statute with incorrect or overreaching interpretation.
- Holding legislation unconstitutional based on a clearly flawed precedent.
- Ruling against judicial precedent in a way that is a radical or unjustified departure from accepted interpretation.
- Selectively using obscure case law or foreign law in preference to more pertinent case law or statutory law.

Judicial activism can violate a judge's sworn allegiance to uphold the constitution because in effect, it encourages judges to write their own constitution. Such tendency could lead to unpredictable rulings making it impossible to obey the law. One possible outcome of this confusion is the threat of frivolous lawsuits. It also violates the principle of separation of powers. Purpose of the judiciary is to interpret existing laws and policies and an action that is not done strictly in accordance with existing law is nothing but an activism. Legislative branch under the Constitution is explicitly empowered to make the laws and the Constitution deliberately has an amendment process. Consequently, any change to the laws or the Constitution outside this framework itself is illegal.

Supreme Court Chief Justice John Robert's disapproval of judicial activism is well known. "Judges are like empires, Empires don't make the rules, and they apply them. The role of an empire and a judge is critical. They make sure everybody plays by the rules. But it is a limited role. No body ever went to a ballgame to see the empire." other famous US Justices Felix Frankfurter and John Marshall opine, "Courts should not intrude in the areas of policy making reserved by the constitution to the political branches. Judges don't commission to solve Society's problems as they see them, but simply to decide cases before them according to the rule of law. When the other branches of governance exceed their constitutionally mandated limits, the courts can act to confine them into the proper bounds. It is judicial self-restraint, however that confines judges to their proper constitutional responsibilities[1].

Dr. Manmohan Singh, Prime Minister said during the Conference of all State Chief Ministers and High Court Chief Justices on 8th April 2007 at Delhi, "Dividing line between judicial activism and judicial overreach is a thin one" This statement was made exactly after two days of the Supreme Court interim judgment staying 27 per cent reservation quota for OBCs in all India educational Institutions is very relevant. The Prime Minister also added," Judicial activism no doubt serves as a corrective mechanism just like public interest litigation, however, it would not be advisable if it is used as a weapon in settling political accounts. Judiciary should restrict itself well within its own limitations."[2]

Upendra Baxi on Judicial Activism

Several decades of political development rendered the bulk and generality of Indian citizens to the status of constitutional orphans. Judicial activism in its defining moments, seeks to restore to them a minimum dignity as citizens with rights. In this, judicial activism emerges as a platform of resistance to the neo-colonial practice of power that seeks to convert citizens into subjects. The Supreme Court is able to close small tannery businesses that pollute the Ganges and yet finds itself unable to take a coherent human rights stance in mega irrigation projects and hazardous nuclear power plants that present long run environmental and human hazards. Indian societal culture decisions arresting environmental degradation continue to be made without much care for those whose right to livelihood stands thus jeopardized. Governmental, social co-operation is notoriously sub optimal for the old and new socially vulnerable sections of Indian society. *Dalit* population which the Constitution anglicizes as the scheduled castes and scheduled tribes constitute the old sections. The new socially vulnerable are the new minorities viz. neo Buddhists, Muslim minorities, converts etc. The future of socially informed Indian judicial activism would be shaped by challenges to fashioning state/ civil society co-operation thus posed[3].

Does Indian Social Condition Influence Judicial Activism?

Former Chief justice P.N. Bhagavati observed, "Since judges are drawn from the class of well to do lawyers, they unwittingly develop certain bias. The members of the judiciary have so far been drawn from the very section of society, which is infected by ancient prejudices and is dominated by notions of gradations in life."

Justice P.B. Sawant also observed in his judgment in the *Mandal case*, "All aspects of life are controlled, directed and regulated mostly to suit the sectional interests of a small group of the society which numerically does not exceed 10 per cent of the total population of the country. This has resulted in concentration of the executive power in the hands of a select social group. It is naïve to believe that the administration is carried on impartially, that the sectional interests are subordinated to the interests of the country and the justice is done to those who are outside the ruling fold. This reveals that typical Indian social system with social gradations and discriminatory social practices since centuries is so inbuilt with the routine life that it has strong potentialities in influencing the judicial activism, since the judges are also human beings.[4]

Judicial Activism at times also contributes in numerous social causes. Conservation of ecology is one of such most notable blessings because of the judicial activism. Various judgements on reservation has also taken note of the prevailing conditions of social discrimination in the country with deep pain. However, sometimes reservation is dragged surprisingly in irrelevant issues too as can be seen in the following case;

Reservation Abused in Famous Best Bakery Vadodara Mass Killing Court Proceedings

The whole nation still remembers with pain the massacre killing in Gujarat during February/March 2002 connected with and after Sabarmati Express Godhra episode. It was altogether a different case of inhuman and enmass brutal killings of the human beings because of the communal hatred. It has as such nothing to do with the aspect of reservation. Surprisingly the Court judgment on this unfortunate Vadodara Best Bakery case, states on page No. 20 Para 59 as under.

'... The provision of reservation was enacted only for ten years. The subsequent increase in the reservation in view of the vote bank is painful. It is a fact that violent riots do take place on account of Reservation. Reservations for disabled are tolerable. But on account of improper reservation, brain drain takes place and youths are tempted to go out of the country. Till date, there is none who can be compared with Chanakya in the field of politics and economics. According to Chanakya, only merit should be the criteria for any appointment. Qualified people are ignored and those without qualification are appointed in the name of reservation, this is against human rights. The only logic in this anomaly is to attract vote bank.'[5]

Best Bakery case was much more than a plain criminal litigation matter affecting the social fabric of the entire society. It was expected of Judicial activism in such highly criticizable inhuman misdeeds to guide with a positive path of duty to the administration and a positive direction to the society, which is miscarried away by unsocial and pretty political elements. Instead, unfortunately, the judiciary in this important case came down heavily on all together a different and irreverent issue of reservation. The comments as found above in the judgment reveals the social bias of the judges are living in the same society and carry with them their own reservations on social aspects which gets reflected particularly during judicial activism.

Judicial Activism Under Novel Terminologies

Basic Structure of Constitution

A conflicting situation between the two vital arms of the democracy i.e. legislature and judiciary is not a new thing. As is recently pointed out by the Supreme Court Chief Justice K.G. Balkrishnan, it is a welcome and healthy phenomenon. The Prime Minister of the country Dr. Manmohan Singh also advised the judiciary to stick to its own limitations.

It is often contemplated while delivering judgements on reservation that constitutional amendments aiming at reversing certain earlier Supreme Court judgments are damaging the basic structure of the Constitution. Herman Belz says in his Article 'Challenge to the living constitution'.[6]

The Constitution embodies aspiration to social justice, brotherhood and human dignity. Indian judicial activism owes an additional role while operating amidst a typical society surrounded with graded inequality to safeguard the interests of the vulnerable section of the country. Indian parliament has resorted to number of recent constitutional amendments for protection of reservational rights which are negated by few recent court cases. It is difficult to digest that limited reservational provisions could upset the whole and so solid structure of the great Indian Constitution.

However, if one studies a series of recent judgments more particularly on reservation issues, a reference questioning basic structure of the Constitution in connection with the constitutional amendments on reservation matters often draws the attention. Reference to Article 14 to center importance of general equality of all citizens and Article 16(1) for equality of opportunity is often put forth while interpreting reservation provided under Article 16(4). And all these three Articles are found quoted with so much of complexities that it will always leave an impression that reservation means snatching away of freedom of equal opportunities and thereby a collapse of concept of general equality as well. The whole text of such judgments is so cleverly put that judicial activism of the clever judges will go unnoticed.

Indian Constitution is so dynamic and flexible that provisions for reservation are one of the foundational aspirations of the Constitution. But the interpretation has to be in the total perspective rather than a gauge of bare interpretation of legal jargons. Constitution itself provides for amendments according to the needs of time and needs of the society. On every occasion when a constitutional matter comes before the Court, the meaning of the provisions of the Constitution will call for interpretation, but every interpretation of the Article does not become a basic feature of the Constitution. There are no implied limitations on the power of the Parliament under Article 368 when it seeks to amend the Constitution. Amendments for giving effect to the directive principles cannot offend the basic structure of the Constitution. On the contrary, the amendments which may abrogate individual rights, but which promote constitutional ideals of ' justice, social, economic and political' and the ideal of 'equality of status' are not liable to be struck down under Article 14 or Article 16(1) and consequently such amendments cannot violate the basic structure of the Constitution. The amendments to the Constitution, which aimed at removing social and economic disparities, cannot offend the basic structure. Promotion has been one of the foremost issues under the judicial scrutiny. Jurisprudence relating to public services do not constitute basic feature of the Constitution and therefore issues regarding consideration for promotion in service matters is not a basic feature.

Merit

Merit is yet a point of strong attack in the matters relating to reservation. Various aspects of merits are discussed in details in Part II at Chapter 8 on 'Merit and Reservation'. Merit in reference to scheduled castes and scheduled tribes has always been construed as anti-meritarian. Application of reservation is always treated as sacrificing of merit. This can never be universally true. Gone are the days when there used to be a long gap in the performance in the competitive tests or promotional examinations of SC/ST *vis-a-vis* general category candidates. Merit in case of clerical posts, other lower cadre posts has to be viewed differently than in case of other technical, professional or jobs needing special skill or where question of human life is very sensitively involved. Unfortunately, this does not happen during judicial review of reservational issues. A common yardstick is taken and that is reservation means always damage to merit. Here comes the judicial activism.

Supreme Court constitutional Bench in *M. Nagraj* notes, 'It is the state who is in the best position to define and measure merit in whatever ways, they consider it to be relevant to public employment because ultimately it has to bear the costs arising from errors in defining and measuring merit'.

Effeciency in Administration

While most of the judgments invariably make a reference that efficiency of administration should not be jeopardized, none contains as to how the lower cadre induction of equally qualified SC/ST would spoil the efficiency. They also keep silence as to what is the present state of efficiency in the state administration and what are the contributory factors for such poor state of affairs particularly in context with the one-fifth presence of employees belonging to scheduled castes and scheduled tribes?

Enabling Provisions

Constitutional Articles pertaining to reservation are in force since 1950. Now these provisions are seen as enabling provisions rather than statutory constitutional requirements on the pretext that the Articles contain the word 'May' in its syntext. If judiciaries perceive social equality provisions like this, the objective to bring about social equalities will be a far-flung dream.

Promotions

Reservation as a general rule is linked with adequacy of representation. Accordingly, reservation in promotion was in force right from 1955 which was also confirmed by the same Apex Court in *Ranghachari case.* The Supreme Court reversed in *Indra Sahney* matter in 1992 its own earlier judgment in *Rangachari.* While on one hand, the supreme court asks for basis of OBC population of 1931, it has never asked in any of the promotion cases either in *Indra Sahney* or railway case of *Akhil Bharatiya Shoshit Karmachari Sangh* or *M. Nagraj case* as to what is the status of representation of reserved category in the government services, whether quota meant for them is adequately represented, if not why and so on. This is reverse judicial activism.

Constitutional Powers vs. Judicial Powers

The issue of reservation is now confronted with one more novel argument i.e. The parliament cannot in the exercise of its amending power, alter the basic structure or framework of the Constitution...The amending power cannot be so exercised as to make the constitution suffer a loss of identity.

Recently a Bench of nine judges of the Supreme Court sat for five days from October 30, 2006 to hear the arguments regarding the scope of power of Parliament to amend the Constitution.

The people of India have created through the Constitution the three organs viz. executive, legislature and judiciary. None of the above organs are above the people and all of them derive their authority from the Constitution. Thus, the judiciary also derives its authority from the people of India. Till 1993, the executive was vested with appointment of judges, which was the executive was vested with appointments of judges, which was since thereafter done by the judiciary itself. In other words, there is no direct or indirect involvement of the people, the ultimate democratic authority.

It is in this context, a question arises; Is it open to the Supreme Court to strike down a constitutional amendment, including an Act put under 9th Schedule, which gives it an additional immunity from judicial review?

Any exercise of such power by the Supreme Court would be destructive of the most important basic feature of the Constitution, namely making India into a Democratic Republic.

Some Court Cases Involving Remarkable Judicial Activism

M. Nagraj and others vs. Union Of India: (CA 61/2002 decided on 19 October 2006)

The judgment in this case states on page 126, " ... We are upholding the validity of the constitutional amendments subject to the limitations. Therefore, in each case, the Court has got to be satisfied that the State has exercised its opinion in making reservations in promotions for SCs and STs and for which the concerned state will have to place before the court, the requisite quantifiable data in each case and satisfy the court that such reservations became necessary on account of inadequacy of representation of SCs and STs in a particular class or classes of posts without affecting general efficiency of service as mandated under Article 335 of the Constitution.

This is nothing but a true case of judicial activism. The judgment assumes the supreme court's role as monitoring rather controlling agency for implementation of reservation. The administration is required to submit quantifiable data in each matter, to satisfy the supreme court in each such case about necessity of reservation in view of inadequacy of representation in each referred case. Is this the job of the apex judicial authority of the country? If the Supreme Court is really concerned about efficient, effective and sensible implementation of reservation, it should have asked at least once the quantifiable data relating to backlog, which unfortunately, it has never done.

OBC Reservation in Higher Educational Institutions

Supreme Court's latest order staying OBC reservation of 27 per cent in all India educational institutions is one more instance of judicial activism.

Reservation upto 27 per cent in educational institutions is in force since 1992 consequent to implementation of Mandal Commission's Report. The Supreme Court in famous *Indra Sahney case* also okayed this reservation in 1992. Since then, this 27 per cent reservation for 52 per cent OBC population have been in force since last 15 years without any dispute as regard the fixation of quota of 27 per cent or adequacy of representation of OBC in education and so on. The Government introduced 27 per cent reservation for OBCs in all India higher and professional educational institutions such as IIMs/IITs etc. for the first time in 2006. There should be no point of dispute or need for opportunity to OBC students for admission in these prestigious educational institutions. The Supreme Court has ordered stay against this proposed reservation questioning the followings:

- How can census of year 1931 be taken as a basis of arriving at OBC reservation?
- Where is the evidence to show that OBCs are under represented in higher education?
- How can we be sure that the mechanism proposed by the government is the best way of redressing these disadvantages? And finally

- What is about Creamy layer? Giving the benefit of reservation on the sole ground of being an OBC, is unacceptable.

Raising question about basis of reservation after post implementation of fifteen years is nothing but illogical and negative judicial activism. Secondly, reservation of 27 per cent for the whole lot of 52 per cent population itself is out of question. It would have been better had the Supreme Court questioned OBC status of certain advanced castes such as Jat, Maratha, Patel, Reddy, Khadayat and Nayar which are at present enjoying the status of OBC as per Mandal Commission Report prepared on the basis of survey carried out in eighties. Supreme Court's questioning the 1931 basis will simply result in deferment of these belated legitimate reservation benefits once again for few more years.

As regards adequacy or otherwise of representation of OBCs in higher professional educational institutions, this is also an unpractical and non-issue question. Adequacy of representation has to be seen in case of recruitment and promotion where category-wise representation or rather possibility of over representation has to be monitored. If the category is already sufficiently represented, quota under reservation has to be accordingly regulated. This is not so in case of reservation in educational institutions. Particulars of OBC students inducted as a general category candidates in the earlier batches of such institutions in absence of reservation has nothing to do with the reservation quota now to be filled. Availability of such statistical information is not possible also.

The Supreme Court has asked as to how the proposed mechanism will be best to redress the disadvantages. Reservation has been in force for SCs and STs since acceptance of the Constitution from 1950 and the same for OBC was subsequently implemented from 1992. The mechanism of reservation in rendering educational opportunities to the oppressed people under this category has brought about significant results. Education is the master solution to all problems and evils connected with economic and social backwardness. Reservation in prestigious educational Institutions to OBCs as proposed is definitely going to bring desired advantages in these communities. The Supreme Court's such question itself is ridiculous.

And finally, issue of Creamy layer. This is a long debatable question. Reservation to OBC or reservation in educational institutions is not being introduced for the first time. OBC reservation in educational institutions is already in force for over 15 years. Extension of reservation now to all India educational institutions is a very small part of the total ambit of reservation. So, pending reconsideration or review of the aspect of Creamy layer, there was no point in withholding the reservation as enacted by the peoples' elected representatives in the Parliament.

Ajit Singh (I) vs. State of Punjab

The Court held in this promotion related matter whether a promotion amounts to reverse discrimination, "Promotion is an incidence of service. Seniority is one of the important factors in making promotion. Right of equality has to be preserved by preventing reverse discrimination. Equality principle requires exclusion of extra weightage of roster point promotion to a reserved category candidate. Without catch up rule, giving weightage to earlier promotion secured by roster point promotee would result in reverse discrimination and would violate equality under Articles 14, 15 and 16. The Court therefore set aside the factor of extra weightage of earlier promotion to a reserved category candidate as violative of Article 14 and Article 16(1) of the Constitution.

Question arises here is that this was a 1986 year matter pertaining to Indian Railways where reservation in promotion is in effect since 1955. The Court nowhere felt to ask why is that reservation backlog is still carried out in lower posts that too for as long as thirty years?

Some Quotes on Judicial Activism

Dr. B.R. Ambedkar

The purpose of a Constitution is not merely to create the organs of the State, but to limit their authority, because if no limitation is imposed upon the authority of the organs, there will be complete tyranny and complete oppression. The legislatures may be free to frame any law; the executives may be free to take any decision; the Supreme Court may be free to give any interpretation of law. It would result into utter chaos."

Shanti Bhusan, Renowned Advocate and Former Law Minister

It was clear that the role of the judiciary was to control the executive and the legislature from exceeding their powers. However, even the apex court was not absolutely supreme and if the people of India felt and expressed their views through two-third majority of Parliament, the Supreme Court could be overruled by resort to the ultimate power to amend the Constitution. In a democratic republic, no non-elected body can claim for itself a power to finally decide the questions of moment for the people.[7]

Justice Krishna Iyer (*Akhil Bharatiya Soshit Karmachari Sangh vs. Union of India*).

Every directive principle is fundamental in the guarantee of the country and it shall be the duty of the state to apply that principle in making laws. It obligates the state to promote with special care the educational and economic interests of the weaker sections of the people and in particular of the scheduled castes and scheduled tribes and shall protect them from social justice and all forms of exploitation, "When Article 46 and Article 16(4) are read together, the luscent intent of the framers of Constitution emerges that the exploited lot of harijans, girijans groups in the past shall be extirpated with special care by the state.

The Judge maintained that the inference is obvious and it is that administrative participation of SC and ST shall be promoted with special care by the state. The real power could be shared by the weakest sections only if the doors of the upper decks were opened to them. The higher echelons are the real controllerates, not the menial levels, hierarchically structured as our society is "obviously Article 16(4) was not designed to get more harijans into government as scavengers and sweepers," the Judge specified, " but as 'officers' and 'bosses', so that administrative power may become the common property of the high and low, humanized and integrated into one community. Social stratification, the bane of the caste system, could be undone and vertical mobility won not by hortative exercises but by experience and shared power."

State of Punjab vs. Hira Lal

The Supreme Court in this case reversed the High Court's verdict saying that the extent of reservation to be made is primarily a matter for the state to decide. By this, we do not mean to say that the decision of the state is not open to judicial review. The reservation must be only for the purpose of giving adequate representation in the service to the scheduled castes, scheduled tribes and backward classes.... The mere fact that the reservation made may give extensive benefits to some of the persons who have the benefit of the reservation does not by itself make the reservation bad.

The length of the leap to be provided depends upon the gap to be covered.

The Supreme Court has come forward in this case in advocating the legitimacy of a socially charged constitutional provision like reservation and also acknowledging the state authority in deciding the quantum of reservation, but at the same time, authoritatively reaffirming its own authority of judicial review in any of such vital matters.

Ajay Kumar Singh vs. State of Bihar (1994)

There is no rule under Article 15(4) that a student cannot be given the benefit of reservation at more than one stage during the course of his educational career. But why not go by your own ruling that persons who have entered a stream and become members of a single class and to treat them differently after that will be to treat equals unequally? And hence, a violation of Article 14 which in turn is a basic feature of the Constitution.

The court however clearly states that "Where to draw the line is not a matter of law but a matter of policy for the state to be evolved keeping in view the larger interests of the society and various other relevant factors.

The Supreme Court in this case has restrained itself by drawing a line between matter of law and a matter of policy, the later being the discretionary domain of the State.

Justice Mathew

"The State can adopt any measure which would ensure the adequate representation in public service of the members of scheduled castes and scheduled tribes and justify it as a compensatory measure to ensure equality of opportunity provided it does not dispense with the acquisition of the basic minimum qualification necessary for efficiency of administration... And government can extend that "**Any Measure** " to scheduled castes and scheduled tribes and confine it to them or it can extend it to OBCs or to all of the three, he said.

Judicial Activism becomes equally important in matters dealt by the administration exercising special judicial or magisterial powers vested in them through statute. This includes land allotment matters and disputes connected therewith etc. Down/troddens become the worst victims particularly in case of disputes against the larger and dominating upper castes masses. The authority also operates amidst various pulls and pressures from higher authorities, political communities and at times unsocial elements. A positive and sympathetic judicial activism only can come to the rescue of these deserted groups under such circumstances.

REFERENCES

1. Avtars of Indian Juicial Activism; explorations in the geography of (In)justice; Upendra Baxi.
2. Dr. Man Mohan Singh, Prime Minister during the conference of all state chief ministers and high court chief justices on 8th April 2007 at Delhi.
3. Avtars of Indian Juicial Activism; explorations in the geography of (In)justice; Upendra Baxi.
4. Justice P. B. Sawant in the *Indra Sahney Mandal case.*
5. The Betrayal : P.S. Rashtrapal, Member of Parliament.
6. Heman Belz; *Challenge to the living constitution.*
7. Shanti Bhusan, 'Restraining Judges', *Times of India,* 16 December, 2006.

14

Some Misconceptions about Reservation

A. PROMOTIONS

This is another area where lot of resentment and controversies in the minds of the people at large prevail. People are heard saying that:

1. Once members join a service, they are one class; to give a permanent advantage to some because of their birth would split them into different classes. That would mean creation of a permanent separate category apart from mainstream; i.e. a vertical division of the administrative apparatus, whether they work or not, they tend to think their promotion assured. This in turn is bound to generate a feeling of despondence and heart burning among open competition members. All this is bound to affect the efficiency of administration.
2. At the initial stage of recruitment, reservation can be made in favour of backward class of citizens, but once they enter the service, efficiency of administration demands that these members too compete with others and earn promotion like all others; no further distinction can be made therefore with reference to the " birth marks".
3. Reservation at promotional level is dubiously dangerous to the efficiency of administration The not so qualified person occupies a chair and finds himself incompetent to deal with matters and a more qualified person forced to work under reservational promotees

gets frustration accelerated and stops taking interest in work.

4. That the position of all sections including these sections would have been much, much better had administrators been selected, posted and backward class employees promoted not because of their birth but strictly on merit. Administrative structure should be steered not into these ditches of jobs and promotions as matters of right, and entitlements, but towards accountability and performance.

And like this, lots of arguments are advocated in expression of feelings against the reservation in promotion. The above contentions besides negating the core objective behind reservation in promotion are also apprehensive of a question on efficiency in government because of more number of employees from the reserved categories. It has also stated that recruitments with no reservation right from the beginning of the Constitution that would have better yielded the task of betterment of these communities targeted to be uplifted. It was also stated somewhere that railway accidents are also the outcome of the reservation policy. At one sight, these all are over exaggerations of reactions against reservation.

Yes, it is true that when a member is taken into a particular service, he becomes class by itself in the cadre, he is inducted and should be at par for all practical purposes. This gets defeated with reservation in promotion. But, this has to be understood in context with the noble objective of the constitution behind the provisions for reservation in promotion. Dr. Ambedkar said in one of his speeches in constituent assembly that aim behind reservation was never simply making of clerks and peons from scheduled castes and scheduled tribes. It was to make them participate in the administration of the country. This could materialize more meaningfully with reservation in promotion. More people of these categories in the higher echelons means better and more equitable sharing of power of administration, which should be a welcome step. Unless the real sufferers of the social inequalities are brought in the decision-making process, addressing the chronic problem of inequality will remain far from being solved.

The Constitution expects adequate representation of the reserved category candidates i.e. 15 per cent in case of scheduled castes and 7.50 per cent in case of scheduled tribes in central government services and nothing more. Reservation in promotion enables to fill up such shortfall if it is at all there. Even while filling up such shortfalls, all the governing norms have to be observed without exception.

As regards efficiency, this is an unnecessary apprehension often used for restricting otherwise a valid and legitimate entitlement. Yes, it is true that fast track promotions for these categories do have taken place during the eighties. This was in view of the negligible representation of the backwards in the higher echelons at that time on one hand and overall large number of promotions taking place in the government set up because of ever expanding horizons of the government administration to meet the aspirations and expectations of the developing economy and rising population in the country. During this period of eighties, reservation in promotion as a felt need was implemented consequent upon constitutional amendment. So, quite for some time, promotions of reserved category employees could be seen disproportionately at higher rate, which was purely a temporary phenomenon. The promotions have since settled to its normal situation in the government sector may be because of saturation, computerization, privatization etc. Numbers of court judgments have also played an important role in restricting application of reservation in promotions under one plea or the other. So gone are the days when a scheduled caste or scheduled tribe person much junior to his fellow general category colleagues, used to be promoted superseding his much higher senior behind him. Besides this, entire promotion system in government set up has undergone a sea change with more stringent norms for any promotion. Under this, comprehensive appraisal system enjoined with other promotion requisites automatically brings about checks and balance norms obviating chances of inefficient feeder cadre person from promotion possibilities irrespective whether he belongs to a reserved category or otherwise since they are evenly applicable to SC/ST/OBC employees as well.

It had been held in *Jagdishlal and others vs. State of Haryana and others* that promotion is a statutory right while the right of the reserved category candidates under Article 16(4) and Article 16(4A) were fundamental rights of the reserved candidate and therefore, the reserved candidates were entitled to the benefit of continuous officiation.

Adequate representation of scheduled castes and scheduled tribes is stipulated in the constitutional provision under Article 16(4), which reads as under;

Article 16 (4)

Nothing in this article shall prevent the state from making any provision for the reservation of appointments or posts in favour of any backward class of citizens, which in the opinion of the state **is not adequately represented in the services** under the state.

Table 14.1 gives an idea about the representation of the scheduled castes and scheduled tribes in central government services at the beginning of the reservation in promotion and now its cumulative position after about 25 years.[1]

Table 14.1: Representation in Central Government Services

As on	*Class I Officers*				*Class II Officers*			
	1974		*1999*		*1974*		*1999*	
	No.	*%*	*No.*	*%*	*No.*	*%*	*No.*	*%*
Scheduled castes	1,094	3.25	5,909	11.29	4,292	4.59	13,306	12.68
Scheduled tribes	155	0.46	1774	3.39	258	0.49	3,512	3.35
Others	32,423	96.29	44,660	85.32	88,970	94.92	88,145	83.97
Total	33,672	100.00	52,343	100.00	93,520	100.00	1,04,963	100.00

Source: 10th Five Year Plan 2002/2007, Vol. II. Sectoral Policies and Programmes, Planning Commission, Government of India.

The above figures reveal that inspite of reservation not only in initial recruitments, but subsequent additional reservation in promotion in 1978, there is no adequate representation of 22.50 per cent in aggregate. This indicates a clear contrast between the concern expressed in the above observations and the obtaining position with regard to representation of scheduled castes and scheduled tribes officers in central government services. The concern about promotional reservations is so roaringly expressed leaving a general impression that all senior higher positions are now being filled through only reserved quota employees in total disregard of seniority, merit and all other requisite norms of promotion.

The above figures reveal that there were hardly 3.71 per cent officers in class I and 5.08 per cent officers in class II services from the reserved categories in 1974, which is far below the required representation of 22.5 per cent. After introduction of effective reservation norms in promotion in 1978, the position could improve to 14.68 per cent in class I services and 16.03 per cent in class II services taking further 25 years till 1999.

Caste consciousness in Indian society has so widely and deep rootedly spread that it operates in every sphere even after the person enters a government job. A person's caste identity is disclosed from the records before his arrival in the office. The persons from amongst the existing staff who belong to the same caste will establish rapport from the day one and new stranger entrant with his unknown caste background will have difficulty in settling in the new atmosphere. This is a common phenomenon irrespective whether person belongs to an upper caste or a lower caste.

Justice Beg has very rightly pointed in *Rangachari case*, **When citizens are already employed in a particular grade as government servants, considerations relating to the sources from which they are drawn, lose much of their importance does not hold good in the Indian society which has still not come out of the stigma of caste discrimination and socially graded hierarchical identities.**[2]

Employees' Appraisal

Performance of government employees is evaluated on the basis of their annual confidential reports (CRs) . The employee's future promotions are considered on the basis of such ratings. While rating a subordinate employee by his next superior under whom he is working, his performance is evaluated on different gradations. It is experienced that caste based social factors invariably influence the person's evaluation. Experiences have shown that scheduled castes and scheduled tribe employees are often victimized during such evaluation. Of course, this cannot be proved with substantive evidences as all this is done on highly confidential basis. But casteism does prevail and operate to the detriment of the lower caste employees. Theoretically, it is easy to say that once a person enters a job, he becomes part of that system and should not be branded with a separate identity such as scheduled caste or scheduled tribe. But the bitter reality is other way round. An employee in the Indian set up carries with him his caste identity not only at his initial place of posting, but also at places of his subsequent postings. Feelings of social compartalisation is so inbuilt in the social set up, that though it has considerably weakened during last fifty years, it still exists that none can deny.

Now the promotions in government jobs requires that the employees' preceding five years' confidential reports are supposed to be at least '**very good**' i.e. above 60 per cent consistently. A slip in evaluation below very good rating even for a single year will debar a person from being eligible for that promotion process. This is mandatory for all the employees without exception to the reserved categories. Now think of those employees working under a boss who is by his own social background or experience is caste bias. Needless to add that this does not happen with all the people. All the superior officers may not be caste bias. But purpose of stating over here is that it is a common social phenomenon in Indian social environment carrying a possibility coming in way of a neutral and bias-free assessment of an employee. This could be other way round also in case of an upper caste employee working under the scheduled caste or scheduled tribe appraiser.

The employees in the government sector have powerful trade union organizations. Though, there is a sizeable strength of scheduled castes, scheduled tribes and other backward class employees in the government sector, it is seen that the leadership of these trade unions still rests with the upper caste leaders though they are handful in numerical strength. How does all this happen? It is dominance of Indian caste system.

Employees after all are drawn from the society and they do not function devoid of social systems. So whatever social beliefs, perceptions, bias are prevailing in the society at large all that go with the person who could be a government employee as well which reflects his attitude, behaviour etc.

As regards railway accidents, it is nothing but an outright exaggeration and a clear bias against the preferential treatment being given to a left out portion of the society, because of the inhuman, illogical and ridiculous social caste hierarchical system prevailing and accepted for over two thousand years. Indian Railway is the world's biggest public sector service undertaking and has earned a big name for its overall efficiency handling the highest numbers of passengers and tonnage of freight. Accidents are connected with the human factor and simply recruitment or promotion of reserved category people in railways should not be blamed for such mishaps. There are certain pubic sector undertakings like Indian Oil Corporation (IOC), Hindustan Petroleums (HP), Hindustan Machine Tools (HMT), to name a few which are considered in the proud list of top most global companies world over. A large number of manpower in these companies belong to the reserved categories since they were inducted in these companies under the reservation provisions in force in these companies long back.

B. ROSTERS

Roster point is yet an another subject of hot debate. A feeling prevails that roster means filling of the vacancy with reserved category putting aside all norms; rosters operate on sub-sub caste basis and so on. Recently, in one of the books on reservation, observation in respect of operation of roster was made as under[3].

"Promotions in government departments came to be determined by an innovation 'The roster system'. By this system, specified vacancies at each level came to be set apart for persons who belonged to such and thus caste i.e. vacancies are being reserved on the basis of sub-sub-castes."

Such incorrect observations leading to lot of misunderstandings and misconceptions with regard to roster system are the outcomes either of lack of legal/conceptual clarity in the matters of reservation/roster or due to extreme negative bias of such observers or opinion makers in reservation matters.

Roster is a set mechanism in the government administration for operation of reservation provisions at the time of recruitment, promotion or any change in the existing composition of the employees/officers etc. Taking an imaginary illustration, suppose, a particular central government administrative establishment has a staff compliment of 100 persons in a particular section. Then, its roster points will roughly spread as under for general category (G), other backward class (O), scheduled castes (SC) and scheduled tribes (ST).

Table 14.2: Roster Point Mechanism

SL	1	2	3	4	5	6	7	8	9	10	11	12	13	14	15	16	17	18	19	20
FOR	G	G	G	O	G	G	SC	O	G	G	G	O	G	SC	ST	O	G	G	G	O

As can be seen from the above, it is purely an arithmetic mechanism ensuring proper composition of all categories of employees viz. General, OBC, SC, ST etc. It ensures adequacy of eligible quota for the respective category. However, there are many misunderstandings prevailing with regard to roster system.

1. Roster Means Filling of the Vacancy with Reserved Category Putting Aside All Norms

This is not so. Roster only stipulates as to whom the next vacancy should go. It is not that roster means reservation and reservation only. It is a chart showing the statutory staff composition in that particular establishment. Suppose, in another establishment having present staff strength of ten persons in one particular cadre, and suppose, more ten are to be recruited or promoted in that particular cadre, the roster helps in deciding reservation/general category wise positions to be made available in respect of new ten incumbents, which will be like this, 5 have to be from the General category, three from other backward classes, one from scheduled caste (If fraction rounded off to one, then two) and one from scheduled tribe cadre

2. Rosters Operate on Sub-Sub Caste Basis

This is also not correct. If a particular roster point is meant for being filled by an OBC category candidate, then the position is supposed to be filled by any candidate irrespective of his sub caste within the lists of OBC category, provided he meets with all the eligibility criteria and all other recruitment, promotion norms are explicitly adhered to.

So it is not so that a reserved category candidate just applies and gets the promotion instantly. Application of reservation in promotions with such limitless relaxations as misconceived, would not have led to huge backlog of class I/II officers even after application of the reservation norms since over 50 years.

Single Post Promotion/Roster

As regards promotion in case of single post situation, lot of misunderstanding prevails. There is a general impression that if there is only one post in a particular cadre e.g. Post Master

General, Chief General manager (Telecom) etc. such post will automatically stand reserved for a backward class. In reality, it is not so. Any post in government or public sector, irrespective whether it is a single post or more, it will be filled as per updated roster point and not from the category of which the post is relinquished. According to roster point, general category candidates will fill in first or single or any of the first six posts only. 7th will be filled in from scheduled caste and 14th from scheduled tribe. Following para is taken from one of the recently written book on reservation.

"In some of the top grades, there are single post in the service. If at any point of time, the incumbent is not a member of the backward class, it would certainly be the case of inadequate representation as regards that post which would mean that such posts which are single may be reserved for all time to be held by members of the backward classes, because if at any moment such a person ceases to hold, there would be inadequate representation in regard to that post."

This is grossly incorrect. Moreover, promotions in government are taking place on the basis of cadre and not the post e.g. Secretary, Addl. Secretary, Selection grade, junior grade and so on. i.e post master general is not promoted, but officers of postal department from various feeder cadres are promoted, some of whom on promotion may be posted as post master general also, managing director, chief general manager etc. are the postings and not promotions. Post is an outcome of promotion.

Justice Fazal Ali says, "The government accordingly has full authority to classify employees in different categories and within a class, institute measures in favour of scheduled castes and tribes and OBCs so as to ensure real equality.

Supreme Court constitutional Bench of five judges in *Arti Ray Chaudhary vs. Union of India* had declared that they were following a line of precedents and held reservation of single post with the help of the roster system was entirely constitutional.

C. RELAXATIONS

Reservation is the prime form of special provision under the Constitution for quota in government jobs, electoral seats and admission in educational institutions. While other lesser types or say supplemental or ancillary provisions under constitutional reservation include exemptions, concessions and relaxations. Article 16(4) has provided for reservation of appointments and posts. So exemptions, concessions, relaxations etc. are enacted through regulatory framework for making reservation provisions more effective. i.e. to ensure that the members of the reserved category fully avail of the reservational provisions in their favour.

Relaxations permissible to the candidates belonging to scheduled castes, scheduled tribes and backward classes are yet one more issue of controversy. It is argued that unlimited relaxations are allowed to backward classes in a drive to fill up maximum vacancies from the reserved categories. This includes relaxation in age, standards of suitability, in total disregard to norms whether the candidates fit into the promotional criteria or not. The arguments are put like this;

Permission to relax minimum standards has become a mandate to grant preference: "If members of scheduled castes and scheduled tribes, can maintain minimum necessary requirements of administrative efficiency, not only representation but also preference may be given to them to enforce equality and to eliminate inequality."

The arguments are far from the reality and the prevailing governments norms in force at present.

Actual laid down provisions/norms etc. with regard to relaxations are as under.

1. Relaxation in Upper Age Limit to SC/ST/OBC Candidates

Five years' upper age relaxation is allowed not only in case of reserved categories, but it is also available to women, ex-servicemen and so on. One will not disagree that the upper age limit even otherwise deserves to be extended in view of the prevailing chronic state of unemployment.

2. Relaxation in Requirement of Experience, Standard of Suitability etc.

There are no relaxations with regard to experience and other norms relating to the job requirement and the candidates' general suitability e.g. minimum requirement for a probationary officer's post in Banking is fixed at first class in any graduation discipline. This is never relaxed even in case of reserved category candidates also i.e. a candidate belonging to a reserved category has also to be with first class for being eligible to apply for the post of probationary officer in a Bank.

3. Principle of Pick Up

There is a misunderstanding that in case of promotion, if a sufficient number of candidates is not available, eligible SC/ST candidate may be picked up "till the bottom of the seniority list for filling up the reserved vacancies."

No, this is also wrong. There were a few relaxations during initial implementation of reservation in promotions in seventies/eighties. These rules have undergone a sea change and promotion rules in all the government departments are uniform for all the employees irrespective whether one belongs to a reserved category or a general category.

4. Bench Mark Relaxations

There is a wrongful notion that where standards of evaluation have been prescribed for promotion, the resevationists not meeting the prescribed benchmark could be promoted provided they were not found unfit for promotion.

The word '**Unfit**' though appears so simple and plain is not so in reality. To be fit in promotion a government employee has to have his preceding five years' confidential reports to be at least '**very good'** and above. Very good means quantitatively 60 per cent and above. Next below it comes. Average/good and lastly unsatisfactory. It means if an employee's C.R. is less than Very Good, even for just one year, he becomes 'Unfit' to be promoted. This statutory requirement is uniformly applicable to all the employees without any relaxations irrespective whether the officer or employee belongs to a reserved category or otherwise.

How is this rating in CRs becomes an invisible but a very powerful weapon for caste biased victimization is narrated in the earlier part of this chapter on wrong notions prevailing about promotion.

So it is not true that a reserved category candidate/ employee just applies and gets a promotion instantly as sensed from the above quoted contentions.

5. 50 per cent Reservation Cap Has Become Mandatory Minimum 50 per cent

This also needs to be clarified. Supreme Court judgment in *Indra Sahney case* stipulated that reservation cannot exceed 50% of the total seats, which the government has already implemented as per directive, wide OM dated 29 August 1997. However, it is possible that a reserved category candidate scoring at par with or higher than a general category candidate, comes under the selection list as a general category candidate provided he also fulfills all other criteria applicable to a general candidate such as no age relaxation etc. So, it is possible that number of SC/ST/OBC candidates could exceed 50 per cent cap.

D. CARRY FORWARD

Carry forward of unfilled reserved vacancies is one more controversial area. Lot of misunderstanding prevails for want of clarity in this regard. Sometimes, it is presented in such a bias way that a rosy picture is created that all the government positions will be fully occupied by reserved category people only. Quite a few government position is quoted where 90 per cent of super scale positions will be occupied by reserved category promotees in next three years and so on.

The very purpose of carry forward is ensuring adequacy of representation in the government services. If unfilled vacancies are declared exhausted for backward classes, the governmental commitment to provide adequate representation of backward classes in services will be frustrated. And therefore, the government has to adopt either of the two alternatives:

1. The State may provide for carrying on the unfilled vacancies for the next year or next to the next year, or
2. Instead of providing for carrying over the unfilled vacancies to the coming years, it may provide for filling of the vacancies from the general quota candidates and add the unfilled posts to the next year quota to be reserved for such backward classes.

Laid down norms in this regard since the launching of the Constitution were like this. If considerable number of suitable candidates of communities, for whom reservation is made, were not available in a particular year, the unfilled vacancies were to be treated as unreserved and to be filled in accordingly by the best available candidates. The number of reserved vacancies treated to have been converted into unreserved was to be added as an additional quota to the number that would be reserved in the next year in the normal course and to the extent general quota of the next year was to be curtailed. This arrangements was to continue for next three years and not beyond.

In this regard there are two famous Supreme Court cases. One, *T. Devadasan vs. Union of India* in the year 1952. The norms as enumerated above came into force thereafter and another one is *State of Kerala vs. N.M. Thomas* in the year 1981. In this case as a result of carry forward rule, 34 vacancies out of 51 in one particular year were to be filled by the scheduled caste candidates. The bench was divided in their respective opinions.

The Court was confronted with another way of getting around 50 per cent limit. This was the "carry forward rule" to which we have just seen references. Assume that this year, 50 per cent seats had been reserved, but that only 30 per cent could be filled as the remaining candidates, even after the relaxation of minimum standards just could not be found. The position was taken that these unfilled 20 per cent shall be "carry forward" to the next year. The result would be that next year, not 50 per cent but 70 per cent seats could be reserved. If again, only 60 per cent of these seats could be filled in that year, in the third year, 80 per cent seats would get reserved and so on.

Special Recruitment Drives

Governments now especially before each bout of elections, go in for "special recruitment drives" in which only persons from the backward classes can apply. So, there is the effect of 50 per cent reservation plus of the "special recruitment drive"; plus of the ruling that those members of these castes who qualify on merit; even though they have availed of relaxations like those relating to age, qualifying marks etc. shall be counted not in 50 per cent reservation quota but in the general category.

This is an extreme illustration of misunderstanding regarding reservation or say myths of reservation. So far arithmetical calculations are concerned, what is mentioned here above is partially correct. Reserved posts not filled in particular year get carried forward up to next three years. So calculation could be like that.

This has to be examined in its totality. Why first of all such reserved posts are not filled in chronic unemployment situation where thousands of reserved category candidates are standing in the long queue of employment seekers is a matter of concern. Second, What is wrong if a post which was supposed to be given to a reserved category candidate this year is reserved for being fulfilled by him next year? What about allotting a post to a general candidate to which he was not entitled and was meant for the reserved category candidate. Is it not an advance release of post this year, to which he i.e. a general candidate was not entitled to this year? And finally, is it not that a line has to be drawn for meaningful implementation of reservation in fulfillment of our upliftment dream of bringing about social equalities in the nation?

To conclude, as regard the carry forward, one needs to refer to following provisions in the Indian Constitution;

Article 16(4): Providing for reservation for the SC/ST until representation of these categories reaches to an adequacy level of 15% in case of SC and 7.5% in case of ST.

Article 16(4A): Reservation in promotion until there is an adequate representation .

Article 16(4B): Backlog vacancies are not to be counted in the 50 per cent reservation ceiling.

The above provisions obviate the possibility of recruiting/promoting the reserved category people in excess of 15 per cent in case of scheduled castes, 7.50 per cent in case of scheduled tribes and 27 per cent in case of other backward Communities as is also decided in the famous *Sabharwal case*. In other words, whatever exaggerations made as above, carry forward will never result in exceeding the stipulated upper limit signifying adequacy of representation in each reserved category.

E. MAINTENANCE OF EFFICIENCY IN ADMINISTRATION

A concern has been expressed that reservation on high scale would jeopardize efficiency in state administration as reservation means inducting people with lesser merit who would not have been otherwise qualified as in Government jobs in absence of reservation.

Chief Justice, A.N. Ray says, "In regard to employment, like other terms and conditions associated with and incidental to it, the promotion to a selection post is also included in the matters relating to employment and even in regard to such promotion to a selection post. All that Article 16(4) guarantees is equality of opportunity to all citizens." He did caution, however, that while reserving a proportion of promotions, government must bear in mind the impact of these steps on the efficiency of administration because it must not be forgotten that the efficiency of administration is of such paramount importance that it would be unwise and impermissible to make any reservation at the cost of efficiency of administration

Article 335 : Maintenance of Efficiency in Administration

'The claims of the members of the scheduled castes and scheduled tribes shall be taken into consideration, consistently with the maintenance of efficiency of administration, in the making of appointments to services and posts in connection with the affairs of the union or of a state'.

The above article has reiterated provisions of reservation embodied in another Article 16(4) putting further a clause regarding maintenance of state administration. Meaning is plain. It goes without saying that the state administration has to be maintained all along undertaking any welfare measure including reservation. It appears that this clause 'maintenance of administration is cleverly caught to defend any thing against reservation. As regards, reservation in employment mainly in two cadres i.e. subordinates, clerical and supervisory, let us examine how could it affect or rather adversely affect the state administration. Subordinate services are out of discussion in this regard.

Clerical Services

As regard clerical services, there is not much to worry about as the work involved is such that it will not adversely affect the state administration. Justice Krishna Aiyer comments as under in the regard in *N.M. Thomas* case on reservation in promotion in the lower posts.

"The posts in question are clerical posts and the way duties are discharged, just cannot have much impact on the efficiency of governance as a whole. He further notes that in *Rangachari case,* the Supreme Court has already accepted reservation in higher posts.

He states, "If in selecting top officers you may reserve posts for SC/ST with lesser merit." He holds, "How can you rationally argue that for the posts of peons or lower division clerks reservation will spell calamity? The part that efficiency plays is far more in the case of higher posts than in the appointments to the lower posts."

Promotional Posts

Promotion of a reserved category is subject to all stringent norms as enumerated earlier in this chapter. Hence expected efficiency required of him maintaining the overall administration would not remain under any vaccum of compulsion. The only benefit of reservation to a reserved category candidate would be that in a promotional avenue where promotion eligibility is minimum five years, he might get promoted after eight to ten years i.e. some one or two years early than a general category employee. i.e. Promotion in government now-a-days takes place after a far long stint of service because gradually reduction in creation of promotional posts because of modifications in service conditions and recruitment rules, changing direct recruitment/promotion ratios, induction of more and more computer savvy personnel at higher level etc. Therefore, it never happens that a reserved category will get promotions after promotions uninturrptedly and reach the top positions superseding all his general category collegues because of the reservations.

Promotions in general in government administration are based on highly pro employee considerations. Restricting a person on mere effeciency ground in general is very difficult in spite of tightened CR requisites, since there is an commonly over liberal tendency in such ratings. Hence apprehension about effeciency in connection with reservation has to be viewed with this realistic consideration.

SC/ST Constitutes only One-Sixth of Total Government Staff

Secondly, 'maximum strength of promotees belonging to scheduled castes and scheduled tribes in the central government constitutes hardly 15/16 per cent i.e. one-sixth of the total strength. Is it possible for such a small fraction to spoil the whole administrative functioning in the government?

Appointments or promotions of people from reserved categories is not the sole ruining factor disrupting efficiency in the administration but host of crucial factors such as employees' mind set because of overly protected service conditions, absence of adequate accountability, excessive political interference, lack of transparency in the admiistration, continued black shadows of British days culture in the administration and above all percolation of deteriorating ethical values and sensibilities in the society at large which all collectively infect the effeciency in the administration. Of course, it is not that hopes for enhancing efficiency in the state governance is lost. The governance shall have to invest in its employees enormously towards on the job trainings, motivational workshops, skill and aptitude improving, introduction of modern tools and techniques, so as to enhance its internal office culture and environment, infrastructure and automation etc.

Present level of efficiency in the government is well to the knowledge of every body in every sphere and therefore need not be elaborated. Blaming reservation and reservation alone for the poor state of governance needs to be introspected within from the bottom of the heart by one and all at large.

Reservation in recruitment and admission in educational institutions have been in force right from the first day of adoption of the Indian Constitution on 26 January 1950. Reservation in promotion was introduced much later thereafter consequent upon 77th Amendment in the Constitution with addition Article 16 (4A), which explicitly allows reservations in promotions also. Thus, reservation in promotion has become a mandatory requirement.

Constitutional Bench in M. Nagraj and others on Article 335

"Efficiency in administration was held to be a constitutional limitation on the discretion vested in the state to provide for reservation in public employment. Under the proviso to Article 335, it is stated that nothing in this Article shall prevent the state to relax qualifying marks or standards of evaluation for reservation in promotion. This proviso is conferring discretionary power on the state to relax qualifying marks or standards of evaluation. Effeciency is a variable factor. It is for the concerned state to decide in a given case, whether the overall efficiency of the system is affected by such relaxation.

Article 335 has also to be read with Article 46, which provides that the state shall promote with special care the educational and economic interests of the weaker sections of the people etc. Therefore, where the state finds compelling interests of backwardness and inadequacy, it may relax the qualifying marks for SCs/STs."

Maintenance of Effeciency in Banking

Indian public sector banking industry introduced a golden handshake like scheme for voluntary retirement to its employees/officers in the year 2000, which was overwhelmingly responded by the staff with substantial retirement of about 20 per cent from this sector. It so happened that most of these voluntarily retiring people were from the general category. With the result that ratio of SC/ST employees/officers in public sector banking shot up all of a sudden to over 30 per cent. This highly dynamic industry simultaneously also underwent revolutionary developmental measures such as innovative banking, total computerization of its operations, introduction of globally available internet banking services at Indian door step and above, all aggressive marketing campaign. All this envisaged excellent productivity, adoption of new and complex technologies, with new business outlook. It is worth noting that the existing manpower on the banking pay roll took up all these new challenges. Every body now acknowledges wonderful inroad in all spheres of developments made by this public sector industry rising above the much criticized governmental mind set. Higher proportion of SC/ST staffs in this industry nowhere posed any hindrance in implementing all above referred to novel professional experiments.

Justice Krishna Ayer on Maintenance of Administration

Justice Krishna Ayer in another matter of *Akhil Bharatiya Shoshit Karmachari Sangh* states; "Trite arguments about efficiency and inefficiency are a trifle phoney, because after all at the higher levels, the harijans/girijans appointees are a microscopic percentage and even in the case of class III and II posts, they are negligible. The preponderant majority coming from the unreserved communities is presumably efficient and the dilution of efficiency caused by the minimal induction of a small percentage of 'reserved' candidates cannot affect the overall administrative efficiency significantly.

It is fashionable to say and there is perhaps some truth in it that from generation to generation, there is deterioration in efficiency in all walks of life from politics to pedagogy to officialdom and other professions. Nevertheless, the world has been going forward and only parties whose personal interest is affected forecast a doom on account of progressive deficiency in efficiency. We are not impressed with the misfortune predicted about governmental personnel being manned by morons

"Unfortunately, the very orientation of our selection process is distorted and those like the candidates from the SC and ST who, from their birth, have had a traumatic understanding of the conditions of acrostic India, in one sense, more capability than those who have lived under affluent circumstances and are callous to the human lot of the surrounding masses,

I divagate and make these observations only to debunk the exaggerated argument about harijans and girijans being substantiated. We may put aside this angle of vision and approach the problem traditionally because every new idea has resistance to encounter before acceptance and every original thought has been branded a heresy."

REFERENCES

1. *10th Five Year Plan 2002/2007*, Vol. II. *Sectoral Policies and Programmes*, Planning Commission, Government of India.
2. Justice Beg in Supreme Court *Rangachari case*.
3. Arun Shourie, *Falling Over Backwards*, 2005.

15

Dr. Ambedkar on Reservation

Bhimrao Ramji Ambedkar popularly known as Dr. Babasaheb Ambedkar was the real architect of the whole, historic and comprehensive structure of the reservation. Hailing from a poor oppressed Mahar family, Dr. Ambedkar experienced the bitter taste of social discrimination at every footing of his whole life right from the tender childhood. It was perhaps this suffering of social hatred and caste oppression that reinforced in this great soul an instinct to fight lifetime in addressing the similar sufferings that his crores of caste fellows were enduring without even murmuring. He faced the experience of physical untouchability not only in the primary school days, but also even after obtaining rare foreign education, when he joined as a Defence Officer in the office of Maharaja Sayajirao Gaekwad of Baroda. All this strengthened him to struggle for the cause of the downtroddens and producing in him a patriot presenting the world best constitution which *inter alia* also brought the provisions for reservation changing the lives for one-fifth population of the nation living in almost a sub human life.

Dr. Ambedkar's Entry to the March Towards Reservation; 1917

Dr. Ambedkar's role as far as the journey of reservation is concerned, came on the forefront from the year 1917, when the idea of social and political rights to the untouchables was mooted out for the first time in the country. In this year, people from the depressed classes organized two separate meetings at Bombay and demanded for the free and compulsory education for their children and also certain other rights such as to elect their own legislatures. These two meetings of the depressed classes created a pressure in the Congress, which sought the help of Dr. Ambedkar. In the meantime, Dr. Ambedkar was also called upon to give evidence before the South Borough Committee where he explained the wretched condition of the oppressed people and demanded **'Separate Electorate'** with reserved seats in the central legislative assembly and provincial legislative assemblies for the oppressed Indians in proportion to percentage of their population. The South Borough Committee recognized separate political existence of the oppressed classes and strongly recommended that measures should be taken to protect their interests.

The South Borough Committee recommendations gave birth to The Government of India Act 1919, which recognized for the first time in the Indian history the politico-constitutional existence of the people from the depressed classes. This made possible nomination of at least one depressed class representative out of 14 non-official members nominated by the Governor-General to the central legislative assembly. This was the maiden historic achievement of Dr. Ambedkar.

Dr. Ambedkar whole-heartedly wanted to initiate the political education amongst the backward classes who were mostly illiterate. Therefore, he argued for the responsible legislatures. He wanted that there should be elected legislatures from the depressed classes instead of nominated one as provided in the Government of India Act of 1919. However, the British Government and Congress refused to recognize the demands of special representation of the depressed classes through election. But, in substance, the Government of India Act 1919 proved as the **'Mile Stone'** in the history of reservation to depressed classes, because it provided representation to this community in the legislature for the first time through nomination.[1]

Before Simon Commission 1930

Dr. Ambedkar appeared before the Simon Commission on 23 October 1928 in Pune for giving evidence. He pleaded that the depressed classes had a separate and distinct entity quite different from other minorities. Hence, they require special protection. He asserted, "The first point, therefore, I would stress before the conference is that we must be regarded as a distinct and independent minority. Secondly, I would like to submit that depressed class minority needs greater political protection than other minorities in British India, for the simple reason that it is educationally very backward and that it is economically poor, socially enslaved and it also suffers from certain political disabilities from which no other community suffers.[2]

It was Dr. Ambedkar only who demanded for the first time reservation in services for the depressed classes on 8 August 1930 during the All India Depressed Classes conference held at Nagpur. He along with Rao Bahadur Srinivasan participated on behalf of the depressed classes in the first historic round table conference, Dr. Ambedkar clearly stated, "The problems of oppressed classes will never be solved unless they get political power in their own hands." While explaining the social condition of the depressed classes, **he stated that they were depressed by the government, suppressed by the Hindus, and disregarded by the Muslims**. We are left in most intolerable position of utter helplessness to which I am sure there is no parallel and to which I was bound to call attention". Dr. Ambedkar was of the view that the orthodox people would not allow the depressed classes to have equality of status and equality of treatment. Hence, he tried strenuously to secure representation of oppressed Indians. i.e. scheduled castes, scheduled tribes, and other backward classes and other oppressed classes i.e. Buddhists, Jains, Muslims, Sikhs, Christians, etc. in the cabinet and the decision-making agencies of the government. The result of the first round table conference was that the whole world came to know that the fate of the Shudras and Ati Shudras in India was worse than that of Negroes in America.

Franchise Committee and Communal Award 1932

The Franchise Committee visited India in 1932 as to ascertain the views of various parties and in respect of position and status of the 'oppressed classes'. Almost all the leaders of the oppressed classes while giving the evidence before the Franchise Committee supported the scheme of '**Separate Electorate**'. Hence, Dr. Ambedkar also changed his earlier stand and exclusively demanded the policy of '**Separate Electorate**'. On the report of the Committee, J. Mac Donald, the British Prime Minister declared communal award on 17 August 1932 i.e. distribution of political power in proportion to the strength of the communities. The award was based on the principle of communal representation that was embodied in the Government of India Act, 1919. The communal award gave 'separate electorate'. According to Dr. Ambedkar, the communal award gave two benefits to the depressed classes as under;

(a) A fixed quota of seats to be elected by separate electorates of the scheduled castes to be filled by them only.
(b) Double vote one to be used through separate electorates to elect their own legislatures and the other to be used in the joint electorates to elect Hindu candidates.

Gandhiji's Fast Unto Death and Reservation Policy

Though the communal award declared the principle of 'separate electorate' to the depressed classes and other backward communities, i.e. the Sikhs, the Muslims, the Indian Christians and the Europeans, yet Mahatma Gandhi and his supporters objected to the policy of separate electorate relating to the depressed classes only. Mahatma Gandhi resented to 'fast unto the death' to oppose the separate electorates of depressed classes. While opposing separate electorates for depressed classes and others, Mahatma Gandhi argued, "Muslims and Sikhs are well organized, the 'Untouchables' are not. There is little political consciousness among them and they are so horribly treated that I want to save them against themselves. If they had separate electorates, their lives would be miserable in villages, which are the strongholds of Hindu orthodoxy. You must understand that I can tolerate the proposal for special representation of the Muslims and Sikhs as a necessary evil. He further explained," Separate electorates to the untouchables will ensure them bondage in perpetuity. The Muslims will never cease to be Muslim by having separate electorates. Do you want the 'Untouchables' to remain 'Untouchables' for ever? Gandhi fully agreed with Dr. Ambedkar's bitterness against Indian social system. In this regard, he stated," I have the highest regard for Dr. Ambedkar. He has every right to be bitter. That he does not break our heads is an act of self-restraint on his part. He is today so much saturated with suspicion that he cannot see anything else. He sees in every Hindu a determined opponent of the 'Untouchables' and it is quite natural. But the separate electorates that he seeks will not give him social reform[3].

Reservation Policy Through Poona Pact

Because of fast unto death by Mahatma Gandhi, some moderates and prominent leaders of the country arranged a meeting between Mahatma Gandhi and Dr. Ambedkar so as to find out some amicable solution. In response to justification given by Mahatma Gandhi for opposing separate electorates provided to the depressed classes, Dr. Ambedkar replied to the Congress leaders, "The fears expressed by Mahatma Gandhi about consequences of arrangements for the representation of the depressed classes are in my opinion, purely imaginary. If the nation is not going to be split up by separate electorates to the Mohammedans and the Sikhs, the Hindu society cannot be said to be split up if the depressed classes are given separate electorates." Dr. Ambedkar finally submitted to the proposal of Mahatma Gandhi in view of the threat to his life. Accordingly, an agreement known as 'Poona Pact' was signed in the Yerwada jail, Pune on 24 March 1932. The Poona Pact is remembered as an another mile stone of the modern reservation policy. Salient features of the Poona Pact were:

- Reservation in Provincial Legislatures in favour of depressed classes.
- 18% Reservation for the depressed classes in the central legislatures.
- Provision of educational grant with earmarking of a portion for providing educational facilities to the members of the depressed classes.

Since Poona Pact nullified the value of double voting, Dr. Ambedkar felt very hurt and he expressed his reaction, "The second vote given by the communal award was a priceless privilege. Its value as a political weapon was beyond reckoning. No caste Hindu candidate could have dared to neglect the untouchables in his constituency or to be hostile to their interest if he was made dependent upon the votes of untouchables.[4]

Dr. Ambedkar came out as Hero of the depressed classes after Poona Pact. The Poona Pact proved as origin of modern form of reservation policy. The reservation in earlier period on communal basis had a hidden agenda to divide the Indians, while the reservations originated through Poona Pact had objective for gradual uplift of the depressed classes. No doubt, had Dr. Ambedkar succeeded in getting the privileges of 'separate electorate' and 'double vote system' implemented, the growth of depressed classes would have been very fast and they would have become the power center.[5]

Reservation Under Government of India Act 1935

Principles agreed in Poona Pact were fully implemented through Government of India Act 1935. It provided the facility of reservations to the scheduled castes in legislative bodies through election for the first time. There were also provisions for different types of reservations in provincial legislatures, Dr. Ambedkar's comment in respect legislatures elected from the reserved seats', "The fact that a seat is reserved for a minority merely gives a security that the minority candidate will be elected. But it cannot guarantee that the minority candidate declared elected will be a person of its choice if the election is to be by a joint electorate. The result is that the legislatures of the minority elected to the reserved seat instead of being a champion of the minority is really a slave of the majority". After independence in 1947, the reservations to Muslims, Christians, Parsees, Sikhs, and Anglo Indians were abolished.[6]

Dr. Ambedkar on Reasonability of Percentage of Reservation

"There are three points of view in which it is necessary for us to reconcile, if we are to produce a workable proposition which will be acceptable by one and all. First; is that there shall be equality of opportunity for all citizens. It is the desire of the members of this House that every individual who is qualified for a particular post should be free to apply for that post, to sit for examinations and to have his qualifications tested so as to determine whether he is fit for the post or not and that there ought to be no limitation, there ought to be no hindrance in the operation of this principle of equality of opportunity. Another view mostly shared by a section of the house is that, if this principle is to be operative and it ought to be operative in their judgment to its fullest extent; there ought to be no reservation of any sort for any class or community at all, that all citizens, if they are qualified, should be placed on the same footing of equality so far as the public services are concerned. Then, we have a massive opinion which insists that although theoretically, it is good to have principle that there shall be equality of opportunity, there must at the same time be a provision made for the entry of certain communities which have so far been outside the administration.

As I said, the drafting Committee had to produce a formula, which would reconcile these three points of view. Firstly that there shall be equality of opportunity. Secondly, that there shall be reservations in favour of certain communities which have not so far had a 'proper look-in' so say into the administration. If honorable members will bear these facts in mind—the three principles, we had to reconcile—they will see that no better formula could be produced than that is embodied in sub-clause (3) of Article 10 of the Constitution; they will find that the view of those who believe and hold that there shall be equality of opportunity has been embodied in sub-clause (1) of Article 10. It is a generic principle. At the same time, as I said, we had to reconcile this formula with the demand made by certain communities, that the administration which has now for historical reasons been controlled by one community or a few communities that situation should disappear and that the others also must have an opportunity of getting into the public services.

Supposing for instance, we were to concede in full the demand of those communities who have not been so far employed in the public services to the fullest extent, what would really happen is, we shall be completely destroying the first proposition upon which we all agreed, namely that there shall be an equality of opportunity. Let me give an illustration. Supposing for instance reservations were made for a community or a collection of communities, the total of which came to somewhere near 70 per cent of the total posts under the state and only 30 per cent are retained as unreserved. Could any body say that the reservation of 30 per cent as open to general competition would be satisfactory from the point of view of giving effect to the first principle, namely, that there shall be equality of opportunity? It cannot be to my judgment. **Reservation must be confined to a minority of seats.**" It is then only, the first principle could find its place in the Constitution and be effective in operation. If honorable members understand this position that we have to safeguard two things, namely the principle of equality of opportunity and at the same time satisfy the demand of communities which had so far no representation in the State, then I am sure they will agree that unless you have some qualifying phrase as 'backward', the exception made in favour of reservation will ultimately eat up the rule altogether. Nothing of the rule will remain. That, I think, if I may say so is the justification why the drafting committee undertook on its own shoulders, the responsibility of introducing the word 'backward' which I admit did not originally find a place in the fundamental right in the way in which it was passed by this Assembly.

Dr. Ambedkar on Social Equality

Dr.Ambedkar said in Constituent Assembly, "On the Social plane, we have in India a society based on privileges of graded inequality which means elevation for some and degradations for the others. On the Economic plane, we have a society in which there are some who have immense wealth as against the many who are living in abject poverty. On the 26th January 1950, we are going to enter into a life of contradictions. In politics, we will have equality and in social and economic life, we will have inequality. We must remove this contradiction at the earliest possible moment, or else those who suffer from inequality will blow up the structure of political democracy which this Assembly has so laboriously built up."

Dr. Ambedkar on Article 16(4)

This important constitutional article embodies the core concept of reservation with an ideological plank of building an egalitarian and secular society. While speaking in Constituent Assembly during finalizing this article, he stated as under.

"It is easier to give power but difficult to give wisdom" Dr. Ambedkar further said, " Let us prove by our conduct that we have not only the power but also the wisdom to carry with us, all sectors of the country which is bound to lead us to unity"

Dr. Ambedkar has tried to convey that mere constitutional enactment would not suffice for ameliorating pitiable condition of downtroddens. Sensitizing wisdom will have to be supported to this noble cause to see its desired fruits.

Dr. Ambedkar on Implementation of Constitutional Provisions

He said in Constituent Assembly: "I feel however, good a constitution may be, it is sure to turn out bad if those who are called upon to work it, happen to be a bad lot. The working of a Constitution does not depend wholly upon the nature of the Constitution. The Constitution can provide only the organs of the state such as the legislature, the executive, and the judiciary. The factors on which the working of those organs of the State depend are the people and the political parties they will set up as their instruments to carry out their wishes and their politics. Who can say how the people of India and their parties will behave? Will they uphold constitutional methods of achieving their purposes or will they prefer revolutionary methods of achieving them? If they adopt the revolutionary methods, however good the constitution may be, it requires no prophet to say that it will fail."[7]

REFERENCES

1. *Dr. Ambedkar on Reservation* by S.K.Biswas, Maha Bodhi Book Agency.
2. *Dr. Ambedkar Writings and Speeches;* Vasant Moon Vol. XVI p. 465.
3. *Dr. Ambedkar on Reservation* by S.K.Biswas, p. 85.
4. *Babasaheb Dr. Ambedkar Writing and Speeches,* Vol. 9 p. 90.
5. *Reservation Policy* by Dr. Ram Samujh IRS Samruddh Bharat Publication, p. 59.
6. Dr. Ambedkar on Reservation by S.K. Biswas.
7. *Dr. Babasaheb Ambedkar Writings and Speeches,* Vol. 13 p. 1210.

PART IV

Reservation in a Wider Perspective

This concluding part attempts to examine reservation in the wider current perspective such as new economic reforms viz. liberalization, privatization and globalization and its special impact on caste dominated Indian society and social justice measures like reservation. This part also incorporates political scenario in context with reservation policy, changing political perceptions and priorities, power equations etc. and it's combined impact of implementation of reservation. A reference of affirmative action experimented at other countries in addressing the problems of social and economic inequalities is made to have a juxtapose in Indian relativity. A few alternatives in substituting reservation are also suggested which include land reform measures, entrepreneurial participation etc. Finally, while concluding, the obtaining position on this vital social issue is summarised and efficacy of reservation in attainment of social harmony and establishment of an egalitarian society is discussed.

16

Liberalization, Privatization, Globalization and Reservation

New economic reforms era popularly known as liberalization, privatization and globalization i.e. L.P.G. is a world wide phenomena and most of world countries have participated in it. This reform process has completed its first phase so far. The World Trade Organization (WTO) a voluntary global organization assisting the smoother international trade and commerce took the lead in bringing togather the member countries at the international forum in 1991 which has since then proved an on-going reform catalyst bringing still the entire global economy closer and closer for the mutual benefits.

These new economic reforms i.e. liberalization, privatization and globalization have far reaching implications on Indian economy as well. So far the Indian economy is concerned, the immediate impact was seen in a sudden activation in the economy. Since independence, the country was no doubt progressive, but the progress was much slow than what was desired for a country crossing its population beyond 100 crores. In some sectors the progress was sluggish and in some others, it was still negative also. Inspite of huge investments from the exchequer, the nation was not witnessing a reciprocating outcome till nineties.

India took an impressive entry in the new economic reforms, right from 1991 with a firm determination of its active and whole hearted implementation. And soon thereafter, there was a sea change in the world's perception of looking at us. The result was that the nation which was perceived as a poor people's land with starvation, doldruming economy and rigid and complex license permit culture is now differently seen as a giant market of 100 crore consumers.

Liberalization, privatization and globalization are the world wide phenomena and as such, we had no choice for its option or otherwise. It has twin effects; positive as well as negative. The first post implementation decade of LPG has brought about marked momentum in the country's economy, which none can deny. The nation undoubtedly have been benefited out of it.

Liberalization

Liberalization means, untying government control over the private sector, or to say process of doing away with the much criticized erstwhile license, permit era.

The greatest advantage of the new economic reforms to the most rigid and beurocratic nation like India is liberalization. The country so far never thought of the need for liberalizing the age old laws, rules and regulations which were in force particularly to suit the British regime, culture and the colonial remote control. Rules and regulations framed by the alien rulers to keep the country in a slavery condition has to be modified by an independent democratic nation for suiting its own people, their needs, their aspirations and so on. But this was never done as it should have been. The new economic reforms policy and its monitoring global agency i.e. World Trade Organization (WTO) impressed upon these member countries to give a fresh thinking with utmost priorities to review and drastically liberalize these rules.

Our policies of liberalizing the tight administration norms going in the direction towards abolition of license permit era has been very timely launched. So far norms pertaining to the industrial sector is concerned, we have brought about a revolution in discarding unnecessary licenses, right from SSI registration to continuously doing away with number of procedural steps, inspection formalities and to some extent taxation simplification also. This is a very encouraging step hoping this pace to further accelerate to have fullest possible liberalization in the country.

Simplification of Few Statutes and Procedures

All this liberalization policies have greatly relaxed the industrial entrepreneurs right from small scale to a giant industrial corporate. It was experienced that the industries people particularly the technocrats and those fastly expanding their business horizons were required to have a section of their staff besides expert consultants exclusively for meeting these procedural requirement. They are relieved now from these worries not fully but to a greater extent. Procedures are not only simplified, but also made transparent so that they can be easily understood to those who have to implement it. This has eased their task enabling them to concentrating in productive and profiteering work.

Similarly rigid land laws have also undergone the liberalization process and have acquired revolutionary changes. It being a state subject, quite a few states have liberalized the rules relating to purchase of agricultural land by existing farmers any where which hitherto was restricted within a radius of 8 km. Similarly, there have been drastic reforms in land laws on old/new patterns, special economic zone (SEZ) all with a view to giving an impetus to overall economic development.

All these rapid land law reforms also carry an inherent threat of possibility of eating away of agricultural lands belonging to the backward, tribals etc. by rich farmers. Economic exploitation of backwards by the upper castes landowners is not a new thing in India. Similarly, there is an enthusiastic trend of land allotment to the corporate sector either for industrial purpose such as SEZ etc. or corporate farming. This is likely to hamper the rural economy. We have land spared exclusively for the village cattles' grazing. Will such liberalization of land allotment not harm old established rural economic structure? Will such corporate invasion in the rural economy not imbalance the rural fabric in any harmful way? Or can there be a planning for involving these new entrants with specific role to play in augmenting the rural economic development and the social justice aspect considering that average half the rural population belongs to backward classes comprising of SCs/STs and OBCs.

The Indian people demand that the industrial sector enjoying liberalization benefits must voluntarily shoulder some social responsibility by creating more job opportunities and all along contributing in national goal of social justice and economic equalities.

Liberalization at apex or policy level will reduce the procedural aspects or exemption from certain cumbersome requirements. But the whole idea of this new concept has to percolate down the level. Unless this happens, the real fruits of liberalization will not be seen. This pre-supposes *inter alia* change in the mind set at the government administrative level.

Privatization

Privatization means allowing free entry to private sector industries in all wide spectrums of economic and industrial activities. In other words, a free hand is now given to the private sector for its growth, expansion, diversification etc.

Till nineties, the public sector was operative on a massive scale in providing essential utilities to the people such as electricity, transportation, construction, telecommunication and so on deploying huge public exchequer funds and employing manpower on a large scale. Under the policy of privatization, there has been a gradual shift of all these public sector functioning to private sector. This has led to large scale expansion of privatization and emergence of more and more corporates. This has also created an environment of steep competition among the private sector which benefits the people at large with better quality, and variety of purchase options Those were the days when a consumer had to wait for years to have an automobile two wheeler of his choice which is now readily available at the show room on terms suiting to his requirements.

Implementation of privatization has far reaching impacts on Indian economy and life. It has led to reduction in government role in economic activities. This shall have twin effects. One, on the employment in the government/public sector which naturally will tend to reduce day-by-day. No doubt, this will on the other hand increase employment in the private sector. However, since the private sector will be subject to no statutory laws to implement reservation policy or similar other affirmative action like obligations. Privatization shall have a negative impact on the interests of SC/ST/OBC. All these aspects connected with privatization are elaborated in Part II at Chapter 11 on 'Reservation in Private Sector'.

Can our policy of privatization bestow upon the corporate sector with some social responsibility towards social justice, social securities and Pay Back?

Globalization

Globalization means opening up of international economic boundaries, inviting entries of globally operating multi-national and trans-national corporates and industries in our country and likewise allowing Indian corporates also to freely operate on global market.

Globalization has not by now remained an unknown area in Indian traditions of global trades. It has definitely provided an appreciable momentum to static Indian economy which was very much witnessed steadily accelerating industrial growth and global recognition for the country in new fields like IT, medical tourism and so on. The large population also had the feel of this new world wide phenomena with quality products, improving hygienic conditions, with all their reflection in improved physical life index (PLI) in the country quite at a very upright rate in the recent times.

However, far reaching consequences of the globalization are as under;

There was a sudden spurt in the entry of globally reputed Multi National Corporates (MNCs), which simultaneously among many other good features also invited latest technologies for the benefits of the Indian consumers. Huge private sector operators created an atmosphere of healthy competition which gave variety with options, cost competitiveness and far improving post sale services to the users. The economic growth momentum was also boosted by the vital role played by international financial institutions such as World Bank (IBRD), Asian Development Bank (ADB) etc. with special thrust on the Indian economy.

Thus, globalization is not merely an economic phenomenon. It has multiple manifestations, such as political, social, cultural and religious. These manifestations are ghastly and gruesome. It involves assaults on local, material, regional, consumer habits, materials products and political and cultural practices.[1]

Impact of LPG on Indian Economy

These new economic policies have also brought about certain major other changes at the government functioning level. The new reforms pre-suppose dispensing with government control in so many aspects with a view to providing a free hand to the private sector. The government started simplifying the procedures and paper formalities, reducing the procedural layers etc. All this resulted into lesser manpower requirement at the government sector. Thus, recruitment at the government sector almost came to a halt, which can be seen, from the following statistics.[2]

Table 16.1: Impact of Reforms (LPG) on Job Composition (In lacs)

No. of Employees	*Pre-Reforms (1990/91)*	*Post-Reforms (1999/2000)*	*Change*
Central Govt.	69.72	66.86	- 2.86
State Govts.	97.71	103.71	+ 6.00
Local Self Govts.	23.12	22.55	- 0.57
Sub Total	190.55	193.12	+ 2.57
Private Sector	76.75	86.45	+ 9.70

Source: National Sample Survey Statistical Abstract, 2001.

The above statistics speak for itself. While there is very negligible rise in the employment absorption in the government/Public Sector, employment increase in the private sector is not only substantial but also spectacularly, four times the government/public sector employment.

Employment

Economic momentum in any country has to respond to the general aspirations of the country foremost of which would be employment generation. The above figures clearly reveal that growth in the national economy does commensurate with the desirable employment growth in the country. No doubt, employment in the private sector has sizably increased which still cannot be considered to be satisfactory looking to the need for increasing job aspirants day-by-day.

Anti-cultural Invasions

The LPG has also led to transmogrification of traditional religious and faith system with disintegration of traditional social fabrics and shared norms by the invasion of consumerism, cyber culture, new fangled religion, social fads and changing work ethics and work rhythms. The most concerning effect of the new policy is rise of a new threat on the globe in the form of extremist, fundamentalist and terrorist tendencies in the third world countries which are intended to destabilize and strike at the root of their civilization and multicultural and pluralist nature.

Consumerism

Globalization on the one hand uproots local communities and pushes them into homogenization. On the other hand, it develops alienation and breeds conflicts of identity. Second, it pushes consumerism and competition onto the center stage of the development paradigm. Third, it erodes traditional bonds and generates social insecurity. The country has vast proportion of people living below poverty line. These new imitative tendencies have more negative impact on the family budgetary aspects of the poor.

Impacts of LPG on SC/ST/OBC

Poor and backward community people particularly scheduled castes, scheduled tribes and other backward classes are the worst sufferers of impact of liberalization, privatization and globalization. Impact of LPG on these groups is multi dimensional.

Impact on Reservation

LPG has led to reducing the governmental role in many spheres of economic and administrative activities. This results in dismantling of jobs on the government pay roll where reservation for SC/ST and OBC is implemented as per the laid down norms. Since these jobs in government are reducing day-by-day due to LPG, scope of representation of SC/ST/OBC in the government jobs will get restricted. The Constitution had set a noble goal for the upliftment of these groups by providing reservation in government jobs. Implementation of reservation has brought about a revolutionary result too. But this mission is still half the way. Unless it is completely accomplished, whatever has been achieved through this vigorous process will go futile. The dream of the nation after all is creating a harmonious society free of inequality and discrimination.

Upon independence, a major governmental and public sector initiative in almost all the sphere of the economic activities was launched. This includes setting up of public sector undertakings, various incentives to the private industrial entrepreneurs, agricultural subsidies and so on. So far, welfare of the scheduled castes, scheduled tribes and other backward castes was concerned, all these policies of major government initiatives opened up job openings on a wide scale in the government departments and public sector undertakings. With introduction of the reservation policy, educated scheduled castes, scheduled tribes and other backward castes youth got large scale opportunity for government jobs because of this. It is a different part of the story that education level in these reserved categories was so low almost to a negligible level that though the statutory provisions of reservation opened up immense opportunities for them, they could not avail it for want of even bare minimum educational requirement. However, inspite of that, the policy of major government initiative was in the best interest of the scheduled castes, scheduled tribes and other backward classes people.

Now with new economic reforms in the name of liberalization, privatization and globalization, there was 'U' turn in the economic policy of the country. Under the new economic reforms, government started gradual withdrawal of its stake holding from public sectors through disinvestments. The initial experiment with its success was further extended to privatization of management of certain essential services such as electricity, telephone communication etc. which were hitherto managed by the governments wherein good number of employees belonging to the scheduled castes, scheduled tribes and other backward classes people got the jobs under the umbrella of reservation provisions. These departments have been converted into private companies under statutes and are also expected to compete with other private operators. Though, the laid down statutory reservation provisions continue in these converted companies as far as interests of the scheduled castes, scheduled tribes and other backward classes people are concerned, it is likely to be adversely affected in future. Now with emergence of steep competition in this sector, pace of development of the government companies will be limited which will restrict the entry of new job aspirants of these categories.

In short, business growth now onwards will not result into corresponding employment growth in the government owned corporates/establishments, where the reservation norms are applicable in view of steep competition, retrenchments, disinvestments, outsourcing, automation etc. This is going to be the biggest loss to the SC/ST/OBC being the potential losers of the jobs.

With introduction of privatization policy, certain public sector industries are closed either under the plea of efficiency or sold as a strategy of disinvestments. The manpower in the public sector which have so far employed substantial people from amongst the reserved categories are gradually losing their jobs through the process of retrenchments or voluntary retirements.

Similarly, privatization policy implemented on the education front has opened a flood gate of private self finance educational institutions. Though, reservation is extended to these institutions after a long legal struggle and then in the parliament, its implementation has posed number of issues operating against the interests of the SC/ST/OBC. Reduction in number of government run and aided educational institutions will narrow down the scope of providing educational opportunities to these communities. It is perhaps education only which has brought these people to their present better condition, which if jeopardized will put these poor people nowhere. Unaffordable fee structure beyond the reach of most of the poor SC/ST/OBC in these unaided educational institutions is also a new curse complimented by LPG.

Equally worst sufferers of LPG are traditional scheduled tribe people. Increasing over exploitation of unprocessed raw materials from forests particularly in the tribal dominating states like orissa has posed a great threat to the subsistence and survival of these poor people. Similarly entry of more and more multinational corporates in the interior parts of the tribal areas have caused involuntary and forced displacements of these communities from their dwellings.

Contract Labour System; A New Form of Exploitation of SC/ST/OBC

Simultaneously, all along with this hurricane of LPG, there has also started a process of reviewing the existing decades old labour and industrial laws of the country. Review of any outdated law is always desirable so as to ensure their objectivity, suitability and simultaneously enforceability in to day' context. New economic reforms should also realign in such a way that it contributes in the social obligation of uplifting downtroddens through the proposed revision/review in labour and industrial laws which should be devised in such a way so as to check possible exploitations under the contract labour system and more importantly considering apportionments of such labour contracts in a way that its positive features go straight for the benefit of the backward classes.

A new contract system has taken shape relieving industrial houses from maintaining their own employed labour force. This contract system though not quite a new in our country, is the other opposite end of the statutorily protected; rather over protected employment system. This system is very much exploitative for unorganized and unskilled labour type work where the major chunk of the manpower comes from the lower backward castes. The country had total labour work force of 39.9 crores of all types i.e. skilled, semi-skilled and unskilled in the year 1999/2000 of which 37.1 crores or say almost 93% is in the unorganized sector. It is the moral responsibility of the state to safeguard the interests of these highly vulnerable section of the society.

Agriculture Sector

LPG basically aims at accelerating large scale economy and big size business and industrial activities. As is seen, ours is an agrarian economy providing to three quarter of this country's vast population half of whom are SC/ST/OBC. **LPG policies are not farm pro-active and rural friendly.**

Nicholas B. Dirks, Vice President of Arts and Science of Columbia University, New York during his recent visit to India said, "The extent with which these kinds of prejudices survives from place to place, it is obvious to anybody looking at contemporary politics of India that no amount of liberalization is going to change the situation. Even affirmative action does not seem to be changing anything. He further added, " I also think that when you have such massive growth in the economy, that's what people are focusing on. We all know that the agriculture sector is not growing; we all know that the urban population still depends on cheap labour and **that the social**

relations of caste are embedded in even the global success of the economy in India".[3]

No Place for Affirmative Action

LPG after all means more business, more velocity of money and so on. Centre point of LPG is profitability by all means. Social justice measures such as affirmative action etc. on voluntary basis has hardly any place in it, unless statutorily made obligatory.

D. Parthsarthi states, "While economic liberalization may 'open up' the economy, it does not necessarily open new opportunities for economic and social mobility for those in need of affirmative action, for those who have been and are discriminated against on the basis of caste, religion or gender. Given the attitudes of those in the private sector towards *dalits* and other backward classes, the limited gains due to **affirmative action policies may receive a set back in the absence of policy measure for greater inclusion**, so that more sections may gain from processes of the new economic changes."[4]

Indian economy in post economic reforms era is sailing on two extreme ends. On one hand, it has started campaigning towards becoming the world economic power with success on all fronts of the progressive parameters. And on the other hand, it carried with it all along black shadows of lacs of scavengers still lifting on their head and hands the human excreta. Can this new economic era with all user friendly global technologies do something in the direction towards removing this shameful dot on the Indian social system and of course the mankind at large?

The globe has perceived this country as the biggest consumer market for their products. Can the winds of globalization within the country bring with them something special for the scheduled castes, scheduled tribes and the other backward classes? It should not necessarily be through implementation of Indian reservation provisions, but can the welfare measures for these poor SC/ST/OBC people re-invented in line with affirmative action, which has been so successful in the developed country like USA.

REFERENCES

1. P. Radhakrishnan, *Religion, Caste and State,* p. 109.
2. National Sample Survey Statistical Abstract 2001.
3. Nicholas B. Dirks, *The Hindu,* dated 15 Jan. 2007.
4. D. Parthsarthi, *Advocacy Internet,* Nov/Dec. 2005.

17

Affirmative Action and Reservation

Social discrimination is a world wide phenomenon in different forms like racial, caste-based, domicile based and so on. Problem of social inequalities is faced by most of the global countries in a varying degree of its gravity. The nomenclature, basis of discrimination and extent of such inequalities may differ from country to country. It is estimated that one out of every twenty five persons on the globe suffers from caste discrimination based on the kind of work they do and their family origins. It comes to around 250/300 million people globally and 179 million in India alone are the victims of social oppressions. Major countries having this problem include, Yemen, Kenya, Nigeria, Somalia, Pakistan, Sri Lanka, Nepal, Bangladesh, Ethiopia, Senegal and Japan. It is pertinent to note that most of the countries are having social inequality problem though the principle religion in these countries is not Hindu, the home of the origin of caste system.

Democracies all over the world have always responded to address this problem either by enacting legislations or incorporating equality clauses in their constitutions. More and more voluntary organizations such as 'World Social Forum' and many others are also coming forward to fight for this cause.

Issue of racial discrimination in USA is well known through out the world. The whole nation vowed during the later half of this century with strong and firm determination for coming out of this national shame. The United States' federal government launched number of measures known as "**Affirmative Action**" which became popular later on as '**Minority Diversity Programme**'.

Concept of affirmative action was introduced for the first time in 1961 by the then President John F. Kennedy. Minority in USA is not religiously connected, unlike the same connoted in secularism philosophy of the modern political Science. Sect and communities under the American minority concept include Negroes, Hispanics and other similar class of people belonging to the neighbouring continents. The US Government defines minority for this purpose as the "**Sufferers of inequality**". Proportion-wise, they constitute 27 per cent of total American population.

Affirmative action in USA, unlike in Indian reservation system is not backed by constitutional sanction or Supreme Court ruling. The affirmative action policy is largely an executive document that expresses a normative concern for enhancing representation and on occasion even promises rewards to those organizations that demonstrate a fair sprinkling of colours in their ranks. In other words, there is no such thing as quota for blacks or hispanic Americans in the affirmative action policy in America.

Though diverse methods and means were used while tackling the issues of discrimination and inequality by corrective laws since last two centuries in America, the same were launched on a firm footing from the year 1864, with 13th and 14th constitutional amendment prohibiting slavery and providing equal protection under law to all United States citizens. Affirmative action got momentum with enactment of the Civil Rights Act, 1964 that provided a comprehensive legislative under the law to protect and enforce against discrimination. The Act also created '**Equal Employment Opportunity Commission**' as an administrative agency to administer and enforce the statues.

The rules under the affirmative action include *inter alia* 5 per cent of defence procurements to be made from the suppliers belonging to the minority through entering into contracts, sub-contracts etc. as may be the case. The minority contractors who are awarded with such contracts are in turn expected to report utilization for all groups that make up the protected class of minorities. US Public Works Employment

Act requires 10 per cent of each federal construction grant to be awarded to minority businesses; Another US statute i.e. The Rail Board Revitalization and Regulatory Reforms Act requires that recipients of financial grants and their sub-contractors establish a goal of 15 per cent of purchases to be awarded to minority businesses; Providing technical and management assistance to disadvantaged businesses; co-ordinating activities among all federal departments to aid in increasing minority business development etc; The US government having felt the need for effective implementation of all these provisions, introduced criminal penalties in 1985 against those companies which injure minority diversity programme.

Mechanism of Affirmative Action

The most interesting part of the American affirmative action is its mechanization of implementation, which is narrated hereunder.

1. Affirmative action has not relaxed the basic quality norms for any job or contract. In other words, quality norms have to be complied by the minority reserved categories also. It is interesting to know how does it operate in USA. A target lot is taken up from the minorities first of all. While deciding the lot, there will be no discrimination on the grounds of race or creed. The authorities while taking such lot, will ensure that admitting such students, the quality of the campus life would not be affected in any way. In other words, the university and college officials shall keep in mind, the well being of the institutions to which they belong when deciding on admissions. Those given admissions have a reasonable chance of pursuing successful careers afterwards. And a comprehensive arrangement of pre-recruitment training of the so taken candidates is made.
2. A subsequent package for imparting skill upgradation to them is also carefully chalked out and then put to implementation on an on-going basis during the training phase and an in-house attempt for total

development of the target lot is made so as to prepare them as per job specifications and skill requirements thoroughly during initial pre recruitment process.

3. All this is done quite honestly and whole-heartedly. The industries have admirably witnessed a miraculous positive result also. The whole implementation has been found so successful to produce thousands of minority aspirants to meet with varied and diverse industries' expectations. Even the world best multi-national corporates have no cause of complaints regarding level of efficiency of these minority candidates prepared under the diversity programme. This would not have been perhaps possible but for the strong and honest determination of the industries for the upliftment of those lagging behind in the race of socio economic development.

Implmentation by American Private Sector

Realising this national call, the American corporate sector responded to it overwhelmingly as can be seen from the performance with regard to implementation of affirmative action by the American private sector.

Exxzone Mobiles

This is the world's No. 1 multi-national company operating in the mobile communication sector. The company is having total manpower of 21,547 of which it has recruited 16.09 per cent in top managerial cadre and 18.08 per cent in other middle administrative level belonging to the minorities. Besides, providing the employment, the company also purchased goods worth US $ 20 crores from the minorities.

Wall Mart

Wall Mart is the world renowned 2nd biggest Multi-national corporate having world wide chain of departmental stores. The company has employed 2.27 lacs persons from minorities out of total 9.78 lacs employees which comes to 23.21 per cent of total manpower.

General Motors

General Motors hardly need any introduction. Size-wise, it is the 3rd biggest Company among the world largest 500 private corporate giants. This Multinational Company has employed 320 Dealers from the minorities. Besides, it purchased goods worth US $250 crores from vendors belonging to minorities.

Twenty three per cent of total manpower at General Motors constitute of minorities out of which 19.2 per cent are in managerial cadre, 17.6 per cent on technical side and 16.3 per cent in marketing.

Ford

Ford is equally such world class automobile giant the 4th biggest multi-national automobile company. The company has total job enrolment of 3,45,991 people of which 18 per cent are represented by the minorities.

And like that there numerous companies of varied operational scale and cross national spread have implemented affirmative action in the right earnest. Merit and employability etc. have never become a hindrance or threat in their maintaining world class name in spite of adapting this social cause.

Affirmative Action as Responded by US Media

Affirmative action does not take care of employment front only, but it also aims at due representation of minorities in the print as well as electronic media.

It transpired in the year of 1975 that representation of the minority communities was as low as 3.95 per cent in media sector. This was soon corrected by initiating special drive through recruitment fairs, training workshops for the non-whites, which wonderfully improved the situation. Within a short span of one year, it was found that representation of minorities shoot up to the extent of 17.1 per cent in Wall Street Journal, USA Today 18.7 per cent, New York Times 16.2 per cent. And so on. Press photographers in US represent 16 per cent belonging to such minorities. 950 out of 1,446 American dailies have accepted the resolution of the American Society of Newspapers for giving due representation to the minorities.

Similarly, four biggest TV Companies viz. FOX, NBC, ABC and CBS entered into an agreement known as "**Diversity Agreement**" undertaking the representation of the minorities in various electronic media related roles such as authors, actors etc. and giving reasonable time slot to these minorities even in the TV programmes.

American Affirmative Action and Indian Reservation; A Juxtapose

Both United States of America and India were facing a common problem of discrimination by a section of their own nationals over another. However, nature of discrimination prevailing in both these countries was different. USA was confronted with racial discrimination, which was existing there for over three hundred years. The Indian problem was caste discrimination, which was as old as over two thousand years.

Affirmative action implemented in U.S.A. is voluntarily righting the historical wrongs of slavery. While reservation in Indian context was a statutory requirement under Indian Constitution without any option.

The reservation in India emerged out of a challenge to national sovereignty claims. It predates affirmative action by several decades, embodies altogether different political proposals and represents the interests of a demographic majority.

As regards, American affirmative action, a number of historical circumstances made it possible for white Americans to constitute themselves into a nation of equals excluding the African American slaves and the native Americans in the first instance. As the U.S. Model evolved beyond its 18th century origin, it subsequently and quite belatedly took the note of these groups through affirmative action and other measures. The political initiative of emancipation came first and was only much later followed by affirmative action in 1960s and 1970s.

On the other hand, when India was binding itself to a constitution and parliamentary democracy in the mid 20th century, blatant exclusion such as in the original U.S. model could not be made without risking its very legitimacy. The reservation was a constitutive necessity for the Indian Republic. While the success or failure of the American affirmative action can and has to be evaluated statistically, the same cannot be said for Indian reservation system, whose function is primarily political constitute and social symbolic. American affirmative action is meant for numerical minority, whereas in India the section contending for the reservation is a numerical majority.

Affirmative Action and Formal Equality

As stated by D. Parthsarthi in his Article on *'Towards a Larger Perspective"* affirmative action programmes act to deliver substantive rather than formal equality. The push towards substantive equality requires that law and administration serve the equalization of economic and social opportunities. It requires a rejection of rational system that merely works towards enhancing efficiency. Merely providing for formal equality of status may result in missed opportunities for those who lack for historical and current reasons of bias and discrimination abilities as arbitrarily decided by the market and dominant social forces to compete with others from more privileged backgrounds. Constitutional provisions and judicial pronouncements in India have precisely relied upon the principle of substantive justice or equality as legal basis for upholding reservation policies. In the era of privatization and liberalization, it is all the more important that we do not lose sight of this very important democratic principle[1].

The Malaysian Experience of Reservation

One of the most successful experiments on reservation is found in Asian country Malaysia. Malaysia too was a developing economy in fifties/sixties like India facing lot of odds and adversities on the economic front one of which was external economic aggression from China. The idea of implementing reservation quota in Malaysia was basically designed to dismantle Chinese monopoly. They launched a reservation policy especially for '**Bhumiputras**' i.e. sons of the soil, the local origins of Malaysia. The reservation policy comprised of:

- reservation in educational institutions.
- preferential awarding of contracts to Bhumiputras, the original Malayasian inhabitants and the target beneficiaries under the reservation experiment.
- fixation of job quota for these communities in the private sector.
- thirty per cent of newly listed companies to be registered for and owned by the Bhumiputras.

As can be seen from the above, Malaysian reservation policy has multiplicity of affords. One; Job assurance in government as well as private sector, entrepreneurial priorities, corporate ownerships and so on.

The experiment has brought wonderful results. The Malaysian origin Bhumiputras who were more or less at par with oppressed Indians in seventies got a big fillip with sharing in the economic development of the nation. Their ownership in the corporate sector which was just meagre 2.3 per cent in 1970 shot up to as high as 23 per cent in the year 2000. This community development got reflected in the overall economic growth of the nation as well recording impressive overall national economic growth of 6 per cent to 7 per cent. Another noteworthy feature of this experiment is that the country did not face any anti Chinese internal civic disturbances, unlike that happened in the south Asian countries including India against affirmative action like reservation etc.

All along this, the country also concentrated on major reforms in the educational system of the country. They also had like us education system suiting to the need of an alien British emperorship. Malaysia brought about drastic changes in their entire education system keeping their country's requirements in mind and with that an objective of making it to suit local and national needs which also augments fostering economic development. They now started indigenously preparing their own graduates from Malaysian institutions as per the specific need of Malaysian economy and society.

The Malaysian reservation policy has two other noteworthy features viz; high-tech sector, foreign firms and globally competitive industries were exempt from the reservation experiment and regulatory provisions were kept quite flexible so that wherever it was absolutely necessary in enforcing any specific requirement that should not pose any adverse consequences in overall economic development of the nation.

REFERENCE

1. D. Parthsarthi in his Article on *'Towards a Larger Perspective"*.

18

Politics of Reservation

The nation after independence was wedded to the democratic system of governance. Under the democratic system people of the country have a place at the top above legislature, executive and judiciary, three functional organs of the pyramid structure of the democracy. People in Democracy were to choose by a voting franchise as to whom to hand over the rein of the governance. Such elected representatives upon completion of their electoral tenure or under any other circumstances have to go back to the people for obtaining a fresh mandate every time for the next term. So far, the question of reservation policy relates, the priorities and sensibilities of so elected legislatures shall have an effect on nurturing and implementation of reservations. This will correspondingly percolate to executive wing which is again not only headed by the People's elected governing body, but also influence in monitoring of such social justice measure like reservation policy.

Thus, role of political bosses become very important in enacting meaningful provisions regarding reservation and its effective implementation, monitoring and grievance redressal. All these call for a strong political will and firm determination of the ruling politicians for establishment of an egalitarian society through the constitutional support like reservation. This again requires sensible awareness of these peoples' representatives about the prevailing social conditions, need for the reservation in the present social context and their own readiness to counter all the protests and odds with a positive mindness and a common consensus. Political leadership during the fifties i.e. at the time of launching of the reservation policy in the country was fully aware of this scenario. The then political generation who themselves were so patriotic, selfless had realized the plight of the slavery days. They had high esteem for the hard earned independence which could be strengthened only by according a top most priority to the cause of social equalities and need for uplifting the downtroddens in absence of which mere political freedom will have no value at all. The people also responded to this cause with all sympathy and a feeling of endurance for establishing social and thereby economic freedom in the country.

Socio-political Position Seventies Afterwards

All this went well till seventies with synergic effects of positive efforts of the political operators and whole hearted co-operation from the people as well. Followed thereafter was a new era of second-generation politicians. With passage of time, value based Gandhian political generation started disappearing from the Indian public life and cognizable political scenario. Political power winning concepts like removal of poverty etc. became redundant. Keeping this new situation in mind, novel ideas, which are helpful in attaining political power, were being either thought of or experimented. And in this process, reservation started becoming a popular vote-pulling tool. There were also other major shifts in Indian public life with symptomic changes started being seen right from sixties. The political ideology gradually started being shifted to the caste considerations with focus on consolidation of voters in communal or caste denominations more particularly from the 1967 electioneering. In seventies, the caste considerations got further and further strengthened because of the deliberate efforts by the shortsighted politicians and their political organizations. The caste based and other sorts of political compartalisation knew no boundaries of reasonableness and disastrous impact of their political games on the social integration process. All the political decisions started being centered now on political gain i.e potential vote profiteering out of it. The citizen was rather being gradually forgotten as a centrally focused point of all developmental process, but now regarded as a subject of polling point.

Nineties brought further sea change in the Indian democracy and polity. Hitherto, the power was mainly dominated by single political party regime barring a small fraction of about 30 months during 1977/80. But now is found a multi party alliance at center and regional party rule at the state level. All this gave rise to new power equations in Indian political scenario.

Emerging Backward Class Politics

Parliamentary democracy with adult franchise has changed the *locus standi* of the backward castes in politics. Backward classes were now emerging out as a center point of political power because of their numerical strength. They started understanding importance of their votes. The political aspirants also saw in these groups of communities a ladder leading to the ultimate political power. In electoral politics, group/ collective action prevails over an individual.

The Parliament and the state assemblies had enacted and modified wherever needed, number of social justice and welfare related laws for the well beings of the poor and backward castes of the country. Such social welfare laws include land reforms, bondage labour abolition act, Minimum Wages Act and hundreds of similar other laws. All these laws aim at social justice. These laws in their applicability are such that its enforcement naturally leads to displeasing a section of the society that have no doubt illegally or immorally enjoyed the accruing benefits at the cost of its real beneficiaries. A politically headed government in the present caste dominated electoral structure avoids enforcement of such laws honestly and in its true spirit. There will be an avoidance tendency in the enforcement of such laws. Individual cases of such unjust partiality on the part of the political bosses appear in large number in the day-to-day newspapers. In short, we have enough of laws aiming at social justice in the country. What is needed is now a strict, impartial and honest enforcement of these laws.

Reservation Centered Politics

Reservation has been a surrogate for caste politics and is being skillfully manipulated by the political parties. Since explicit caste based communication is forbidden by the Constitution, reservations have become a via media to influence castes. The social justice pedigree of reservations gives this communication a progressive veneer.

The sway of caste identities in influencing voter groups has intensified with the collapse of the hegemony of the national political parties and the emergence of regional parties and the rise of coalition politics. Reservation centered politics is played along three dimensions: One; Demanding reservation for certain social groups e.g. *Dalit* Christians, Backward Muslims etc. Two; Backing demands by certain castes to get included in the reserved categories, and Third; Inciting demands for a split in the quota by certain sub-castes in a conglomerate reserved category e.g. Madigas in Andhra Pradesh. All these invariably create inter-caste conflicts, which are manipulated by the parties to their advantage. Relevance of this politics can be seen from recently erupted Gurjars' agitations in Rajasthan.

After the basic schedules for the SCs and STs were prepared in 1936, there have been many subsequent inclusions of caste groups within them. Meenas who constitute 10 per cent of state population were included in the ST schedule in 1954 and are virtually monopolizing the ST reservation. Gurjars constitute 7.5 per cent population and have now emerged as an important political presence. Their demand for ST status was articulated in 1981 during the then Congress rule. During 2003 elections, Bharatiya Janata Party (BJP) upheld this demand by promising ST status to Gurjars. When the BJP led state government failed to do anything about fulfilling its promise over the past three and half years, the other political party i.e. Congress grabbed the opportunity to fan the Gurjar anger. Now when the Gurjar agitation has provoked the other party i.e.

Meenas, both these political parties viz. ruling BJP and opposition Congress have been vacillating in their stand. Other small political parties have also voiced their support for the Gurjars.

This is how reservation is used as a weapon for political gains.

Political Role in Implementation of Reservation Policy

Role of responsible and sensible political masters is very important in democratic system of governance more particularly in implementing and monitoring reservation related statutes and rules. The political environment is characterized by lack of sincerity and even outright indifference in the matters of scheduled castes and scheduled tribes. The issues of action plan for development of SC/ST/OBC, caste discrimination and atrocities have not been significantly figuring in the manifestos of major political parties except some headlines therein without any clarity, focus, emphasize or concentration of action proposed. Perhaps political community do not find SC/ST cause as an attractive slogan of political mobilization either at the time of election or subsequently. The issues of SC/ST do not form a sizeable part of the questions asked in central and state legislatures and discussions/debates therein. Of course, when major incidents of atrocities against scheduled castes or scheduled tribes take place, voices are raised in the parliament or assemblies and outside largely to embarrass the government and at times to extract a commitment for specific measures to be taken to prevent such occurrences. But expression of concern for scheduled castes and scheduled tribes on such occasions remains short-lived.

There are various other reasons for poor political attention to the cause of scheduled castes and scheduled tribes. It is found that larger political process remains preoccupied with other political problems. Major political parties have very inadequate representation of scheduled castes and scheduled tribes in important decision-making positions. Even the representation of scheduled castes and scheduled tribes in politically held government positions in pursuance of constitutional requirements and various bodies and political formations is more a symbolic rather than real empowering to the political process and cannot use it for any effective advocacy of their agenda.

Reservation Perceived as a Negative Discrimination Against Upper Castes

But then started some murmuring against the reservation particularly from beginning of the eighties. There were several reasons for opposition to reservation. With good priorities given to the education through out in the country, the new generation of youth came out with aspirations of making good career in the field like medical, technology, where in seats were available in limited numbers. This created an atmosphere of steeper and steeper competition for admission in such courses. Naturally, this raised up admission percentage in such courses so high. Students who are otherwise with very good percentage had occasions to miss their admissions just for few marks ahead. As against this, students under the reserved category could get such admissions with lower percentage than their counter parts. This was the beginning point of dissatisfaction amongst youth who were not at all aware of the chronic social situation of past discrimination, hatred and untouchability and hence the need for such reservation. While on the other hand, the simultaneous expectations of social integration and realization by the upper castes about the age old plight of their own counter parts brethren could not percolate in a way it should have been. Had this taken place in the Hindu society, on an on-going basis, the dire need for the reservation and the possible sacrifice to some extent by a fraction of the society could have been accepted in the people. Instead of that, started being seen the negative role of politics of reservation. The issue was tossed politically exciting the people against the reservation boomeranging against the ruling political power at that time.

The eighties also started witnessing of situation of unemployment and arising there from general unrest against the governance. Soon after, independence, the nation started with massive economic plannings. Public sector undertakings and so on. All this provided huge employment avenues to the youth during first thirty years. But since then, while on one hand manpower requirement started diminishing and on the other hand, growing population and education created more demand for the employment. So youth in an increasing number was found unemployed. As against this, people under the reserved categories were getting jobs because of the operation of provisions of reservation. This naturally created a sort of dissatisfaction amongst the youth who as stated earlier was not at all aware, if somewhat aware, then, was not ready to accept it as to why the reservation has to be provided for.

Electoral Casteism

The nation adopted the democratic system of governance after independence with one person having value of one vote. Political party or alliance with majority will rule for the given tenure under this system.

The selection criteria of candidate by the political parties during the fifties was party loyalty, party work etc. Element of staunch patriotism in those new post-independence days had its positive impact in the electoral politics on both the sides i.e. Voting citizens as well as the electorate aspirants. This was seen in the notable presence of stalwarts in the first and the second seating parliament. One cannot think perhaps of the prospects of their being elected in the present day political deteriorations.

All political considerations then started being centered around or based on caste consideration starting right from selection of a candidate in the election. If a particular constituency is having majority of a particular caste, then the candidate has to be from that caste only in utter ignorance of his merit, or utility or education and so on. The only consideration is caste, caste and caste. The voters also responded to these political calculations accordingly as well. They have also now a tendency to vote their own caste fellow irrespective whether he is fit or competent for the job involved.

This does not end even here too. Going further, caste became dominating factor in every respect in the political terrain. It has not stopped at the main caste; sub-division of Indian castes into number of sub-castes and so on will actively operate here too. Numerical strength of a particular sub-caste or still further a sub-sub-caste will bring political position in their fold.

Caste consideration does not remain restricted to electoral decisions only. Political organizations are commonly taking caste equations, combinations, and representations into consideration. Caste dominates in political organizational hierarchy right from top to bottom. Surprisingly, top most position has invariably to go by all probabilities to the caste having highest numerical strength. This does not stop here. Following, the first position, the next one shall be claimed by another dominating caste or sub-caste numerically. Similarly, all other positions have also to be shared on the basis of majority/minority, territorially north or south etc. Going still further, the political parties have now formed separate cells such as scheduled castes, scheduled tribes, OBCs, Minorities, Linguistics, Some ambitious political organizations have gone still further with formation of particular caste-wise Cells such as Thakors, Maldharis, etc. The quarrels of occupying various organizational position sharing goes on for months together.

Where will all this lead to? All our empirical studies are carried out on the plea that education in the country is going up by leaps and bounds. Therefore, it has presumably narrowed the caste barriers, caste stigma and so on. Position above reveals the picture other way round. The caste consciousness is getting stronger and stronger. All the efforts in the direction of social integration and social harmony are reversed by this new political characterization.

Casteism politics and shortsightedness are the inharent and inevitable present day characteristics of the entire political community in the modern democratic system that we have accepted upon independence unanimously. Our democracy in spite of all this, has withstood amidst all adversities and is undoubtedly now recognized as the strongest democracy on the earth. Politicians are the very byproducts of this system. If this political community could not come up to the nation's expectations, it is altogether a separate matter of self-introspection rather than simply blaming the democratic system as solely responsible for all evils including the negative counter effects of reservation system.

Politics of OBC Reservation

The Government of India appointed the first backward classes commission in 1953. The commission submitted its report in 1955 identifying 2399 castes as socially and educationally backward. Majority of the members recommended reservation for the OBC among other things in government jobs and educational institutions. The government did not accept the recommendations on the ground that the commission had not applied any objective tests for identifying backward classes. However, by the early 1960s, it was difficult for the ruling Congress Party to ignore the clouts of some of the backward castes in north and south India. The socialist party in Hindi speaking belt mobilized OBCs. In 1967, the monopoly of the Congress which was ruling the country since independence uninterruptedly was challenged and the party lost power in several north Indian states. This was also the time when the naxalite movement was at its height and the land grab movement had mobilized the backward castes against exploitation.

The Congress Party split in 1969 into Congress (I) and the Congress (O), the former led by Indira Gandhi being more radical than the later. It evolved a strategy to win over the OBCs. The Congress in its manifesto of 1971 declared its pledge to promote with special care the educational, employment and economic interests of the weaker sections.

At the state level, in the early 1970s, several state governments appointed social and economically backward class commission (SEBC) to assess the conditions of the various groups and report as to which sections of the society should be treated as OBCs. These commissions were also asked to recommend what special treatment and/or concessions similar to those enjoyed by SC/ST should be granted to the OBCs.

At the National level, the second backward class Commission under the chairmanship of B.P. Mandal was appointed by the Janata Party Government in 1978. However, the Janata Party Government lost its power before the Commission could complete its report. The Commission in December 1980 submitted the report. It was placed before the parliament after lot of protests and fasts by the backward class members of parliament. There was no action to the report for almost a decade. Then was the regime of National Front Government. This government was facing lot of problems from beginning itself such as Punjab and Kashmir violences, Ram Janmabhumi issues, price rise etc. Here comes the politics of OBC reservation.

The National Front Government Prime Minister V.P. Singh once a critic of Mandal Commission Report announced on 7th August 1990 that his Government has decided to implement the first phase of the Commission's recommendations i.e. providing 27 per cent for reservation in jobs for socially and economically backward classes in all central government departments, offices, undertakings including banks and other nationalized financial institutions. Surprisingly educational institutions were kept outside the purview of this reservation in view of the anti reservation agitation in the educational institutions.

The OBC reservation had constantly remained under one controversy or the other. Upon resistance from beginning itself, services related to science, technology, space and atomic energy were exempted from operation of the reservation. Later on, military services were exempted. Further, the central government made the option of acceptance of Mandal Commission recommendations at the discretion of the respective state. If the list of OBC castes enumerated under the Mandal Commission and the state's own OBC list differs, the state list would prevail. Then was the addition of economic criteria, which rests with the recent application of reservation in educational institutions like IITs and IIMs.

Tamil Nadu Politics of Reservation

Tamil Nadu is a typical illustration to understand the politics of reservation in our country.[1]

Tamil Nadu was the first state in the country to introduce reservation in the year 1921. At present also it is a state with highest reservation of 69 per cent far in excess of what is stipulated by the Indian Supreme Court. It is also a unique state in reservation provision with highest modifications/ revisions etc. in its state reservation policy. The chronology of these game chased from one end to another is as under.

1921 Anti-brahmin movement spearheaded by Justice Party, communal reservation introduced for the backward classes with 16 per cent of the total seats.

1951 16 per cent reservation for SC/ST and 25 per cent reservation to other backward castes (OBC)

1971 Santhanam Commission recommended introduction of Creamy layer and altering reservation per cent for other backward classes to 16 per cent and separate reservation of 17 per cent to Most backward classes (MBC)

The ruling DMK government increased OBC reservation to 31 per cent and SC/ST reservation revised to 18 per cent making total reservation provision to 49 per cent.

1980 ADMK government introduced the concept of Creamy layer in the OBC reservation against the protests from the opposition.

The Creamy layer concept was subsequently withdrawn with simultaneous increase in OBC reservation to 50 per cent. Total reservation stood at 68 per cent.

1989 Statewide Vaniar Sangh launched roadblock agitations and demanding 20 per cent reservation in the State Government and 2 per cent reservation in central government exclusively for Vaniar caste.

DMK split OBC reservation with 30 per cent for OBCs and 20 per cent for MBCs. Separate reservation of

1 per cent was introduced for the scheduled tribes. Total reservation now stood at 69 per cent.

1992 Supreme Court put 50 per cent cap in Mandal judgment and Creamy layer to be excluded from the reservation entitlement.

1994 The Supreme Court instructed Tamil Nadu to follow 50 per cent cap in reservation in the case filed by K.M. Vijayan.

1994 69 per cent reservation since exceeding Supreme Court 50 per cent verdict, put under 9th Schedule.

Caste cum reservation profile of Tamil Nadu is as under[2].

Table 18.1: Reservation Profile of Tamil Nadu

Category	*% of Total Population*	*% of Reservation*
Backward classes (OBC)	46.14	30
Most backward castes	17.43	20
Denotified Communities	3.44	
Scheduled castes	19.00	18
Scheduled tribes	1.04	1
Upper castes	12.95	31
Total	**100**	**100**

Source: 10th Five-Year Plan 2002/2007, Vol. II. Sectoral Policies and Programmes, Planning Commission, Government of India.

As per Advocacy Internet November/December 2005 published by National Center for Advocacy Studies, Pune. "The experience of reservation as above has been very positive and that is why there is wide spread support for it in the state. The government healthcare system in Tamil Nadu is better than most of the states and one reason has been the quality doctors that the system produces, a factor attributed to reservations. Many of them also opt to serve in rural areas. Not surprisingly the Tamil Nadu chapter of Indian Medical Association supports reservation quota.

Now comes the political battle. 69 per cent reservation in the state was clearly defeating the Supreme Court verdict in

Indra Sahney case that aggregate reservation should not exceed 50 per cent to which Central Government already started implementation wide its OM dated 29 August 1997. This naturally rendered the Tamil Nadu reservation of 69 per cent void before the law. In a special session of Tamil Nadu Legislative Assembly held on 9 November 1993, it had been unanimously resolved to call upon the Central Government to take steps immediately to bring a suitable amendment to the Constitution of India so as to enable the State Government of Tamil Nadu to continue its policy of 69 per cent reservation in government services and for admission in educational institutions as at present. An all political party meeting had also been held on 26 November 1993 in Tamil Nadu urging that there should not be any doubt or delay in ensuring the continued implementation of 69 per cent reservation for the welfare and advancement of the backward classes. All political parties keeping their political differences aside unanimously resolved continuance of existing reservation of 69 per cent in the state.

Tamil Nadu Government enacted a legislation, namely Tamil Nadu backward classes, scheduled castes and scheduled tribes (Reservation of seats in educational institutions and appointments or posts in the services under the State) Bill, 1993 and forwarded it to the Government of India for consideration of the President of India in terms of Article 31C of the Constitution.

In view of the importance and sensitive nature of the matter, the Union Home Minister convened a meeting of all the leaders of all political parties on 13 July, 1994 to discuss the provisions of the Bill. The general consensus among the leaders was that the Bill should be assented to. Accordingly, the president gave his assent to the Bill on 19th July 1994.

Tamil Nadu Government accordingly notified the Tamil Nadu backward classes, scheduled castes and scheduled tribes (Reservation of seats in educational institutions and of appointments or posts in the services under the state) Act, on 19th July, 1994.

The matter did not rest even at this juncture also. The Tamil Nadu politicians in their strong quest to put this matter free from all future vulnerability of reservation being tossed here and there found out the safest place for it. Tamil Nadu Government now requested the Government of India on 22nd July 1994 that the aforementioned Tamil Nadu Act 1994 be included in the 9th Schedule to the Constitution of India for the reason that; the said act relies on the directive principles of state policy enshrined in Part IV of the Constitution. Therefore, once it is brought under 9th Schedule, it cannot be challenged as violative of any of the fundamental rights contained in Part III of the Constitution. Accordingly, Indian Parliament acceded to The Tamil Nadu Assembly's unanimous resolution requesting Tamil Nadu Reservation Act for being put in the 9th Schedule by passing 76th constitutional amendment in 1994.

If one looks at the chain of events leading finally to putting this most controversial act in the safest shelter of 9th Schedule, a strong political will cannot remain hidden. 1992 *Indra Sahney* Court judgment restricting reservation maximum upto 50 per cent; Tamil Nadu's special legislative assembly resolution for continuance of 69 per cent reservation in the State, Central Government all political party meeting in July 1994 for discussing this Tamil Nadu meeting. The President's consenting the bill immediately thereafter within 6 days; Passing 76th constitutional amendment on 22 July 1994 putting the Act in the 9th Schedule i.e. three days after President's consenting the bill.

With gradual ascendance of primordial politics and the tendency to think of vote banks along caste lines, the necessity for critically assessing reservations has been put aside. No doubt, this requires a serious intellectual engagement that does not quite fit in with the exigencies of populist short-term politics. This is why, for the most part, reservations have become a kind of holy cow in public circles. Nobody dares any question its relevance and what is worse many are more than willing to extend reservations to cover other groups by arguing that they had also been victims of some kind of historic injustice.

While the educated elite has found little to say in its favour, preferential treatment has proved durable if not popular amongst the politicians. Of course, members of the beneficiary groups remain generally favourable. In fact, while every commission set up to review the scheduled lists (SC/ST/OBC) has recommended some de-listing, the parliament/assemblies have invariably ended up adding to the lists. Part of the fear that the reservation regime may become a runaway one derives from this historical memory.

REFERENCES

1. Advocacy Internet Pune, Nov./Dec. 2005.
2. 10th Five-Year Plan 2002/2007, Vol. II. Sectoral Policies and Programmes, Planning Commission, Government of India.

19

Reservation: As a Social Equality Measure

One of the controversies attached with reservation is that it creates a divide in the society mainly into two broad vertical walls i.e. Pro-reservationists and Anti-reservationists. Some go to an extent that it divides the society into many more small caste compartments based on the vested interests attached to reservation.

A question that arises here is: **Was an Indian society one, undivided and integrated before implementation of reservation?**

Answer is **'Certainly not.'**

The Indian society was already divided into so many castes and sub-castes compartments since time immemorial. In fact, reservation was thought to be one of the measures for bringing about national integration, social harmony and equated economic development in the country by uplifting those left behind. Caste is a fundamental reality of contemporary Indian life. Caste culture is so deep rooted that only a few persons will be out of it in their thoughts and action. It is an undeniable reality because caste consciousness exists to day also. It is a common experience that persons of different economic levels and occupational groups belonging to the same caste feel close to each other without making much conscious efforts, whereas one has to make consistent efforts to be closer with the members of other castes. In Indian society, the kinship ties have not broken.

It was anticipated that modernization, westernization, industrialization and advanced education would help in gradual destruction of caste system. However, the experience of subsequent post-independence years have proved that caste system continues to operate deep in the Indian psyche. **The Indian caste system has shown tremendous capacity to withstand against or adjust with the new forces and it has done so now with the so called modernization and industrialization of today also.** In fact, the very function of the caste system is to accommodate new emerging ambitious elements in the old system and maintain the *status quo* otherwise.

Casteism; Removal in Principle; Denial in Defence; But Operative in Practice

Those who indicate the change in rituals, formal contacts, food, clothing and neighbourhood as breaking of caste consciousness are in reality misjudging the spirit of casteism. Many of those who deny it in principle, operate it in practice. Life moves in the frontiers of caste and cultured men speak in soft tones against the system of caste, while its rejection in action just does not occur to them.

No doubt, some of the contents of the caste system have weakened, but the spirit of casteism very much exists. Since casteism, in its essence is a state of mind, it gets reflected at two levels; one, the consciousness exhibited in the mentality of people and second; the external behaviour. These two have historically been complimentary components of social reality, one of which is present in Indian society till today, the other accompanying it as its vogue yet vital shadow. This brings us to the psychological aspect of the caste system, which is real and distinguishes people from 'we' to 'they'. It is at this level that economic factors move within the boundary of the caste system. The 'ascriptive' status of individuals thus continues to be the order of Indian society.

There is a widespread impression among educated Indians that caste is on its last legs and that the educated, urbanized and westernized members of the upper castes have already escaped its bonds. But these impressions are wrong. The Indian social system has not changed its inherent characteristics. **Some apparent changes in people's behavioural manifestations should not be considered as caste disappearance from society.** Apparent hostility towards caste system has not weakened core casteism. Rather, the new economic and political interests have discovered in it an important vehicle to consolidate new values of caste identities which hitherto were supposed to be getting eroded and beginning to disintegrate.

How can the Goal of Social Equality be Attained?

With this scenario of Indian social reality, social justice demands that the prevalent social consciousness must be discounted for while moving towards social equality. There are three logical basis for achieving effective meaning to social equality. These are; (1) Existence of an equally open system; (2) Equality of opportunity, and (3) Equality of results. An equally open system is one, which is based on formal competitive norms. In India, there are public institutions for such purposes authorized by the Constitution of the country and assumed to be neutral and secular. Essential features of a competitive examination are that the competitors are unaware of their place in the society that a bias contingency of social circumstances is non-existent and that selection is natural and neutral. Social justice in such situation is the result of a fair bargain. But in Indian situation, none of these assumptions is valid because of the structural and psychological constraints imposed by the social system.

The provision for additional facilities to those deprived is advocated on the ground that the disadvantages can be removed by meeting the initial shortcomings, which make differences possible. The historical, social and economic fortunes are advocated to be remedied by providing infrastructures necessary to mitigate the unequal start. The provision for recovering the disadvantages in the beginning of a competition accepts the elimination of social differences in order to assure an equal start but justifies unequal result. Equality of opportunity can be overshadowed by the dust of inbuilt bias prevalent in society and thus remains arbitrary.

What is needed to make social equality a reality is to built up a base on equality of results. For this, we are left with a different principle if we wish to set up the social equality in society. Such a policy would incorporate three considerations. First, equality of results would require unequal treatment for the initially disadvantaged so that they eventually wind up equal in resources and rights. The disadvantaged inevitably are identifiable largely in group terms. Second, the principle of social equity must be linked with the principle of quota representation in the positional areas of social landscape. And third, the disadvantaged inevitably be identified in-group terms, which in the context of social equity is nothing else than caste groups. It should be understood that the Indian society being beset with caste realities, the unit for implementing equality of results could not be 'individuals' since society is beset with historical social distortions and the existing caste bias. Since difference refers to group as opposed to individuals, even if the conditions are made equal in course of time, **a stop gap arrangement may be helpful and that is what the policy of reservation is all about**. In a caste ridden society, the achievement of social equality requires that policy of equal opportunity must concentrate on equality of results on social surface. Otherwise, benefit of additional opportunities created through the overall development will go only to the upper castes making social surface still more uneven. The goal of social equality therefore, demands a policy of reservation in jobs and education on social grounds.

Democratization of Power

While examining the advisability of reservation in India, the social base of power generating structures in India needs to be understood. In addition to political authority, the governmental positions acquire to influence the entire life in society. Since the marginal jobs in the modern sector and in the government are acquired through modern education, this is an essential ingredient to be included in the power structure system. The social composition of those controlling educational system therefore is equally significant. In India, the entire power generating structure has been dominated by members of the upper castes. This is not a random phenomenon, but a patterned one. A restructuring of this monopolistic hold is an important aspect for a society constitutionally wedded to equality.

The political system in the country and the emerging order of the Indian economy have brought a new phase in the functioning of the bureaucracy. The regulation of political, economic and social activities has given a new dimension to the power of those in the government since the points of interaction between government and the public have enormously increased. This has resulted in the subordination of people under the mercy of those controlling the state apparatus. With increasing number of laws passed by the government, the power of obstruction has also been increasing even though power to sanction and decentralized power of obstruction have made the common man much more miserable in modern society.

The discharge of power in the best interest of society as a whole presupposes the neutrality on the part of government officials. This requires that they are free from any bias. This is possible when social contingency have had no role in shaping their career or is irrelevant in determining their future. This also requires a check on them by the neutrality of political authority having control over them. But in a caste-segmented society, this may be rare. In a stagnant society, particularly, neutrality is difficult to be presumed to be given. Moreover, when political and economic interests twist and win the power of bureaucracy, its neutrality is not only jeopardized, but also takes a particular social pattern. If a snapshot of what is expected from the people in the position of power and what they actually perform is taken, there cannot be much difficulty in visualizing their bias performance. The political and economic movements are testimony to this aspect of bureaucracy. **It is a common experience that Indian bureaucracy has not got rid of ascriptive personality and thereby has failed to discharge function as a neutral agency of the State.**

An examination of social composition of the white caller profession in general and the top bureaucracy in particular becomes relevant for an understanding of what is happening in our society and how to resolve this in the long and the short run. Table 19.1 provides a glance of the caste composition of the top bureaucracy in the country. This indicates that the upper castes have a monopoly over the administration and it is because of the policy of reservation that some scheduled castes and scheduled tribes have found a place in it.[1]

Table 19.1: Composition of Class I Officers in Central Government

Caste Category	*Population Share (%)*	*Share in Class I Services (%)*
Upper castes	25.34	89.63
OBCs	52.10	4.69
SC/ST	22.56	5.68
Total	**100.00**	**100.00**

Source: Mandal Commission Report, 1978.

There is a similar monopoly in higher and technical education of the country. Since all India statistics are not available, a sample illustration in respect of Rajasthan is shown here under with a view to drawing an idea about overall general approximation of the position in the country.[2]

Table 19.2: Composition of Rajasthan University Teachers, 1993

Caste Composition	*Natural Science*	*Social Science*	*Total*
Upper caste	88.3	81.5	84.3
Intermediate castes	1.7	5.7	4.0
Lower castes	—	0.7	1.2
Minorities	1.7	0.7	1.2
No Response	8.3	11.4	10.1
Total	**100.00**	**100.00**	**100.00**

Source: Prof. Y Singh, Essays on Modernization.

The educational institutions manufacture graduates and determine the life chances of those educated. It is academic institutions which build an army of bureaucrats at the helm of governance, teachers imparting knowledge and culture in the society and also executives, managers managing vast resources in the society. Though imparting knowledge is a positive behaviour, awarding distinctions is a normative act. It is in the later role that the social composition of teachers becomes an important element in determining life chances of those educated.

These two highlight the basic features of dominance and control over Indian society. The top bureaucracy and the university teachers being composed of the upper castes and thus, the power generating structures are socially unbalanced. This exhibits that a small section of population has perpetual monopoly of power in society. There happens to be only a marginal difference between the traditional structure of control apparatus in old traditional Indian society and the post-independence society, which is supposed to be moving towards social equality.

This explains why the economic benefit and political supremacy have been in correspondence with the social hierarchy of Indian society.

There may be two ways to remove the monopolistic situation in the power structure of our society. The first is that the medium and with it the culture associated, of instruction from the educational system has got to be changed from the foreign and feudal language i.e. English to Indian vernacular languages. This can stop breeding the hereditary slaves in Indian society and usher idealization in its place. And second; a change in the composition of the entire bureaucratic apparatus in correspondence with the social composition of the Indian society. The later part of solution rests on making the bureaucracy, a somewhat structural representative of different segments of society.

There are various advantages of demolishing the monopoly of a small section over education and modern jobs. First; the success of Indian democracy demands a decentralized system. But this will have narrow meaning of the initiative and control do not emerge from below. Political democracy must base on social democracy. It must be a representative system. Otherwise, political democracy and the caste system being dichotomous, only the later can survive, given the resilience in the caste system. For dealing with the monopolistic power structure, education and bureaucracy must resemble the structural form of Indian society. In other words, **advantage of reservation is that it makes a representative bureaucracy commensurate with political democracy**. Second, the patterned ill being on the lower castes will evaporate once the monopoly of the upper castes is brought to check centuries old social subjugation which has been the prime cause of deprivation in society, economic misery is a small part of it. If the bureaucracy represents all sections of the society, the severity of atrocities will surely be much less. The socially unbalanced bureaucracy is partly responsible for the deteriorating law and order situation since in society is rarely neutral. The result is that those who commit atrocities do not get proper punishment partly because of their caste similarity with structure of bureaucracy. And third; there will be a change in the outlook over the social surface of society. If all castes have educated people and bureaucrats in reasonable proportion, the left behind population may develop identity of interests. The dividing parameters may change from social similarity to other interests common to all those feeling disadvantaged and deprived. Taking all those factors, demolition of the monopolistic hold should be an essential item on the agenda of the scheme of transformation of Indian society.

Reservation not a Communal Demand, but a Secular Approach

Reservation in jobs and education is a secular move towards an anti-caste strategy rather than a caste consolidation device. This becomes clear when secularism is defined in the proper context of the existing social realities and the perspective of society. Secularism is an enlargement of mind by overpowering prejudice through the consolidation of reason. In India, a perpetual domination and control of a very small minority over a large majority is an act of communalism. It is only the prejudice of mind, which supports this state of affairs. This is tantamount to the rejection of an idea that men are born equal. If we believe that men are born equal, any support to the cause of domination by a small section over the entire society is a communal approach. Reason demands establishment of a society in which men are not accepted, not only as being born equal but also not treated as equal. Thus, the removal of domination of the upper castes over lower ones is a secular act. **The policy of reservation is an effective instrument to demolish the monopoly of a small segment of people over the affairs of society.** If the lower castes get relieved from the domination and the implicit injustice and exploitation exercised through monopolizing power structure, it will be victory of secularism and will open a new era of social justice and harmony. **The policy of reservation, therefore is not a communal demand but a secular approach.**

Results of last sixty years of post-implementation of reservation also supports this conviction that reservation has rather strengthening castes divides helped in social integration process through upward mobility. No doubt, it has been gradually resorted to be used as a political agenda, which induce a few castes particularly among the OBCs for their inclusion with an only objective of availing reservation benefits. But that does not prove the core concept of reservation turning out to be communal. Evils of casteism have entered other spheres such as political dominance, territorial development and sometimes even caste based localities also. All these are the attributes of years old caste consciousness living in innermost nerves of the Indian society, which sometime circumvents reservation also.

REFERENCES

1. *Mandal Commission Report*, 1978.
2. Prof. Y. Singh, *Essays on Modernization*.

20

Beyond a Reservation Percentage

The issue of upliftment of entire backward communities is a multi-dimensional social issue calling for an honest and sincere concern with a long-term vision. Reservation was resorted to upon independence as an urgent and immediate measure, which did work well during all these years having brought about a significant positive and clearly visible result that none can deny. But, now with changing time and mixed experience of implementation of reservation policy during last sixty years, circumstances now demand something beyond a single measure of mere reservation of few jobs here and there for them which too are diminishing day by day. One will have to go in the total diagnosis of this deep rooted social pathology in its totality to find out the obtaining condition of these classes and the required treatment as a relief and thereafter for its permanent prevention. A socially charged disease having its home in the body for thousands of years will on being attacked, not only resist teeth and nail, but will also remain unresponsive to the initial dosages of treatment, notwithstanding with whatever sincerity and thrust, it might have been launched. This is what exactly is also happening in the treatment of this very unique and symptomatic social disease of discrimination. The treatment has to have twin motives, one-caste stigmatic solutions and other general social hygienic improvement solutions.

While caste stigmatic solutions aim at specific upliftment of the suffering backward communities through statutory support like reservation in educational admissions, jobs etc. Reservation was resorted to as a commonly structured master solution meant for all the target beneficiary backward communities. It did work well also in the initial period. But the time has ripe now to work out with a approach and specific measures for total upliftment of these groups. No doubt, it is a Herculean task in a vast and highly diversified country like ours with thousands of layers of caste gradations. This once again recalls for set objective behind reservation i.e. Mitigating social inequalities. This will have to be viewed keeping the present position with regard to social discrimination, social assimilation and connected therewith and resulting there from position of economic inequalities. It may be noted that all the three target beneficiaries of the reservation i.e. SC/ST/OBC have different set of socio economic situations as under.

Scheduled Castes and Scheduled Tribes (SCs/STs)

These communities were the real sufferers of the social discrimination and caste hatred for the centuries. Reservation for them has been provided right from the beginning. Number of Supreme Court judgments in the recent is centered around the basic query about continuance of reservation. However, in almost of such highly debated judgements, the judges have endorsed felt need for continuance of reservation for scheduled castes and scheduled tribes taking into account the Indian social scenario for these people. Specific problem with regard to scheduled castes is caste discrimination which is not so in case of scheduled tribes. In case of scheduled tribes, the specific problem being faced by them is their isolation from the mainstream society and because of that, natural outcomes would be obviously miserable poverty and lack of even basic education. They suffer social discrimination to some extent, but not of the type of untouchability, the scheduled caste people are facing. Common among both these target communities i.e. scheduled castes and scheduled tribes is social backwardness, a fraction of them who have been fortunate enough to extract the benefits of reservation are well-off. But that's not all. Majority of them living in large rural areas and urban slums still need a lot to be done to bring them up for their assimilation with the remaining masses. Their problems have to be fought with a long-term strategy. Economic misery is their biggest enemy. The first and foremost impact of this is on the education of their kinds. Therefore quality education with good hostel and teaching faculty is required for them. This infrastructure is already established by the social justice departments of the state government with additional grant of the central government also. But so far condition and quality of this government provided educational facilities are concerned, least said is better. Either they are highly inadequate or are run for the sake of their running. They lack almost every thing, which is a must for making a row boy into an alround youth well equipped with competing in the present day world. This will not come by mere launching of schemes or construction of cement concrete set ups. It needs to be manned by sensible and dedicated people at the helm of the affairs, which would make it possible to see the fruits after so many years' hard toiled labour.

Other Backward Classes (OBC)

Other backward classes consisting thousands of castes from the lower strata of the Indian social network is the other set of the target beneficiaries of the reservation. However, their problems are to a major extent different from those of the scheduled castes and scheduled tribes. The common among all the three target beneficiary categories is economic backwardness and inadequate educational progress. Other backward classes do not suffer from caste discrimination and caste hatred, though they are treated as lower in social hierarchy by the upper castes. While scheduled castes comprise of lowest Hindu castes and scheduled tribes comprise of Hindu Tribals as well a fraction of converts, the other backward classes also comprise of besides various Hindu castes, sizeable number of Muslims and Christians i.e. non-Hindus also. Moreover, criteria of inclusion of a class or caste in OBC is still a matter of controversy even after these many years which is coined in one of the recent Supreme Court Judgments on reservation in admission in courses of IITs, IIMs and other all India educational institutions.

This has again created two more problems in the present day situation. One; more and more castes are rushing for being recognized as backward and their inclusion in OBC with the sole motive of availing reservational benefits. This has created a feeling of bias and hatred for the word 'reservation' itself. Reservation never intended to strengthen the caste walls; it was with the humble intention of creating a casteless society in the nation. Therefore, immediate need of the hour is to patch up these loopholes of class/caste criteria, which is working negatively against the reservation. This has created such a feeling of very high magnitude that the reservation is very bad. It is not so. Reservation is still relevant and required. What is required is to make it free from virus of such vested interests. As against SC/ST population of about 23 per cent distributed in comparatively very few castes/communities, OBCs are comprising of more than half the population, distributed in thousands of castes and sub-castes with high complexities of their identification from state to state.

Economic upliftment measures for them have to be chalked out keeping in view the above realities in mind. Mere 27 per cent reservation for these approximately 52 per cent of population will not serve the purpose. Measures have also to be initiated in light of the fact that their social acceptance is not a problem in the Indian society. At the same time, economic condition of many of them are worse than the poorest of the scheduled caste and scheduled tribe persons.

As regard universal Indian problems of poverty, education and economic upliftment which affects the whole Indian population including scheduled castes, scheduled tribes and other backward classes are discussed later on under suggested measures such as social hygienic improvement solutions which inter alia include land reforms, assets redistribution, skill compensation etc.

Social hygienic improvement solutions aim at upbringing of the entire poor and starving masses of the country, a big chunk of which belongs to the scheduled castes, scheduled tribes and other backward classes. This has to be done by just and equitable sharing of land, labour, capital and entrepreneurship, what is known in the economic terminology '**Factors of Production**'. Of these four, labour i.e. employment part is covered in Part III at Chapter 12 on 'Constitutional Provisions', others two i.e. land ownership and capital i.e. assets redistribution are incorporated herein afterwards.

A. LAND REFORMS

Reservation basically aims at bringing up unequals who are alienated due to social inequalities, economic injustice and denial of human freedom by main social stream. Article 46 of the Constitution expects protection of scheduled castes and scheduled tribes and other weaker sections of the society with special care. Thus, a duty has been imposed upon the State to endavour in every respect to take special care of the SC/ST/OBC. The pretext of this special care includes many measures for the ultimate attainment of harmonious society in the nation.

Reservation in jobs as an immediate available recourse was resorted to since inception of the Constitution, which did work well as long as the demand, and supply condition of employment market was posing equilibrium. As the time passed, with manifold increase in population, development on education front and host of other demographic factors, reservation in jobs alone was not adequate for the care to be taken for the scheduled castes, scheduled tribes and other backward classes as envisioned in the Constitution.

The real India lives in its over six lacs rural and interior villages spread to the length and breaths of this vast country. 70 per cent of the nation's population lives in this real rural India. In spite of massive industrialization, the country has still preserved its original identity as agricultural economy with lion's share contributed from rural India which is also witnessed in major economic parameters such as GNP, GDP, etc. Coming back to the present condition of scheduled castes, scheduled tribes and other backward classes in rural India, it is abysmal in spite of planned efforts during last fifty years. There is a felt need of social justice and economic empowerment of SC/ST/OBC marginal farmers, and landless labourers in rural places.

And for this, land reform is the most powerful source of ensuring both social justice and economic empowerment.

Experience has proved that past movements with land reforms and land redistribution has brought about revolutionary progress in drastically changing the old established social gradation ladder in the rural social hierarchy The land reforms has brought marvelous improvement in the condition of a few cultivating communities belonging to upper caste but living in a poor state of affairs in the fifties. Land ceiling measures and movements like Bhudan i.e. land donation have brought a revolutionary shift of the social hierarchy. Certain landless families among Patidars, Chaudharis etc. in fifties after being benefited by land redistribution measures have miraculously progressed. These communities who were considered much lower in social hierarchy than Rajputs and Banias in the fifties are now considered above them with their influential presence not only in the social and economic spheres, but also on the political fronts as well, thanks to land reforms. Thus, land holding plays a very important role in addressing the problem of social inequalities.

Can that successful experiment once again be extended in case of marginal farmers and landless labourers belonging to scheduled castes and scheduled tribes?

Front Line, India's one of the leading weekly notes as under in its publication of 29 December 2006

"Almost all the studies and reports on the *dalit* issues have highlighted the need to bring the land reforms issue to the fore, because *dalits* account for the largest number of landless people in most of the parts of the country. Studies have shown that *dalits'* access to the cultivable land, whether through ownership or otherwise has come down substantially between 1961 and 1991. The NHRC report said 'increase in the percentage of scheduled caste agricultural labourers shows that many of SCs who owned land earlier have lost them, a single most depressing indicator of their worsening economic situation which directly reflects their vulnerability.[1]

The pre independence slogan of "**Land to the Tiller**" could have led to provision of land to every rural *dalit,* which would have released the SCs/STs from their age old agrestic thralldom. But the various land reform acts are enacted and implemented half heartedly. Limited land distribution could not bring the constitutionally mandated qualitative change and economic and social liberation. Similarly scheduled tribes were also being increasingly deprived of land and have in many cases, been reduced to landless poors in their homelands. Their lands are casually developed, rarely irrigated and poorly integrated with the market, leaving the field open to exploiters and middlemen. Moreover, they are also the worst victims of modern large-scale project displacements.

As per the available statistics of 1991 in respect of scheduled castes, 13 per cent of them were landless labourers while 70 per cent were with land holding below one acre which is as good as no land holding. It means nearly 80 per cent rural *dalits* having no possibility of livelihood from their own landholding have to wonder here and there as low paid agricultural labourers. Figures in respect of the other categories i.e. scheduled tribes and other backward classes were not available. However, it is also likely to be more or less some thing at par with that of the scheduled castes only. Further shockingly, landholding of scheduled castes has gone down by 5 per cent during 1991/2000, the decade of world over new economic reforms i.e. economic reforms have led to snatching away of landholding of backward classes viz. SC/ST/OBC.

Unequal Land Ownership

Seventy five per cent of Patidar families, 34 per cent of Koli an OBC community and 31 per cent of scheduled castes and 23 per cent of scheduled tribes families possess more than 5 acres of land. Thus, majority of higher land holding was with the upper caste Patidar community. Equipmental facilities and advancement of agriculture farming techniques will be having a vast difference in respect of a Patidar farmer than a Koli cultivator possessing the same amount of land holding in view of the general economic and educational differential between these two castes.

One third of the OBC families depend for their livelihood on agriculture farm labour and other allied labour work. Of course, 7 per cent of Patidars, 5 per cent of Banias and 4 per cent of Brahmin families are also engaged in such similar agricultural labour work.

The nation has vast areas of surplus available land on one hand while there are lacs of SC/ST/OBC people on the other hand working as landless labourers. Can these two ends not be abridged i.e. allotment of these surplus unutilized agricultural land to these landless backwards? These poors are living in such a pitiable condition that education is out of question and all along this, want of other requisites for availing reservational benefits, scope for the job reservation in government for these misfortunate masses is a mere foul offer for them. Allotment of small piece of land will be more than a reservation to this poor family in their struggle of coming out of economic miseries. If this is done, many more avenues will automatically get opened for them such as education in the family, freedom from bonded agriculture labourship etc. The nation has with a view to boosting further the cycle of liberalization, privatization and globalization has been so generously allotting such unused land to the industrial houses for special economic zone (SEZ) development, corporate farming etc. Why can't this policy of land allotment under LPG/ SEZ etc. be redesigned in such a way that a fixed percent of such land be automatically reserved for being allotted for such social cause? This will undoubtedly contribute in establishing social equalities with much at a faster pace.

Agricultural Labourers

Sizeable population belonging to scheduled castes and scheduled tribes are landless agricultural labourers. They are the real cultivators of land and have acquired appreciable skill also for such job. Unfortunately, these poor labourers are paid very low wages much less than the minimum wages framed under the statute. The reason for such exploitation through very low wages is primarily because the task is performed by so called polluting and low castes. This has also led to devaluating an important skill required for society to survive. If they were paid at least subsistence wages, their socio-economic situation would have improved over a period of time and their children would have been better educated. But because of the strongly preserved and maintained social discriminatory practices, a certain section coming in the lower strata of the society continues to be exploited and kept living in the same deprived conditions. We need to realize the dignity of labour and that minimum wages are being given to every worker for a society to progress. In Indian rural economy, a vast majority does not get enough even for self-subsistence and we justify arbitrarily imposing different values on different skills.

Of the total agricultural labourers' workforce, 49 per cent belongs to scheduled caste, 32 per cent scheduled tribes and remaining 19 per cent belonging to other backward castes. The further perturbing feature is that there has been a phenomenal quantitative rise of 3.28 crores agricultural labourers from year 1991 to 2001. It is a matter of probe to know the reason for such a big rise in the ten years of post economic reforms era. Is it only the population growth, or schooling droppage or mismatching of rural demand supply position of employment or the failure of the LPG? Is this trend not a threat to a desirable balanced and equated socio-economic development? If it persists, where will this lead to?

Table 20.1: Land holding Pattern of Scheduled Castes in India

	1982 (%)	*1992(%)*
Landless	12.62	13.34
Less than half acre	47.97	47.50
Between half to one acre	9.53	8.89
All up to 1 acre	70.12	69.73

Source: Untouchability in Rural India by Ghanshyam Shah and others.

Figures in respect of other categories i.e. scheduled tribes and other backwards classes are not available. The above figures shockingly reveal that number of landless scheduled caste persons have increased. May be because of their compelling circumstances. The National Human Rights Commission (NHRC) report further said; "Despite distribution of the ceiling surplus and other land, the percentage of landless households among the SCs have increased from 12.62 per cent in 1982 to 13.34 per cent in 1992. The poor implementation of land reforms, particularly in the states where scheduled castes constitutes a large percentage of the population, has deprived them of access to this asset to improve their economic position and reduce their vulnerability.[2]

Implementation of Land Reforms Laws/Measures and Backwards

Number of landless labourers continues to be sizeable in almost all the states in spite of existence of land redistribution policies of the governments and in contrast to consistently going up overall economic growth of the nation. The states where the position has gone down from bad to worse in number of landless SCs are J&K from 0.66 to 4 lacs, M.P. from 18.11 to 20.53 lacs and Tamil Nadu from 14.50 to 19.21 lacs. As against this, there are also noteworthy states where position denotes encouraging improvement i.e. reduction in number of landless labourers belonging to SCs. They are Bihar from 35.58 to 19.73 lacs, Karnataka 14.52 to 10.69 lacs and West Bengal from 19.13 to 12.02 lacs[3].

It is pertinent to note about eye-catching improvement recorded by Bihar where number of landless SCs have come down from 35.58 lacs to 19.73 lacs, i.e. reduction of landless scheduled caste labourers by 50 per cent. This could happen due to allotment of total 7,964.55 acres surplus land to in all total 10,057 landless labourers. Of these, 4,687.96 acres or say 68.86 per cent land was reallotted to landless scheduled castes beneficiaries during the years from 1999/2000 to 2003/2004 as reported on page 66 of the above referred to National Scheduled Castes Commission Report.

The implementation of land reforms in the country as a whole has been termed largely a failure except for patches of success in respect of some measures in few states. **The implementation of land reforms has been subverted by the absence of political will, lack of bureaucratic commitment, loopholes in laws, poorly maintained land records, tremendous manipulative power of the landed classes and excessive interference of courts.** Therefore, land redistributive strategy for the benefit of the landless and marginalized labourers to change agrarian relations and break the caste and class nexus has not been succeeded.

In this pessimistic scenario, it is likely that scheduled castes and scheduled tribes have received substantial benefits from the limited enforcement of laws and programmes related to land. Most of the scheduled castes could not benefit from laws on tenancy reforms which conferred ownership rights on the tillers of land and these poor people had no proof or record of their cultivating status. The ceiling on land holdings offered a remarkable realistic opportunity to scheduled caste landless persons to have fortune of now owning some land and thus acquire dignity and status. The impact of this distribution of land is not large considering the magnitude of landlessness among them and the per capita area distributed to them being slightly less than one acre. SC/ST people were also distributed land, which belonged to the government or panchayat or was donated under Bhoodan campaign in view of the priority assigned to them in all land distribution programmes. But the benefits which could accrue from all this redistribution has also been snatched away from a number of scheduled castes/tribes beneficiaries on account of non-delivery of possession over allotted land, forcible dispossession, litigation and alternative claims made by erstwhile land owners and other vested interests, etc. scheduled caste people affected by these problems have been wandering from pillar to post for resolution of these problems but all in vein.

The *dalits* also lost out in land reforms in other ways. Some of them have tried to reclaim vacant/waste lands belonging to government, panchayat or other public bodies which they have been cultivating for a long time. Under the existing instructions/ rules of state governments, such cultivating possessions are usually regularized and leases are issued to them unless the land is reserved for public purpose or is under common use. But due to apathy, negligence and even bias by revenue machinery, they have failed to get rights in respect of these lands. Sometimes, the lands they have been cultivating are allotted to others, while, at other times, powerful landowners manipulate to prevent such allotment. Thus, they face the threat of eviction hanging on their head.

Caste Subordination in Utilizing Free Natural Resources

The downtroddens also face restrictions on use of state owned lands for common use imposed by caste Hindus having large landholdings in respect of grazing of cattle, collection of fodders, right of trespassing and easement and use of water resources etc. This creates immense difficulties for them in livestock farming which is virtually the only subsistence activity, they rely in absence of access to land and capital. These restrictions are no doubt not supported by any law or regulation, but are simply expressions of social power of landowners on one hand and extreme vulnerability of poor scheduled castes on the other hand.

Many scheduled castes and scheduled tribe people in absence of having land for construction of their house, prepare a mud hut with thatch roof on the land of big landowners under whom they work as labourers. This dependence often creates a situation of bondage labour. There are laws for regularization of such houses, which are not implemented because of the nexus of administration with the landowners.

Land has right from the primitive days, remained as the prime source of mankind's livelihood. A person derives most of his basic requirements from piece of a land. Inequalities by way of land holding have substantially led to economic exploitation and social discrimination.

B. ENTREPRENEURIAL PARTICIPATION

The state has to perform a parental role for the people. And a parent has to pay little more concern for its weaker children. It is always welcome when a nation's GNP records consistently upward growth. Such growth or say quantitative increase in its economic prosperity has to be equitably distributed by and large amidst its cross sections of total population at large. That too not merely in arithmetical term. No doubt this is a tough task. The economists' and planners' wisdom lies in meeting such challenges. But the core objective has to be that the assets so created out of upward and consistent GNP growth should be generally distributed in an equitable manner. Measuring the development of the nation should not be viewed from the increase in number of multi-millionaires but number of families coming out of the miserable socio-economic plights.

Number of government jobs are shrinking day by day. A new concept of BOT i.e. Buy, Operate and Transfer has been increasingly adopted by the government for providing public utilities and infrastructure in the present privatization days. This has created diversified opportunities for the youth in place of conventional employments. More and more tasks are now entrusted under contract or tendering or whatever new names given to the system. This has created avenues for self-employment and entrepreneurships. All these opportunities have to be thought of so as to provide due share to the youths belonging to the scheduled castes, scheduled tribes and other backward classes. The whole concept of employment has started being vanishing with its place taken out by new contracting, sub-contracting, bidding and so on. Why cannot this youth be given a suitable piece of this big cake of large number of jobs by sorting out the operational problems amicably? This has been most successfully experimented by countries like Malaysia and USA.

Malaysian Experiment of Asset Redistribution

In this connection, Malaysian experiment is worth noting. Malaysia has similar problem of social inequalities in their country. The backward community in Malaysia is known as *Bhumiputras*. The country like us decided for their total upliftment in seventies i.e. almost 20 years after implementation of reservation policy in our country. Their policy was unique in a way that rather than simply awarding job quota to these communities, they made a comprehensive policy which emphasized more towards equated assets redistribution. This was implemented through preferential awarding of contracts to *Bhumiputras*, 30 per cent of newly listed companies were to be registered with ownership of *Bhumiputras* only, and similar number of other measures in the direction of ultimate empowerment of this community were launched. The experiment has brought wonderful results. *Bhumiputra* ownership in the corporate sector went up from 2.3 per cent in 1970 to 23 per cent in the year 2000 i.e. 10 fold increase in just thirty years. Simultaneously there was also recorded an impressive overall national economic growth of 6 per cent to 7 per cent during this period in the Malaysian economy.

Not Impossible in India

India is proudfully having the highest proportion of youth i.e. 58 per cent of total Indian population are in the working young age group. Preparing these youth for entrepreneurship talents is not a difficult task. This will subside the burden on the employment situation in the country. We have got few world's best entrepreneurship institutes such as EDI, IIMS, SISI etc. and similar other youth training institutions. Can we not tie up all these available infrastrucral facilities and a selected lot from among the SC/ST/OBCs who can be equipped to take the challenges now available as narrated here above?

Incidentally emerging NGOs are exceedingly contributing well in youth related entrepreneurial and other developmental social services. Can some coordination be established in this direction with some specially package thrust for trainning, grooming and deploying scheduled castes, scheduled tribes and other backward castes youth?

Provision of housing reservation is a striking example. Government directly as well through various housing agencies have been constructing new housing colonies, a percentage out of which are earmarked for being allotted to the poor people belonging to the reserved categories. There are also exclusively low cost housing colonies constructed for such people out of the land apportioned for such purposes in posh areas too. This has enabled shifting of backward class families from the slums to better localities. This results in upward mobility of such slum dwellers who get an opportunity to live in a better locality. This has so many advantages for the backward class communities. One; They become owners of such appreciating immoveable assets. Second; they get opportunity of living in upper caste localities, which enhances the scope of their children's cultural mobility and better education.

The economic momentum is catching growth at a much faster rate. Newer and newer experiments of privatization are found successful such as out sourcing, labour contracting etc. which can be considered for being entrusted to the backward class entrepreneurs or their cooperatives. There could be some teething troubles and the so chosen people may not render the output or services at the desired level initially. But they will have to be developed with little social perseverance initially for some time. Similarly, something can be thought of in the direction of allotment of space in commercial complexes, allotment of providing various ancillary services in the new concepts such as special economic zones (SEZ), private ports, private railways etc. of course without necessitating any monetory stake on these communities which they will not be able to manage. What is required is a strong and determined will for the upliftment of these communities who have remained behind in the today's economic progress race.

American Experiment

U.S. Public Works Employment Act, 1997 has a minority business enterprises clause which provides that 10 per cent of the U.S. federal funds granted for local public works projects must be used by the state and local grantees to procure services or supplies from entrepreneurs owned or controlled by minority group members such as blacks, hispanics etc. The purpose behind provisions was obviously as a part of the affirmative action in U.S.A. This provision was challenged on the ground that it is running counter to the equal protection clause provided under the 14th amendment of the US Constitution. However, this arguments against limiting private contractors' choice was rejected by the US Supreme Court. The court upheld the validity of the legislation because it contained the provisions designed to uplift socially and economically disadvantaged persons to a level where they could effectively participate in the US economy.

A Will Will Find a Way

The Indian Government can also prescribe such conditions as a part of their disinvestments programme. To start with, a percentage say 10 per cent may be prescribed either by sub-contracting, executing some other works, etc. for the weaker sections i.e. scheduled castes, scheduled tribes and other backward classes. Indian Supreme Court is more sensible towards the cause of social justice than the US Supreme Court. There is no reason for it to reject an initiative similar to that passed by the US legislation 1997. The overriding question is whether there is a political will and determination at the center and in the states to implement them.

C. CAPACITY DEVELOPMENT

This is a new prerequisite of career building for any youth in the post-economic reforms era. In the present time of steep competition and multiplicities of career options, skill possession has special significance besides qualification. Unfortunately our education system though with little improvement has still not come out to abridge the gap between the college classroom imparting knowledge on one hand and shop or factory floor i.e. industry or market requirements on the other hand. This has necessitated initially skill acquiring and further to skill sharpening.

Microsoft Minority Diversity

Here, a unique attempt of skill improvement adopted by the world's biggest computer giant 'Microsoft' is worth noting. The Company has devised a '**Minority Diversity**' scheme for the backwards in U.S.A. who are identified as minorities. Under this scheme, the Company recruits potential youths right from the tender age. The Company looks after this lot just like a responsible parent right from their under graduation study onwards. Along with this, they also start their computer teaching on them. They arrange in house as well as outside vigorous trainings not only for their technical education but also for their skill development. The whole exercise takes years together at Microsoft Campus before finally getting a skillful, confident and all rounder computer professional. The Microsoft's experience of years reveals that the so produced professional out of originally inducted raw boys/girls gives best output and most satisfied customers for the Company for a long tenure.

Is it also not in line with preparations of newly recruited civil services officers (IAS/IPS) by the Government of India? The fresh lots start their learning right from their orientation to Missouri, then in their respective departmental academic institutions, followed by vigorous on the job exposures, next to it, Bharat Bhraman i.e. tour across the whole country for their overall development and finally again summing up at the academies where from they started their induction learning before commencement of their actual working in the state administration.

Such Skilled Work Force Proves a Permanent Investment

Skill here has to be taken in a broader perspective. It should not suffice only with efficient and effective application of knowledge, but also attitudinal responsiveness with result orientation and cultural acquaintances of modern day corporate world. This will be grossly lacking in the youth of the backward classes because of variety of reasons such as their social brought up and background, inferiority complex developed in them over a period of time, lack of getting such environment around them. The position in case of youth with rural background will be additionally vulnerable. Of course, this will not be formally even in all the youth. The position in respect of children of the educated, as also those serving in government jobs and staying in the cosmopolitan culture will not be so.

It would also not be out of place to mention that a time has ripe when the whole issue of upliftment of these masses have to be considered through a holistic approach, which includes improvement of their health and hygiene, specific issues relating to rural poor backwards including in particular agricultural labourers etc. This will have to be viewed not from bare statistical yardsticks like so much of increase in the per capital income of the people, or reduction in number of families below Poverty Line living as per the government definitions, but looking at the peoples' real welfare as perceived in the society at large.

REFERENCES

1. *Front Line,* Weekly of 29 Dec. 2006.
2. *Untouchability in Rural India* by Ghanshyam Shah and others.
3. National Commission for Scheduled Castes, *Annual Report 2004/ 2005.*

21

Conclusion

Issue of reservation thus is not confined to apportionment of few jobs here and there, but a socio-economic upliftment measure for those who have remained behind for centuries because of the typical social conditions prevailing in the country. The nation cannot prosper ignoring the chronic social inequalities prevailing in social life.

Issue of reservation cannot be perceived in isolation but it has to be linked with the overall social condition of backwards at large and more particularly scheduled castes and scheduled tribes who are the worst sufferers of social fad. It is not that nothing has altered in the last five decades of independence. India's freedom struggle and nationalist movement charged the government of independent India with a mandate for equality and social change. This mission further reinforced by initiatives of Dr. Ambedkar has resulted in significant changes through empowernment laws and affirmative policies. The socio-political landscape of India has also been transformed by the growing strength of SC/ST/OBC electoral power. In addition, the urbanization process has created new opportunities for migration and mobility allowing some of these people to escape the stifling environment of rural caste society.

According to **D. Parthsarthi** notable **Sociologist**, "The policy of reservation is not the only or even the best option for development in the context of a hierarchically placed society like India. Other options include provision of free or cheap good quality education in schools which is accessible to everyone, land reforms by giving land to the actual cultivator, strict implementation of minimum wages, and a complete stoppage of all kinds of discriminatory behaviour whether in villages or in corporate sector. If all these were successfully implemented, there would be no need for reservations for any section of population now. Not just western countries, but also the east Asian tigers such as South Korea, Japan, and China have been very successful in implanting the above measures. That is why they are much ahead of India as far as social and economic indicators are concerned. If we were successful with the measures above, along with a properly designed and implemented policy of reservations, there would soon be no further need for such policies for an indefinite time. We have failed on these fronts and more so it is a deliberate failure. Since such failures benefit the already privileged groups, reservation remains to be an inevitable and justifiable option.[1]

Need for a Holistic Approach

Abuse of Child Labour

Similarly child labour is yet an another chronic problem of the country. There are about six crores child labourers employed in the country in spite of existence of all statutory, prohibitory and punitive labour and security laws. Forty per cent of them belong to scheduled castes and scheduled tribes. Figures in respect of the other categories are not available, which is also estimated certainly at a high scale. The work being carried out by them includes carriage of dead animals and human ascreations, washing of clothes in the rural and urban areas and bondage type labour work in the factory plants in the industrial areas. These are all the citizens of tomorrow's India who will represent real India and also shape the country's fate. They are striving to contribute to their starving families at the tender age when they are supposed to have at least some minimum education so as to be called literate. Is it not a shame for a country like ours', which is now claiming to be as the globe's most powerful economy in the third world? Reduction in labourers' migration with providing alternative source of their livelihood would enhance school going children in families, which would in turn mean a concrete step towards addressing not only economic but also socially charged problems attached with Indian social system.

Upliftment of the Poorest Irrespective of Caste Consideration

These masses live in very economic miseries almost in a starving condition, striving to match the two ends. They represent all castes and communities in varying proportion from different social segmentations. A common programme free from governmental target worries is required to be launched. We have got a Below Poverty Line (BPL) mechanism in the government for chalking out the economic plannings for the people of the last bracket of the society. If one looks at the figures showing the trend or say graphical picture of the BPL, it shows a satisfactory and ever improving condition. But one when goes amidst the slums and chawls of such BPL defined people, the picture does not correspond to what is boasted in the government declarations, pronouncements, publicities, attractively exhibited computer graphs and charts. These poors are found in entirely a different world of scarcities and starvations, wants and what not. It warms the cockles of one's heart as to what is correct? One what is seen with naked eyes or that submitted in the attractive folders, Nets, E-Governance containing nicely worded and beautifully power pointed notes/reports submissions to the bureaucratic Bada Saabs and political bosses?

In the initial years after independence, a voluntary scheme of earmarking 10 per cent out of profit of business/industrial houses was appealed by the government for being spent for the welfare of weaker/backward class of the society with all financial and schematic flexibilities being vested in the hands of such business/industrial houses. This was theoretically found to be a noble idea and was well appreciated publicly including business and industrial corners as well, but when the question of its implementation came, it was opposed teeth and nail by the very private sector and their representing organizations and the whole scheme disappeared ultimately without implementation.

Recently published J.J. Irani Committee Report on examining reservation in the private sector has awakened an optimism that big corporate houses will work out some strategies for skill improvement and enhancing employability of the backward classes as suggested by themselves for these needy groups.

Literacy rate of the country was 5.35 per cent in the year 1901, which went up to 9.50 per cent in 1931 and further to 21.96 per cent in the fifties and now touching to 69 per cent in 2001. Inspite of this growth, much is still left to be done. These are the figures as per the government parameters, which also needs to be reviewed with its present day relativity. Our budget allocation after education was 1.2 per cent in the year 1981, which though raised, is still less than 3 per cent in the recent years, which is one of the lowest if globally compared to. Amartya Sen, the Indian based nobel prize winner economist has suggested it to be at least around 15 per cent.

Sensitizing State Administration

The fact that as India's socio political ambience is still caste ridden, caste is still a millstone round the neck of many officials in the administration and their mindset militates against rising above caste, ironically by imitation effect and because of resentments rooted in the history, wherein lower castes officials are also no exception. Event if some officials are genuinely committed to their calling and to the implementation of the constitutional provisions, fears are likely reprisals from the upper castes bureaucratic and political bosses deter them from their commitments.

Constitutional provisions *per se* are like a rule book. If officials go by its alphabets and letters without understanding the spirit underlying the provisions, they cannot do much, and what they do may even be detrimental to the spirit of Constitution. This may be so more particularly in case of lower echelon burecraucy.[2]

When the communal government order (GO) was in force in Madras Presidency during British Rule since 1927, the colonial government scrupulously followed its implementation by insisting on periodic returns from the concerned departments. In case, where the GO was not implemented, or the posts were not filled according to roster, the government used to call for explanation and where necessary, initiated corrective action. It is doubtful if such practices are prevalent now particularly considering mounting backlog year by year. The very provisions in the Constitution stand on the premises that the state would usher in the conditions necessary for implementing them.

Untouchability in Its Newer form and Shape Needs to be Removed

While *dalits* have mobilized socially and politically, and have secured significant state support, in the form of progressive legislation, most of them, not all, still continue to subsist in conditions of abject poverty and literacy, and are victimized by untouchability and atrocities across the country. Clearly, much more is needed for the majority of the *dalits* to achieve the rights guaranteed to them under the Constitution. The state needs to launch a concerted and focused initiative involving a wide range of measures. This must include a campaign against untouchability in the public spaces, starting from pre-school feeding centres etc. More empowered and secured *dalits* can only stand for their rights, if the state systematically provides basic provisions and services in *dalit* settlements, especially the outreach of health and literacy programmes. A campaign against untouchability requires that the state promote legal literacy and mobilize the masses for legal action, undertakes stronger penal and judicial interventions, provides legal aid guarantee to the survivors, initiates a reorientation of the law and order government machineries to create strict accountability and conducts public sector judicial reforms at all level. In addition, it is imperative that bond between traditional 'unclean' occupations and caste be permanently severed. At the same time, it must be recognized that *dalit* empowerment is crucially dependent upon their access to productive resources such as agricultural land and remunerative wage employment as discussed earlier. The country's larger question of poverty and inequality must be addressed in order that *dalits* are able to exercise their rights in a substantive and meaningful way.

Over the years, reservations have become the standard format for groups demanding equality of results. There is a great degree of political pressure to extend reservations to include communities other than scheduled castes and scheduled tribes. On the other hand, there is little attempt to reflect upon what reservations were meant to achieve and indeed to review this policy, which has been in operation for over 50 years. In order to accomplish this task, it is necessary to contextualize reservations within the framework of democratic governance. Only then, we can adequately plot its future"[3].

Socio-Economic Engineering

What is our national goal? Our national goal is undoubtedly to accelerate the process of upward mobility of more and more backward castes/class families. We want a casteless and non-secular society. But mere thoughts of ideologies will not create by itself such a society. The state and people will have to take up the task of socio-economic engineering. This will have to be followed by necessary responsive planning, result oriented strategies and time bound economic programmes. These strategies and programmes shall have to be continuously monitored and modified as and when needed. Such a thousand year old problem cannot be solved in its own natural course simply by implementation of reservation provisions only. Here two things are worth notable. One; the society never remains static over a period of time. Its aspirations, values etc. go on changing constantly. And second; a single measure or programme may have been successful at one point of time, but it does mean that it shall be ever successful in any social dynamics. Ground realities have to be evaluated in its right perspective, which could give entirely a different picture much averse to the expectations.

There are few caste amongst the scheduled castes and likewise a few tribes amongst the scheduled tribes which have progressed exceedingly well and have also come out of the caste stigma. But they have alienated themselves from their caste fellows. Amongst the other backward castes, there are a few castes, which are far behind in education even to the scheduled castes. But this is not because of the caste backwardness. There are few other castes amongst the other backward castes, though by definition, they are not untouchables, but are so neglected by the society for the centuries, that they are almost in the category of the untouchables. In other backward castes (OBC), there are no conscious and definite efforts for the annihilation of castes. There have been numerous instances of caste conflicts between the other backward castes (OBC) and the scheduled castes (SC).

Hraday Parivartan; Change of Heart

The reservation system when introduced was supposed by itself an effective instrument in removing social inequalities. The experience of these fifty years has shown that this objective has certainly contributed in fulfillment of this objective. But of late, this important tool was perceived as vote catcher device by the shortsighted politicians. This invited all evils, which started posing threat in fulfilling this expectation. Therefore, it is the high time for its overhauling review. This won't materialize merely by arguments for and against the reservation continuance. It has to be instrumental in breaking caste barriers, and provides the maximum benefits to the left out fraction of the oppressed. On the other side, there are no chances of *'Hriday Parivartan'* in a vested interest section among upper castes on a required big scale. Mahatma Gandhiji was well aware of the Indian mind set on the caste stigma. Therefore, he has instead of relying on Hraday Parivartan of the Indian society, accepted the indispensibility of role of the state for removal of untouchability.

Education in any society plays a miracle particularly in the aspects of the social reforms. Unfortunately Indian education system has also failed in its duty to contribute in this highly sensitive Indian social problem comprising of social neglect, untouchability, hierarchical castes gradations etc. A document ' Education for Our People' prepared by an expert committee of 43 prominent people headed by Justice V.M. Tarkunde as desired by Jay Prakash in 1977, states that it is not correct to say that the present education system really educates the people. It's objective is not the spread of education, but it is a merciless mechanism creating a range of people with certain privileges exclusively for them. They will act in such a way to have newer privileges for them. They work with discrimination in such a way that they can easily continue enjoying the privileges and at the same time, they act in such a way that the task of entering this arena of the privileges become more difficult and limited for the oppressed and neglected people of the society.

We have three types of educational institutions. One, government run schools, colleges. Second, private schools particularly for the lower middle class. And Third, private schools and colleges for the upper middle class and the rich. Experience has shown that this present education system has undoubtedly widened the gap of social inequalities. As regard the quality of education in these educational schools/colleges under first category mentioned above, lot much needs to be done. The student teacher ratio in the country is 71:1, which is on a much high side than what is found in the other countries.

Concern Expressed by Various Veterans

Govind Vallabh Pant in his speech moving the resolution for constituting the advisory committee on fundamental rights said, "We have to take particular care of the depressed classes, the scheduled castes, the scheduled tribes and the backward classes... We must do all we can to bring them up to the general level... **Strength of a chain is measured by the weakest of its all links** and so until, every link is fully revitalized, we will not have a healthy body politic".

Supreme Court Justice A.P. Sen, "The state must pay heed to both the objectives of the Constitution, namely efficiency of administration and equality for all persons. The preamble, shows the nation's resolve to secure to all its citizens: Justice—Social, Economic and Political to all its citizens." He warned, "The state's objective of bringing about and maintaining social justice must be achieved reasonably having regard to the interests of all. Irrational and unreasonable moves by the state will slowly but surely tear apart the fabric of the society. It is primarily the duty and function of the state to inject moderation into the decisions taken under Articles 15(4) and 16(4), because justice lives in the hearts of people and a growing sense of injustice and reverse discrimination, fuelled by unwise state action will destroy, not advance social justice."

"The Constitution does not contemplate that representation of a class in governmental services shall exactly correspond to its share in the population; it aims just at securing adequate representation" the judge emphasized.

Swami Vivekanand, great Indian saint and philosopher of Hinduism, "Greater help must be given to him, whom the nature has not endowed with an acute intellect from birth. If a Brahmin is born clever, he can educate himself. If the others are not born clever, let them have all the teaching and the teachers they want. That is justice and reason, as I understand it."[4]

Dr. Ambedkar said in Constituent Assembly; " The political power in this country has too long been the monopoly of a few, and the many are not only beasts of burden, but also beasts of prey. This monopoly has not merely deprived of them of their chance of betterment; it has sapped them of what may be called the significance of life. These downtrodden classes are tired of being governed; they are impatient to govern themselves. This urge for self-realization in the downtrodden class must not be allowed to develop into a class struggle or class war. It would lead to a division of house. This would indeed be a day of disaster. For, as has been well said by Abraham Lincoln, a house divided against it cannot stand very long. Therefore, sooner the room is made for the realization of their aspiration, the better for the continuance for its independence and the better for the continuance of its democratic structure".[5]

Sardar Vallabhbhai Patel on the Parliament floor, "Now our object should be as soon as possible and as rapidly as possible to drop these classifications and differences and bring all to a level of equality".

Justice Krishna Iyer, "The real solution to the issue of reservation lies in 'GROWTH' i.e. to enlarge the size of the cake. The vast human potential of the Harijans and Girijans, the one-fifth of the Indian people goes to thistles and every communal effort to twist the politics of power for promoting chances of getting jobs becomes inevitable, caste being a deep rooted pathology in our country.

Justice Sawant,"Political power does not bring real power. Political power has to be actually exercised to banish the disadvantages and backwardness of socially, educationally and economically deprived sections. The only known medium of exercising power is the administrative machinery. If that machinery is not sympathetic to the purpose of the exercise, the political power becomes ineffective and at times is also rendered impotent. The reason why, after these many years of independence and of vesting of political power in the hands of the people, the same section which dominated the nation's affairs earlier continues to do so even to day, lies here."

Conclusion

How shall this be possible? By throwing the buck on the politicians? By finding faults with the present reservation system?

The policy of reservation should be judged on the ground of prevailing social realities in Indian society. The caste system is impediment to the progress of our nation. The removal of the bondage of caste can help to achieve liberation of individuals, essential for the system of merit to work and the classes to be formed. What is needed is that for a social change, the power generating structure like education and administration must be equitably distributed over the whole social surface rather than being clustered, through one system of legitimization or the other, within the limited segments of society. Caste being a reality of Indian society and a terrifying force of stability, the strategy of social action must base itself on the criteria of caste. It is not a redressal of sentimental grievances around historical deprivation rather a scheme of equitable distribution of the very scarce social positions and educational opportunities, determining status, power and privilege in society. By adopting caste action to abolish casteism, a broad based participation will be possible; a more efficient system for determining merit will emerge and a homogeneous social surface congenial for class formation will be created.

Social tension in the country has been accentuating with the gradual realization of frustration of those deprived and of a sense of loss to those entrenched. The violent reactions in the country have been deepening on caste lines, which are bound to have serious implications for Indian society. The intolerance of the upper castes and the aspirations of the lower castes are glaring indications that the Indian road to social equality is bound to be marked by bloody clashes between different castes, if a definite design of policy is not attempted to achieve balance in society. The days of false promises and rosy hopes are over. The future would be difficult if imperceptible discrimination is not checked in time and with commitment. The demand for reservation concerns only the distribution of educational opportunities, modern jobs and national resources within a democratic political system. This is a just demand through non-violent means. If this is not conceded, it may not be of the boundary of possibility for those who have grievances of being deprived, to aspire for the realization of their rightful place in power structure even though violence, if the inbuilt social discrimination is not tackled through democratic procedures.

The tensions in the country around the policy of reservation are likely to be resolved only when there is a spirit of accommodation specially among those who oppose reservation because of having vested interests in the on-going order of society, must change their heart and work for a social order in which the monopoly of certain castes over the power structure is made non-existent. This would give meaning to a democratic system and usher in a balancing order of society. This is in the best interests of the nation since the caste-segmented society cannot allow the economy to move rapidly on the road to economic development. Justice in a democratic society demands a socially representative power structure. Seen in this perspective, the long run national interest can be protected through internal adjustment which depends upon as to how understandingly the ruling high castes handle the legitimate aspirations and rightful demands of the lower castes who have historically been kept out of the power system of Indian society and whose recovery is impossible under the circumstances without preferential treatment on caste lines.

Justice Krishna Aiyer on Spirit of Constitution

We, as Judges dealing with a socially charged issue of constitutional law, must never forget that the Indian Constitution is a national charter pregnant with social revolution, not a legal parchment barren of militant values to usher in a democratic, secular, socialist society which belongs equally to the masses including the Harijans, Girijans millions hungering for a humane deal. After feudal colonial history's long night."

"These forces nurtured the roots of constitutional values among which must be found the fighting faith in a casteless society, not by obliterating the label but by advancement of the backwards, particularly that pathetic segment described colourlessly as scheduled castes and scheduled tribes to recognize these poignant realities of social history and so to interpret the Constitution as to fulfil itself, not eruditely to undermine its substance through the tyranny of literality, is the task of judicial patriotism to relevant in third world conditions to make liberation a living fact."

"We could not apprehend the social dimension of the stark squalor of SC and ST by viewing Article 16(4) through a narrow legal aperture but only by an *aperçu* of the broader demands of social democracy without which the Republic would cease to be a reality to one-fifth of Indian humanity."

"Our Constitution is a dynamic document with destination social revolution. It is neither anemic nor neutral but vigorously purposeful and value laden as the very descriptive adjectives of our Republic proclaim where ancient social injustice freezes the genial current of the soul."

Constitutional questions cannot be viewed in vacua, but must be answered in the social milieu, which gives it a living meaning. After all, the world of facts enlivens the world of words. And logomoachy is not law but a fatal, though fascinating, futility if alienated from the facts of life."

"A constitutional instrument is *sui generis* and obviously and necessarily, its interpretation cannot always run on the same lines as the interpretation of statutes made in exercise of the powers conferred by it. A Constitution like ours, born of an anti-imperialist struggle, influenced by constitutional instruments, events and revolutions elsewhere, in search of a better world and wedded to the idea of justice, economic, social and political, to all, must receive a generous interpretation so as to give all its citizens the full measure of justice so proclaimed instead of the austerity of tabulated legalism."

"The Indian Constitution is a great social document almost revolutionary in its aim of transforming a medieval hierarchical society into a modern, egalitarian democracy. Its provisions can be comprehended only by a spacious, social-science approach, not by pedantic, traditional legalism."

Our Constitution is unquestionably unique in its character and assimilation having its notable aspirations contained in 'Fundamental Rights' through which the illumination of constitutional rights comes to us through an artless window glass but refracted with the enhanced intensity and beauty by prismatic interpretation of the constitutional provisions dealing with equal distribution of justice in the social, political and economic spheres.

Though forty five years from the commencement of the Indian independence, after the end of British paramountcy and forty two years from the advent of our Constitution have marched on, the tormenting enigma that often nags the people of India is whether the principle of equality of status and of opportunity to be equally provided to all the citizens of our country from cradle to grave is satisfactorily consummated and whether the clarion of equality of opportunity in matters of public employment' as enshrined in Article 16(4) of the Constitution has been called upon into action ?

With a broken heart, one has to answer these questions in the negative....

"The Founding Fathers of our Constitution have designedly couched Articles 14, 15 and 16 in comprehensive phraseology so that the frail and emaciated section of the people living in poverty, rearing in obscurity, possessing no wealth or influence, having no education, much less higher education and suffering from social repression and oppression should not be denied of equality."

"The undignified social status and sub-human living conditions leave an indelible impression that their forlorn hopes for equality in every sphere of life are only a myth rather than a reality..."

REFERENCES

1. D. Parthsarthi, *Advocacy Internet* Nov./Dec. 2005.
2. P. Radhakrishnan, *Economic and Political Weekly* 16 February 2002.
3. *Economic and Political Weekly* 2nd May 1981.
4. *Concept of Equality*: B.N. Ganguli.
5. *Dr. Babasaheb Ambedkar Writings and Speeches*, Vol. 13 p. 1217/18.

ANNEXURE-I

Court Judgements

Sl. No.	*Chapter*	*Matter*	*Year*	*Page*
01	1,8	Akhil Bharatiya Shoshit Karmachari Sangh		29,267, 272
02	1,12,14	M. Nagraj and others	2006	26,145, 266,293
03	3	State of U.P. *vs.* Pradip Tandan		61
04	8,9,12	Indra Sahney *vs.* Union of India	1992	25,45, 149,168, 196,244 251
05	12	Ashok Kumar Gupta *vs.* State of U.P.		226,248
06	12	S.Vinodkumar *vs.* Government of India	1996	250
07	16	Union of India *vs.* Virpal Singh Chauhan	1997	246,255
08	8	Vasantkumar *vs.* State of Karnataka		166,195, 196
09	11C	A'bad Xavier's Col. Soc. *vs.* Govenment of Gujarat	1974	226
10	11C	P.A. Inamdar *vs.* State of Maharashtra	2005	227, 241
11	9	Janki Prasad Parimoo *vs.* State of J&K	1973	159
12	13	Ashok Kumar Thakur *vs.* State of Bihar		188
13	10	Delhi Transport Corp. *vs.* DTC Mazdoor Cong.	1991	193
14	14	N.M. Thomas *vs.* State of Kerala	1981	291
15	20	State of Punjab *vs.* Hiralal		273
16	20	Ajay Kumar Singh *vs.* State of Bihar	1994	273
17	12,14,20	Jagdish Lal *vs.* State of Haryana		255
18	14,20	Arti Roy Chaudhari *vs.* Union of India		278, 284
19	14,20	T. Devdasan *vs.* Union of India		288

ANNEXURE-II

OBC Population As Per Census 1931

(in Per cent)

Sl. No.	*Group Name*	*% of Total Population*	*Total %*
I.	Scheduled castes and scheduled tribes		
	A.1 Scheduled castes	15.05	
	A.2 Scheduled tribes	07.51	22.56
II.	Non-Hindu Communities, Religious Groups etc.		
	B.1 Muslims (other than STs)	11.19 (0.02)	
	B.2 Christians (other than STs)	02.16 (0.44)	
	B.3 Sikhs (other than SCs and STs)	01.67 (0.22)	
	B.4 Buddhists (other than STs)	00.67 (0.33)	
	B.5 Jains	00.47 (–)	16.16
III.	Forward Hindu Castes and Communities		
	C.1 Brahmins inclu. Bhumihars	05.52	
	C.2 Rajputs	03.90	
	C.3 Marathas	02.21	
	C.4 Jats	01.00	
	C.5 Vaishes-Banias etc.	01.88	
	C.6 Kayasthas	01.07	
	C.7 Other forward Hindu castes groups	02.00	17.58
	Total (I+II+III)		**56.30**
	Remaining backward Hindu castes and Communities	43.70	
	Backward Non-Hindu Communities	08.40	
	Total OBC Population as per 1931 Census	**52.10**	

ANNEXURE-III

State-wise Reservation Percentage

Sl.No.	*State*	*SC*	*ST*	*OBC*	*Total*
1.	West Bengal	22	6	7	35
2.	Kerala	10	—	40	50
3.	Uttar Pradesh	21	2	27	50
4.	Bihar	15	1	34	50
5.	Assam	7	15	15	37
6.	Jharkhand	11	27	12	50
7.	Karnataka	15	3	32	50
8.	Uttaranchal	19	4	14	37
9.	Delhi	15	7.5	27	49.5
10.	Maharashtra	13	7	32	52
11.	Andhra Pradesh	15	6	25	46
12.	Gujarat	7	15	27	49
13.	Rajasthan	15	7.5	27	49.5
14.	Madhya Pradesh	16	20	14	50
15.	Haryana	15	7.5	27	49.5
16.	Tamil Nadu	18	1	50	69
17.	Orissa	15	7.5	27	49.5
18.	Himachal Pradesh	15	7.5	5	27.5
19.	Chattisgrah	15	18	14	47
20.	Punjab	20	5	22	47
	All India	15	7.5	27	49.5

Index